Inclusion and Early Years Practice

Inclusion is a difficult, complex issue for which there are no off-the-shelf answers. To be an effective practitioner it is necessary to identify what makes each situation and circumstance unique and use this knowledge to develop strategies and approaches that are appropriate. This timely new text examines the key perceptions, perspectives and concepts around inclusion in the Early Years. Drawing on real-life experiences of practitioners, it considers the questions practitioners are likely to come across in their professional lives and how they might genuinely go about meeting the needs of all the children in their care.

Inclusion and Early Years Practice covers all aspects of inclusion including special educational needs, gender and sexuality, multiculturalism, multilingualism, Roma and traveller communities and well-being. Most chapters feature:

- case studies to develop reflective thinking
- reflective practice boxes to illustrate key points
- questions to promote discussion and debate
- annotated further reading lists.

With case studies drawn from current research and thinking points which encourage reflective practice, this book will be essential reading for students on early childhood studies programmes and Early Years Foundation degrees who wish to become reflective and critically aware practitioners.

Kathy Brodie is an Early Years consultant, author and lecturer. She delivers training on planning, observations, schema, working with under twos, outdoor play, EYFS sustained shared thinking, profiles and special educational needs. Kathy has also been an Early Years professional assessor and mentor for NW Early Years Transformation Group, Chester, Liverpool Hope and Cumbria Universities, and previously lectured on the University of Chester's Early Childhood Studies course.

Keith Savage taught in primary schools and colleges for more than 20 years before retiring. He is currently a councillor on the High Peak Borough Council in Derbyshire.

Inclusion and Early Years Practice

Edited by Kathy Brodie and Keith Savage

Routledge
Taylor & Francis Group

LONDON AND NEW YORK

First published 2015
by Routledge
2 Park Square, Milton Park, Abingdon, Oxon OX14 4RN

and by Routledge
711 Third Avenue, New York, NY 10017

Routledge is an imprint of the Taylor & Francis Group, an informa business

British Library Cataloguing-in-Publication Data
A catalogue record for this book is available from the British Library

Library of Congress Cataloging in Publication Data
A catalog record for this book has been requested

ISBN: 978-1-138-01729-0 (hbk)
ISBN: 978-1-138-01730-6 (pbk)
ISBN: 978-1-315-78010-8 (ebk)

Typeset in Palatino
by Book Now Ltd, London

Printed and bound in Great Britain by
TJ International Ltd, Padstow, Cornwall

Contents

Contents

Figures

Tables

Contributors

Sue Aitken is a senior lecturer in Early Years at Manchester Metropolitan University. She gained her first degree and MA with the Open University and had a successful career in a range of Early Years settings before becoming a lecturer in Further Education. In addition to teaching she has also worked as a consultant for Cheshire and Staffordshire local authorities, helping to design better support services within Early Years settings.

Jo Basford is a senior lecturer in Early Years and Childhood Studies at Manchester Metropolitan University. She began her career as an infant teacher and then specialised in the Foundation Stage. Jo has worked with the private, voluntary and independent sector in various roles as both an advisor and strategic manager in a local authority. Her research interests are concerned with assessment and policy implementation. This is the focus of her doctoral research which explores how Early Years professional teachers are mediating their practice and pedagogical beliefs with dominant assessment policy discourses.

Kate Beardmore graduated from Manchester Metropolitan University in 2012 with a degree in Early Years and Childhood Studies. After working with young adults, she returned to MMU to study for a post graduate certificate in education. She is now a primary teacher in Staffordshire.

Jackie Braithwaite began her career in education, supporting learning in Key Stage 1 but soon developed a keen interest in Early Years, where she successfully led a pre-school setting before becoming a lecturer in FE and HE. Jackie has taught extensively on the Foundation Degree in Early Years and is currently lecturing at the University Centre, Stockport College, on Foundation Degrees in Early Years practice and children and young people. She has a particular interest in citizenship and participation in Early Years settings. Jackie's Master's dissertation focused on children in an Early Years setting participating in their own assessments by becoming photographers and reporters of their learning.

Kathy Brodie is an Early Years consultant, author and lecturer. She delivers training on planning, observations, schema, working with under-twos, outdoor play, EYFS sustained shared thinking, profiles and special educational needs. Kathy has also been an Early Years professional assessor and mentor for NW Early Years

Transformation Group, Chester, Liverpool Hope and Cumbria Universities, and previously lectured on the University of Chester's Early Childhood Studies course.

Sean Creaney is a senior lecturer in Applied Social Sciences at the University Centre, Stockport College. Sean is the unit leader for the research module on the Foundation Degree in Early Years Practice and the BA (Hons) Childhood Studies. He is a Fellow of the Higher Education Academy and a PhD student at the School of Humanities and Social Science, Liverpool John Moores University. He sits on the executive committee for the National Association for Youth Justice and is a member of the Editorial Advisory Board for *Safer Communities* peer-reviewed journal.

Sharron Galley started work as a class teacher in a challenging inner-city primary school, led numeracy in the school and was also a 'lead maths teacher' for the local education authority. During her eight years lecturing in HE childhood studies Sharron achieved her Master's degree in education. Her research interests include how to support BA students with their academic writing, evaluating the study skills provision of HE institutions and creating positive learning environments for children with EAL. Sharron has recently returned to teach in the primary sector.

Gill Mills is a senior lecturer and programme leader in Health and Social Care at the University Centre, Stockport College where she has taught across a range of courses since 2010. Prior to that, Gill taught at all levels from GCSE to final year undergraduate in Manchester and Norfolk. Her background is in psychology, with her current interest in the well-being of children and adolescents, which is a subject that Gill is currently researching with a view to developing projects with local schools that benefit young people.

Zoe Nangah is currently a senior lecturer in the Applied Social Sciences School at the University Centre, Stockport College, lecturing on the BA (Hons) Health and Social Care, BA (Hons) Childhood Studies and Programme Leader for the Foundation Degree Working with Children and Young People. She has been lecturing in Higher Education for eight years. Her previous work experience was with children and young people across primary schools (Teaching and SENCO roles), secondary schools (counselling) and working as a residential care worker within a pupil referral unit. Her interests are in mental health, well-being, inclusion, and supporting children/young people and families within education and social care areas.

Gill Pritchard has 12 years experience working with children and young people with disability and special needs, including specialist training. Much of her work was devoted to gaining access for students to mainstream college, training or work opportunities. Gill's main interest is inclusion and equality of opportunity for those with special needs and/or disability. This was promoted during her 14 years teaching at Stockport College, both in FE and HE. This drive has gained momentum, more recently, due to Gill becoming a grandparent to the most wonderful and captivating little person who has the determination (and hopefully the opportunity) to achieve all that Gill would wish for her.

Cora Rooney has worked as a qualified social worker since 1992 and is a qualified teacher in post-compulsory education. She has been an associate lecturer at the University of Bradford and Bradford College. She has been a lecturer on the BA (Hons) Social Work and BA (Hons) Childhood Studies programmes. She currently lectures on the Foundation Degree in Early Years (sector endorsed), Foundation Degree Working with Children and Young People and BA (Hons) Health and Social Care at the University Centre, Stockport College. She is an associate lecturer on the BA (Hons) Social Work programme at Manchester Metropolitan University.

Keith Savage taught in primary schools and colleges for more than 20 years before retiring. He is currently a councillor on the High Peak Borough Council in Derbyshire.

Karen Taylor has worked as a qualified social worker since 1993 and is a qualified teacher in post-compulsory education. She has been a programme leader and lecturer on the BA (Hons) Social Work programme. She currently lectures on the Foundation Degree in Early Years (sector endorsed), Foundation Degree Working with Children and Young People and BA (Hons) Health and Social Care at the University Centre, Stockport College. She is an associate lecturer on the BA (Hons) Social Work programme at Manchester Metropolitan University.

Acknowledgements

KB: My sincere thanks to Lily's family who generously gave their expertise and time to explain the family's perspective, and many thanks to Lily for being our inspiration. My heartfelt thanks to the students who kindly gave their perspectives on multiculturalism. None of this would be possible without the support of Ian, Chris and Robs. Thank you, guys!

KS: To the memory of my parents, Eileen and Arthur, and with thanks to Helen, who makes all things possible.

JB: I would like to thank Barbara Pickford and Alison Ricketts for their time and expertise.

SG: Many thanks to the teachers who gave up their time to be interviewed for this chapter, their insights have been invaluable.

ZN and GM: Our thanks and gratitude go to our families for their time and patience while we were writing this chapter. Thanks too, go to the students for their research contributions and to Kathy Brodie for her support and guidance throughout.

SC: I would like to thank the students who took part in the focus groups for volunteering their time and providing great insight into their role working and researching with children. I would also like to thank the Editors, Kathy and Keith, for helping to conduct the focus groups with the students. I would particularly like to thank Keith for reading through earlier drafts of this chapter and providing very constructive feedback. Finally, but certainly not least, I would like to thank Leanne, my partner and my beautiful children Callum and Ella for their love and continuing support.

1

Children, young people, inclusion and social policy

Keith Savage

The aims of this chapter are:

- To focus on the meaning of terms such as inclusion, social exclusion, participation
- To develop a framework for evaluating the effectiveness of 'inclusive' policies
- To encourage reflection on the dimensions of inclusion
- To review a political context for policy-making
- To consider how inclusion is about social processes as well as outcomes.

Introduction

Ben Goldacre used to sell a T-shirt on his Bad Science website (Goldacre, 2014) and it carried the message, 'I think you'll find it is a bit more complicated than that.' Every time I tried to complete a thought or a paragraph in this chapter that says something about what we mean or understand by the term 'inclusion', or what might be done to ensure that more of us are 'included', then I pictured that T-shirt.

One of the reasons for 'inclusion' being 'more complicated' is that there is no single way of looking at it or thinking about it. If I stand on a hilltop, I can see the whole panorama around me; from the bottom of the hill only a fraction of the landscape can be seen. To create the whole picture it is necessary to walk around the hill, constantly stopping and observing, and then trying to join up those fragments. If we want to understand what 'inclusion' means in practice, we shall need to look at our practice from as many angles as we can. That is what we try to do in this book, and this is our first stopping place.

The word 'inclusion' should not be a problem in itself. Its opposite – 'exclusion' – helps reinforce our understanding that 'inclusion' is very much about being a part of something. But once you start to go beyond that, all sorts of questions should occur to you. Some are listed here. As you read, think how you would answer them. (At this stage, it is not necessary to confine your thinking to Early Years care and education.)

- What is it that we might be excluded from – or want to be included in?
- Why are some people excluded but not others?
- What factors make it more likely that we will be excluded (or included)?
- Must we be 'included' or should we feel free to opt out if that is what we choose?
- If we are 'included', does that mean we have to give up some of our individuality to fit in?
- What can be done – and by whom – to make inclusion more likely to happen?
- How can we make inclusion more than just a right?
- How can we work to make it something that people 'do' in an active way?

The questions above are some of the points that this chapter will encourage you to think about in more depth. Before you read on, make some initial notes on how you would answer some of these questions at least – or other questions that occur to you. As you continue reading, return to these initial notes and add ideas as you think of them.

Some language and some definitions

The words 'inclusion' and 'exclusion' have already been used several times. Before we go much further, we need to clarify what we mean when we use them and think about why they are significant ideas in Early Years practice. Since they are ideas and not concrete objects, it is more likely that each of us will think of 'inclusion' in different ways. We have different understandings of how physical, concrete, everyday objects look and feel. Imagine a chair – now ask a friend to describe the chair that they imagine: there will be some similarities in your 'chairs', but there will also be differences. How much more different will be the ways in which we think about 'inclusion' which is an idea, an approach, a principle – but not a tangible thing that we can hold?

While ideas might be abstract in themselves, we tend to apply them in real situations and then they take on an apparent life and meaning. 'Happiness' is not something that we can touch or measure – though we think we can see it sometimes. Until we are familiar with a detailed event – the birth of a baby perhaps – we cannot really appreciate what 'happiness' might be; and it will probably be a different experience for the mother, a grandparent or the midwife.

Similarly, throughout this book when you read about 'inclusion' or 'inclusive practice', it will be in connection with some real event or situation. Our understanding of what inclusion means will be helped by the context in which it is used. The possibility of using the idea in connection with the way in which we learn a language or to read; in relation to the different life experiences of

Travelling families or same-sex parents and their children; and as a tool to help us develop our professional research and reflective practices, shows that 'inclusion' is an idea with multiple uses and purposes. In a kitchen we use different knives for cutting bread and vegetables; as Early Years practitioners, we will find we use 'inclusion' in slightly different ways, according to our needs and purpose.

Away from the immediate world of Early Years practice, in terms of social policy, the notion of 'inclusion' has come increasingly to be defined and understood by reference to other, more quantifiable factors. Over the past 20 years or so – certainly after the election in the UK of Tony Blair's New Labour Government in 1997 – more specific terms and language have developed. 'Social inclusion' and 'social exclusion' have become common in any social policy considerations. Kay *et al.* (2006) make the important point that social inclusion is about being enabled to take part – having any barriers to involvement lowered if not totally removed – but having a right to join in is not the same thing as actively participating. 'Inclusion' can be seen as a passive step; 'participation' is active.

There is nothing in law to stop women becoming Members of Parliament in the UK but after the 2010 general election of the 650 MPs, only 146 were women – that is less than a quarter. So what is it that stops more women from participating – being truly included in high-level political life? (At this point you might want to go back to our initial set of questions and add any further ideas.)

There is a presumption behind all of this that 'inclusion' and 'participation' are 'good'. They are something that should be worked for, because their absence in some way or another makes the world and our lives the poorer.

Some of you may have written workplace policies or guidelines about inclusion. Don't look up those policies, don't do a quick internet search, but do try to think of just three positive reasons why it is important to strive to develop inclusive practice.

We try to work here in a way that is inclusive because:

1. _____

2. _____

3. _____

If you are you sharing this book with other practitioners, compare your lists with someone – try and find a third and fourth person to share with.

Can you expand this list of reasons for working inclusively? It is important that you can be strong and confident in your answers because there will be times when you will find that some people will question and dispute your practice.

As Early Years practitioners, the more involved you become, the more responsibility you take for a practice that claims to be inclusive, the more likely it is that you will come across others wanting to make distinctions between 'integration' and 'inclusion', though some people seem to use the words interchangeably. Advocates of the term 'inclusion' usually assume that those being included take their place as equals. Though this assumption – like all others – should be questioned and challenged. There will be situations or circumstances where it may well feel that inclusion is not really working in an equal way and that some do seem to have privileges not open to all. Or it may be that despite a clear policy statement upholding the rights of all children to equal access, you might observe that a group of boys dominate the outdoor play area or that a child with impaired sight tends to be marginalised at story time.

The concern that some have about the notion of 'integration' is the apparent assumption behind it that in some way those who are outsiders, or who are excluded and in need of 'integrating', are in that position because of some failing or inadequacy on their part. If I am excluded primarily because I have limited mobility – I am slow in my movements and am sometimes clumsy – some, more mobile, people might feel sorry for me but might also conclude that I can never really fit in. Once we start talking about, and requiring, integration, we accept that there is a majority group, or a dominant set of behaviours and beliefs. It follows that any minorities must either come to accept, or defer to, the expectations of the majority. By requiring integration on those terms, we expect the newcomer or outsider to change who they are if they are to become accepted or acceptable; to become integrated means to give something up. Of course, it might prove impossible ever to integrate fully in the eyes and ears of some people. I may work hard to learn a language, but my accent and my vocabulary may always betray me to others. If we limit our ambition to integration, it means we allow others to define and put labels on what they see as our failings or inadequacies.

As ever, though, 'it is more complicated than that'. In many situations we choose or want to be part of a group and to find acceptance. It might be in work or a social setting. We know that the group has rules or standards of behaviour. Some we might not be entirely comfortable with but we accept them as part of the price for joining. We want to be an active participant but this may require some compromise on our part. We might also hope that in time the group will recognise qualities and skills that we have, and the group adjusts in some way to accommodate what we can bring. There should be a fluidity and dynamism, which allows change in all involved. For that to happen, all who are involved must be prepared to adjust. This can put particular responsibilities on the shoulders of those with a leadership role as a group changes the way in which it works and relationships within it are redefined. This is something that we return to in the final chapter of this book.

The Alliance for Inclusive Education argues that some degree of integration may be a necessary precondition for subsequent inclusion, which can then remove barriers to participation and allow all participants to engage as equals (Alliance for Inclusive Education, 2014). For all participants to be treated as equals, however, they need to be equally heard and able to voice their concerns and feelings, confident that they will be taken seriously and will have an impact on any decision-making. It is likely that in any community populated by adults, such as workplaces, that not everyone will be heard or taken seriously. In schools, for example, teaching assistants commonly report that their views about a child's development or needs are not sought, even though they may work most closely with the child.

Children and young people are almost routinely discounted when it comes to serious consideration about major decisions that affect their lives. Adults – politicians, pressure groups, employers, businesses, parents – may be heard when it comes to deciding about creating new schools, reforming school curricula or examinations, but when and how are students involved in the decision-making? Hallett and Prout (2003) argued passionately for children's voices to be heard and listened to, but there is still little evidence that this is happening consistently. This is especially true in the Early Years sector.

At this point, pause and consider these questions:

- Why might the views and experiences of young children not be heard or – if heard – not taken seriously?
- What examples of practice in Early Years settings can you recall that went some way to making sure that the voices of the least confident and least articulate children were heard?
- If you have any examples of ways in which children expressed their unhappiness about their time in an Early Years setting, what was (or might have been) done to improve things?

So if we sum up what we mean by inclusion, here are some key elements to any definition that we are likely to find practically useful and widely acceptable.

- Inclusion recognises that people are individuals with a whole range of characteristics that make them different.
- Inclusion assumes that those personal differences should not prevent any of us from taking part fully in social, cultural and economic life.
- Inclusion values difference among people and regards acceptance of difference as a healthy instinct in a strong, confident society.
- Inclusion requires that people not only have the right to take part – they should feel confident about joining in on the basis of their own choices.
- Inclusion insists that if people are to have the choice to be included, then their voice must also be heard and taken account of in the worlds that they wish to be part of.

> Before continuing, look again at the minimum of three reasons for wanting inclu-
> sive practice that you set out earlier. Are the five bullet points above reflected in
> your reasons? If not, do you want to add to the list that you might use in your
> professional role?

Social exclusion

The notion of 'inclusion' tries to make a positive statement about our lives
and how we are treated by others. It is sometimes aspirational; it is hard to
know or to measure the degree to which someone is included or excluded.
As a possible remedy to this problem, the notion of 'social exclusion' is useful. In much of Europe, and certainly in the UK, the idea of 'social exclusion'
took hold at the end of the last century. The Labour Government
(1997–2010) was quick to establish the Social Exclusion Unit (SEU). In part,
this was out of recognition that there were not isolated social issues that
described the lives of children and families. Rather it assumed that housing, crime, unemployment, drug use, education, unemployment, poverty,
and so on were connected or 'joined up', to use the language of the day
(Percy-Smith, 2000).

In terms of social policy, the government argued that it must follow that
'joined-up' responses were required, these issues – previously seen as separate problems – could not be tackled one at a time and the SEU was expected
to deliver a coherent policy response. In defining the terms of reference for
the SEU, one of the helpful consequences was the development of a list of the
different dimensions of social exclusion. If the drive towards inclusion
helped outline appropriate attitudes when making policy, the examination of
exclusion helped clarify the ways in which people and communities might
come to be marginalised or denied access to resources or control over their
own lives.

In broad terms, when policy-makers talk about how social exclusion presents
itself, it has been suggested that it can be seen in terms of access to resources,
participation in economic and cultural life and the overall quality of life. The
Bristol Social Exclusion Matrix (Levitas *et al.*, 2007) helpfully develops and
expands these headings to 10 more specific points.

When it comes to resources, it identifies:

- material and economic resources;
- access to services;
- social resources.

In the sphere of participation, it offers:

- economic participation;
- social participation;
- culture, education and skills;
- political and civic life.

With regard to quality of life, it includes:

- health and well-being;
- the living environment;
- crime, harm and criminalisation.

Look at the 10 bullet points above and enlarge on how you understand them. For example, when we talk about 'economic participation', this is likely to include:

- whether or not someone is in paid work;
- whether that work is full- or part-time;
- whether the work is permanent with guaranteed hours;
- whether the work is for an employer in the private or public sector or whether or not it is self-employment;
- what sort of position or standing someone has in the workplace;
- whether someone is financially independent or reliant on the support of friends, family or some sort of insurance or benefit scheme.

As you make your notes, share your ideas with another professional and ask yourself: 'How does this affect the way in which we see and treat children and their families?', 'What instances are we aware of where we value or respect other people more highly because of where they live, their appearance, the jobs they do or their educational background?'

As governments across Europe focused on social exclusion, what they were considering was the clear and undeniable link between poverty and social disadvantage. The poor in societies suffered from worse health, were less successful in educational terms, died younger, and lived in worse housing – all of this was well known but no amount of policy-making or government initiatives seemed to change these connections. If you talk to older people, they may well say, 'No one knows what poverty is, these days.' In a world where 'everyone' has mobile phones, takes foreign holidays and eats in restaurants, how can we talk about poverty? While, fortunately, it is rare for anyone to die in the UK of starvation – and in that sense there is little absolute poverty – in social situations, people do compare their wealth with others. In relative terms, there remain vast differences between the richest and poorest and the UK is still one of the least equal societies when it comes to wage rate differentials between the top and bottom (Wilkinson and Pickett, 2009). Further, even the most sceptical must be alarmed at the massive growth in dependence – no matter how short-term that need might be – on food banks. A report published in June 2014 showed that over 20 million meals had been provided in one year by food banks – an increase of more than 50 per cent on the previous year (Oxfam, 2014).

The reports of the Living Wage Commission (2014) make for alarming reading (though some will argue that the Commission is not politically neutral and essentially sides with Labour, but few, if any reports, are neutral). It reported – and this key finding was largely unchallenged – that 'for the first time the majority of people in poverty in the UK are working'. So many people are working at below the 'living wage' (more than 20 per cent of those in work) and with the costs of key parts of the family budget (typically food, gas and electricity and increases in VAT) rising far faster than wages, many children are living in 'relative poverty'. For Early Years practitioners, this will be of concern because of the consistent evidence that shows that children from families on low wages soon 'fall behind' their peers in terms of their assessed development. We shall return to the importance of poverty and inclusion later in this chapter.

You may feel slightly overwhelmed by these lists and 'dimensions'. As Early Years practitioners you have limited powers and spheres of influence. Certainly no one is suggesting that it is the role of the Early Years workforce to fix all of society's shortcomings; but we do need a sense of where the failings are and where we can begin to make a difference to our own lives and to the lives of others.

The politics behind the policies

In UK elections the percentage of people who vote has declined slowly since peaking at 84 per cent in the 1950 general election. Among the reasons people give for not voting for politicians or their parties it is commonly reported that 'It doesn't make any difference. They are all the same. They don't keep their promises.'

It can be argued that there is not as much difference between the main political parties as they would sometimes like to make out. For most of us, the only British prime minister that we can identify who disturbed the political consensus of the time was Margaret Thatcher who led a Conservative Government from 1979–1990. The Conservatives continued in power for a further seven years led by John Major who was a less controversial figure. Even if the practical differences between the Conservatives and Labour are not always that pronounced it is still worth examining the supposed distinctions between the two main governing parties. Such an examination will help us better to understand the choices open to policy-makers.

The political labels 'right-wing' and 'left-wing' originated in the French parliament after the French Revolution of 1789. Historically right-wing parties have tended to defend the social and political status quo. The Conservative Party in the UK (and the Republicans in the USA) argue that individuals should generally be 'free' to pursue their own interests. Politicians on the Right argue that as individuals we have life chances and life choices and that by making the best of those possibilities we benefit ourselves and those around us. In broader, economic terms right-wing parties want to see businesses – large and small – and industry as free as possible to act in their own interests. For the Right, personal and business taxes should be low and the government should intervene as little as possible in the lives of people and business. A natural consequence of this is that some people will accumulate wealth and, perhaps, power and others will be poorer and weak. For the political Right, this is an inevitable fact of social life.

Socialist parties are left-wing. There are some commentators who dispute that the British Labour Party (or the American Democrats) are socialist in intent but most European countries still have parties happy to accept the label. For socialists, the key ideas are equality, fairness and shared responsibility. They start from a recognition that what a society or community achieves is the result of collaborative effort. Companies may be owned by individuals and families but a car is not built by one person; a bank is not the product of a single individual. We all use roads and schools and we should all share in meeting the costs. Those who can afford to should pay more than the least well-off. Finally, social structures are not inherently fair in the way that individuals are treated. People can have advantages just because they are born into a wealthy, well-connected family. For socialists, governments should act to help iron out social inequalities and injustices.

The education policies of the Coalition Government formed as a result of the 2010 general election help illustrate some of the differences between the Right and the Left in policy terms. In the years since the end of the Second World War (and that is 70 years now) most British children have gone to schools administered by local education authorities (LEAs). In our larger towns and cities or at county level, Manchester or Lancashire, for example, part of the role of the elected council is to run local schools. The education authority manages overall funding and provides practical support for school staff and governors. This way of providing a service – in this case, education – fits well with left-wing ways of thinking. It is about sharing costs and responsibilities in a bid to provide equally good schools for all. If the system works well, the richer areas should not have better schools than the poorer ones and social inequalities should not be perpetuated.

Since the introduction of the National Curriculum, and the establishment of Ofsted 25 years ago, politicians (Conservative and Labour alike) have expressed a determination to improve education standards and pupil achievement. For the Coalition Government, led, until 2014, in education policy-making by Michael Gove, a key element has been to reduce the size and significance of education authorities and to increase the role of independent schools. In Gove's view, the quality of education provided by local authorities had not improved quickly enough – or in some cases not improved at all. He concluded (and he sought confirmation from Ofsted) that some council-led education services were not providing good enough educational opportunities for all students. From the earliest days of the Coalition Government (dominated by right-wing Conservatives), the establishment of independent free schools and academies has been promoted. Over 4,000 such schools were open in England in August 2014 – about one in six of all schools. They have been funded directly by central government with the result that fewer schools are in the overall management of education authorities and the authorities themselves have smaller budgets.

For Gove, this approach made sense because it removes influence and control from large organisations (education authorities) that he viewed as wasteful, inclined to atrophy and slow to respond to the needs of fast-changing communities. For Gove and his education team, free schools and academies represent a way of 'freeing up' money and resources and transferring real influence away from cumbersome bureaucracies towards smaller, self-motivated and self-managed schools.

Michael Gove attracted as much criticism as any Coalition Government minister and many educational professionals were quick to cheer when he lost his government post as Education Secretary. The political Left accused him (among many other things) of re-creating a two-tier education system in which free schools and academies were given advantages over LEA-managed schools. Free schools were criticised because they were allowed to recruit untrained staff to teach in classrooms and were allowed to be selective in choosing students. The suggestion was that they would not select students who might be difficult to teach or manage in some way.

Multiculturalism

It is important, in this context, to acknowledge the political argument and debate around the notion of 'multiculturalism'. To say that the UK is a multicultural society is a truism. In the 2011 census about 60 per cent described themselves as Christian, 30 per cent said that they had no religion or declined to answer the question and nearly 10 per cent said that they followed a non-Christian religion (mostly Muslims, Sikhs, Hindus, Jews or Buddhists). The same census showed that for more than 90 per cent of the population English was their only or first choice of language. Dozens of other languages are spoken – Polish, Punjabi, Urdu, Bengali, Gujarati and Arabic being the most common. Of course, this variety of nationalities, languages and religions is not spread evenly throughout the country. It tends to be the case that some larger towns and cities are homes to migrant communities. Leicester is often held up as the most multicultural town in England (if not the world).

The political argument is about how should policy-makers respond to the multicultural facts. Unfortunately this strand of the social policy debate has become entangled with what is usually described as the 'radicalization' of a small number of young people. In the aftermath of the attacks of 9/11 in New York and 7/7 in London, some, from the political Right most often, have said that these tragic events are evidence that 'state multiculturalism' has failed. It is argued that state policies have allowed a degree of separatism to develop and that some people who were born and grew up in Britain do not identify with the land of their birth. On the contrary, they are hostile to Britain. It is claimed that for a small proportion of those non-white British descent (and this is nearly always about radical Muslims in the end), there is no real connection with Britain. Politicians will then go on commonly to argue that people must subscribe to 'British values' – a vague notion that has something to do with respect for the rule of law and a striving for equality. Though what is uniquely British about this is unclear.

This, in part, is a re-run of the inclusion/integration/assimilation debate outlined already (and is taken up in greater depth by Kathy Brodie in Chapter 9 of this book). This is a dilemma for education professionals and there is likely to be continuing political pressure applied. On the one hand, it is not doubted that if people from different cultural, faith and language backgrounds are to live together, there needs to be some basic sharing of knowledge about those different lives. On the other hand, some will want to put a limit on the extent to which those distinct lives can be led, requiring adherence to 'British values'. The apparent assumption made by those critics of multiculturalism as a policy framework – rather than a fact – being that to be authentically British requires surrendering a part of your own cultural heritage.

Inclusion in the Early Years

What has any of this to do with inclusion and inclusive practice in the Early Years though? I recently met with a group of experienced Early Years practitioners and we talked about what 'inclusion' meant to them. They gave me a number of practical examples to illustrate their understanding and approach.

Research results

Jess: Inclusion? It's something that we take for granted. It's what we do.

Emma: Inclusion in practice is about not focussing on or highlighting differences. Children are much more accepting than adults and it is important not to label or mark out children as 'different'.

(Continued)

(Continued)

Marie: There are some things that need to be managed very discreetly. I have one girl with a rare skin condition. As part of her care I need to 'pop' blisters and help her wash and dry with her own soap and towel. There are safeguarding issues here and this is not for public display.

Anne-Marie: On the other hand, I work with a boy who has to wear tinted glasses at all times to protect his eyes. This is a fact of life that can't be hidden. He answers other children's questions very directly. 'If I don't wear dark glasses outside the sun will burn my eyes.' So we need to support him sometimes if others persist in questioning him.

Clare: It can be difficult developing consistent care throughout the setting. I work at an after-school club where there are very different expectations about behaviour compared with the school. Shouting at after-school might be tolerated, for example. One of the things I'm required to do is to pass on messages from school staff to parents about their children. These messages are often negative and usually I was not a witness to the original incident. Partnership in all of this is important but it isn't easy.

Sarah: We have a 15-minute team briefing at the beginning of each day – to share news or observations about children and to update each other.

Marie: It is important to us that having agreed a care plan for a child that we share it with other members of staff. It is important, for example, that the mid-day meals team know about how to respond to children on the autistic spectrum. Some needs are more obvious and visible – though that doesn't mean that our response is obvious – but some children might get labelled 'naughty' just because their needs are not properly understood.

Sarah: It isn't always easy to build partnerships with parents and carers. We need to earn their confidence and this takes time. Meanwhile we might not know things about a family that could be significant. For example, we were caring for children who had been adopted but the parents didn't want to tell us that – they were concerned that their children might be stigmatised in some way. But had we known from the outset it might have helped us understand the children better.

Marie: Some children 'stand out' – they get noticed and get attention. As adult:child ratios get worse, it is more likely that the children we see and hear most easily get our attention while 'hidden' children don't get the care they need from us. It can be, of course, that quiet or withdrawn children need more from us than those who appear to be self-confident.

Sarah: Sometimes our planning is quite long-term – other times we need to be more flexible and pro-active. When a Polish-speaking child came to the nursery, we needed to find an interpreter because the EYFS requires that we assess his competence in his first language.

Ann-Marie: We always mark and celebrate a range of Festivals from the major faiths. We mark Hanukkah or Diwali, for example, whether or not we have Jewish or Hindu children in the group. We think it is important that children are aware of events and festivals that are significant to others – and understand that there is not a single belief system.

Sarah: In the same way our use of bilingual books or the display of scripts in languages other than English is not dependent on having speakers of those languages in the class. Inclusion should be a way of life – not a response to what may be seen as 'unusual' or some sort of crisis.

Pam: About 50 per cent of our children use English as an additional language. The interpreters encourage the children to use both (or all) languages they know at home and in school. Sometimes the parents say they want their children to use only English in school – 'That is why they are with you, to learn English.'

Emma: Most parents are OK about other children. Sometimes you hear people talking about the use of 'foreign languages' – and is it necessary? Or the fact that 'funded children' from low income families have nursery places alongside high-earning professional families.

Before you read on, take a few minutes to make notes of your own about what inclusion and inclusive practice means to you. If you are working in a group, compare notes and experiences. When you have made your notes, refer again to the Bristol Social Exclusion Matrix – the 10 bullet points – and see if you can find examples to match each of the 10 points. If you have any gaps can you, on reflection, think of an instance in your practice, or that of others, to fill the gaps?

It is evident from what these practitioners say that 'inclusion' is multi-faceted. Yes, it can be to do with physical ill-health and disabilities that affect people physically and emotionally – sometimes crudely summed up as Special Educational Needs (SEN) – but it is quite as likely to be about cultural and linguistic diversity. Just as there are many aspects to inclusion, so it is evident that there can be no single response – sometimes confidentiality and discretion is called for, at other times it may be appropriate to share with other children and families. What does come through from the comments of these practitioners is that whatever inclusive practice is, it must involve partnerships – with other professionals and with families. If creativity, flexibility and imagination are needed to find successful ways to include children and families who are otherwise on the margins of society, then it follows that whatever the answer is it won't be written down anywhere. We will have to find our own answers. However, that is not to say that we have no help and guidance.

One starting point is to look at what the law says. Laws might not tell us what to do in any given situation – but they should make clear what our responsibilities are, and what rights and entitlements children and their families have.

The law on inclusion and education that applies in England

For comprehensive and up-to-date information, you are urged to consult the Campaign for Studies in Inclusive Education Website – www.csie.org.uk.

There are some key bits of legislation that are relevant to supporting particular aspects of inclusive education. (Most of the legislation was enacted by different Labour governments and is evidence of the political Left's view that the state and government have a responsibility to iron out social inequalities.) The Equality Act 2010 was an attempt to bring together and update anti-discrimination legislation that had been agreed over the previous 40 years or so. Much of the Act was about employment rights but Part 6 focuses on education. It makes it unlawful for any education provider to discriminate between pupils on grounds of disability, race, age, gender reassignment, pregnancy and maternity, religion or belief, or sex.

This is undoubtedly a significant piece of legislation but it is unable to address one of the key issues when it comes to inclusion, access and participation: the significance of poverty. Undeniably it is the case that people of all ages and all social classes experience discrimination because of, for example, their race or sex but, as we have considered earlier, a key factor behind social exclusion is material poverty. The links between poverty and ill-health and educational under-achievement, for example, are well documented and form the roots of the creation of the Welfare State in the years after the Second World War. So while someone may experience discrimination because of what the Equality Act terms 'protected characteristics' – and may, therefore, have recourse to the law – being disadvantaged because of material poverty is not something that is legally recognised.

The Special Educational Needs and Disability Act 2001 (SENDA) made disability discrimination in education unlawful. Schools must not treat disabled pupils less favourably than others. They must make 'reasonable adjustments' to ensure that disabled pupils are not at a substantial disadvantage.

At the international level the UK is bound by two United Nations Conventions. The UN Convention on the Rights of the Child was agreed in 1989. Article 29 states the 'education of children shall be directed to:

- the development of the child's personality, talents and mental and physical abilities to their fullest potential;
- the development of respect for human rights and fundamental freedoms, and for the principles enshrined in the Charter of the United Nations;
- the development of respect for the child's parents, his or her own cultural identity, language and values, for the national values of the country in which the child is living, the country from which he or she may originate, and for civilisations different from his or her own;
- the preparation of the child for responsible life in a free society, in the spirit of understanding, peace, tolerance, equality of sexes, and friendship among all peoples, ethnic, national and religious groups and persons of indigenous origin;
- the development of respect for the natural environment.

This is interesting and should make any English-based Early Years practitioner think about the extent to which the Early Years Foundation Stage (EYFS) and the education offered in Key Stage 1 really matches the purposes outlined in Article 29.

> At this stage, read the bullet points above carefully, and think about how they might affect inclusive practice in your setting. Buried in the middle of all this, for example, is a statement about respect for 'national values' of the country of residence and origin – but what if those values seem in some way contradictory? In any case, as any debate about 'British values' seems to show, no one knows what those distinctive values actually are.

There is a second UN Convention – On the Rights of Persons with Disabilities – agreed in 2006. Article 24 of the Convention requires that signatory states ensure that children with any disability be guaranteed free and equal access to education and that 'support measures are provided in environments that maximize academic and social development, consistent with the goal of full inclusion' (United Nations, 2006).

The UK Coalition Government wrestled long and hard about what might be done to provide educational support for children with disabilities and their families. The Warnock Report of 1978 had led to a radical rethink on the education of those with special educational needs. Indeed, the term 'Special Educational Needs' and the process of 'statementing' come directly from that Report and subsequent legislation. Over the next 25 years or so the number of children identified as having additional needs grew as we developed a clearer understanding of conditions such as dyslexia and autism. It reached the stage where up to 20 per cent of students were identified as having additional needs at some time in their school lives – though only around 2–3 per cent of children had statements written for them.

The process of identifying the appropriate nature of support for this small percentage of students was judged to be cumbersome and resulted in delays. The Coalition Government began consultations in 2011 but it was not until 2014 that the Children and Families Act passed into law. This will see the end of 'statements' and the introduction of education, health and care (EHC) plans. These are intended to meet all needs, adopting a holistic approach. The legislation has received a cautious welcome from those most affected – but while it might improve outcomes for the 2–3 per cent who eventually have EHC plans, there are concerns that those with additional needs will not get the support required.

Apart from the law what compels us?

Early Years practitioners have over the past 20 years or so become accustomed to government direction on how to set about their work. Curricula have been written and rewritten, assessment guidelines and targets have been set and amended. Ofsted inspections have been used to shape required practice. Some critics (crucially Peter Moss and his colleagues Pat Petrie and Gunilla Dahlberg) have argued that this has reduced professionals to the role of technician – left to follow prescriptions rather than make use of their training, experience and judgement. More than that, Moss (2006) insists that a key purpose of UK government intervention in education policy over the past 25 years has been to prepare a docile yet flexible workforce – education exists to prepare young people for the world of work rather than to provide opportunities to learn and discover. Further, he asserts that children's services exist essentially to contain children – to provide a space where they should be safe rather than agents in their own learning.

This might be seen as a purely political point but it is significant in the context of this book. If Early Years provision is primarily about delivering an affordable service for parents, it could be that the emphasis is on playing things safe and focusing on the response of the parents. At the very least this could result in missed opportunities in terms of providing spaces where children have more say when it comes to determining what happens. It is more likely that we have a curriculum and provision that reinforce and transmit the dominant world-view – and this makes a challenging, inclusive practice more difficult to develop.

Moss (2006) makes connections between inclusion, democracy and children as agents in their own experience and argues that if we are serious about Early Years care and education that challenges the existing ideas that marginalise and exclude so many, then we need to rethink how we use the spaces we have. He cites the Reggio Emilia children's centres in northern Italy as possible starting places for the sort of practice that could make inclusion more than a policy or a set of guidelines.

This is no longer an unfamiliar argument for British Early Years workers, indeed many will be weary of being told how other practices offer so much more. The challenge remains, however. There are many aspects of our working environment that are beyond our control. What governments do, how Ofsted presents reports – let alone the impact of advertising on family lifestyles or the pressures of globalisation on employment prospects – these things are outside our immediate grasp. As reflective practitioners we can look hard at what happens within the walls and fences of our own workplaces and we can take responsibility for what happens there.

The following chapters focus on specific aspects of Early Years care and education and spell out some of the choices open to you in more detail. Careful and thoughtful reading, drawing on the case studies and the honest observations of other practitioners who have contributed to focus groups should help you and your teams to reappraise your work and be much clearer about how you bring inclusion to the heart of what you do.

References

Alliance for Inclusive Education (2014) *Integration is not Inclusion*. Available at: www. allfie.org.uk/pages/useful%20info/integration.html (accessed 10 August 2014).

Goldacre, B. (2014) *Bad Science*. Available at: www.badscience.net (accessed 10 August 2014).

Hallett, C. and Prout, A. (2003) *Hearing the Voices of Children: Social Policy for a New Century*. London: Routledge.

Kay, E., Tisdall, M., Davis, J.M., Hill, M. and Prout, A. (eds) (2006) *Children, Young People and Social Inclusion*. Bristol: The Policy Press.

Levitas, R., Pantazis, C., Fahmy, E., Gordon, D., Lloyd, E. and Patsios, D. (2007) *The Multi-Dimensional Analysis of Social Exclusion*. Bristol: University of Bristol: Department of Sociology and School for Social Policy.

Living Wage Commission (2014) *Working for Poverty*. Available at: http://livingwage commission.org.uk/wp-content/uploads/2014/02/Living-Wage-Commission-Report-v2_f-1.pdf (accessed 10 August 2014).

Moss, P. (2006) From children's services, to children's spaces. In E. Kay, M. Tisdall, J. M. Davis, M. Hill and A. Prout (eds) *Children, Young People and Social Inclusion*. Bristol: The Policy Press.

Oxfam GB, Church Action on Poverty and The Trussell Trust (2014) *Below the Breadline*. Available at: http://policy-practice.oxfam.org.uk/publications/below-the-bread-line-the-relentless-rise-of-food-poverty-in-britain-317730 (accessed 10 August 2014).

Percy-Smith, J. (ed.) (2000) *Policy Responses to Social Exclusion: Towards Inclusion?* Maidenhead: Open University Press.

United Nations (2006) *UN Convention on the Rights of Persons with Disabilities*. Available at: www.un.org/disabilities/convention/conventionfull.shtml (accessed 29 June 2014).

Wilkinson, R. and Pickett, K. (2009) *The Spirit Level*. London: Allen Lane.

2

Documenting and assessing learning

Including the voice of the child

Jo Basford

The aims of this chapter are:

- To ask what is the purpose of assessment and documentation in Early Years settings
- To discover how practitioners attempt to reconcile their values and beliefs with the assessment policy of their settings
- To understand how practitioners endeavour to ensure the voice of the child is included in their assessment practice.

Introduction

This chapter intends first to provide an overview of competing theoretical perspectives that can underpin the documentation and assessment of learning. It then explores some of the issues practitioners have encountered, when assessing a child's development, in trying to reconcile their professional beliefs and identity with the policy expectations and the culture and practice of their workplace setting. A case study is provided of a particular incident a practitioner observed that provided her with an opportunity to reflect upon some of the dilemmas that other practitioners may encounter when they are endeavouring to include the voice of the child in their assessment practice.

Assessment and documentation: two competing perspectives?

Assessment practice: working with the 'familiar'

There are two broad approaches to how learning takes place. Some see it as essentially a collaborative, social process. Others emphasise the individual struggle to make sense of the problems encountered in the world around them. Here we will explore how these different perspectives connect with the policies and practice that we commonly encounter everyday in English Early Years settings.

The first English statutory curriculum framework in the field of Early Childhood Education was the *Desirable Learning Outcomes* (Department for Education, 1996) and there have since been four variations. Each framework has seen an increased emphasis on a play-based approach to learning, and a greater consideration of the role of the adult in supporting learning. Research such as the EPPE (Siraj-Blatchford *et al.*, 2003) and REPEY (Siraj-Blatchford *et al.*, 2002) projects have been particularly influential in informing practitioners about the significance of the relationship between the adult and the child in the learning process.

The practice of 'sustained shared thinking', for example, defined as an 'effective pedagogic interaction, where two or more individuals 'work together' in an intellectual way to solve a problem, clarify a concept, evaluate activities or extend a narrative' (Siraj-Blatchford and Manni, 2008: 7) has become familiar pedagogical territory for the early childhood practitioner. Such approaches to supporting learning tend to sit within a sociocultural perspective of learning. A sociocultural perspective values the process of learning within a group rather than on an individualistic basis and sees learning within a social, cultural and historical context (Carr, 2001; Rogoff, 2003). When, as practitioners, we plan activities, we are likely to adopt a sociocultural stance. What happens, however, when we move from planning activities to assessing understanding, learning and development?

Close examination of policy guidance related to assessment practice does not necessarily mirror a sociocultural view. Rather it seems to be situated within a Piagetian (constructivist) framework. The Piagetian view of the child depicts him/her as a 'young scientist'. In practice, we could therefore imagine the child as an active learner, whose capability to acquire and adapt knowledge is hierarchical and sequential in nature, and happens in isolation of others. This idea of understanding learning as something that happens in set stages, or sequences is illustrated in the current *Statutory Framework for the Early Years Foundation Stage* (DfE, 2014). Practitioners are advised to observe children in social, playful situations to provide evidence of children's learning interests and capabilities, in order to 'understand their level of achievement, interests and learning styles, and to then shape learning experiences for each child reflecting those observations' (ibid.: 10).

The term 'level of achievement' is particularly pertinent. Children's level of achievement is defined as identified learning behaviours and capabilities that sit along a developmental continuum. They culminate in 17 outcomes that are expected to be achieved by the end of the Reception year – these outcomes are known as Early Learning Goals (ELGs). However, a child who has not yet reached the expected level will be labelled as 'emerging', and the child who exceeds the level will be awarded the title of 'exceeding'. Note that these judgements are made on an individualistic basis.

For practitioners who work with younger children, they too are required to make judgements about development by undertaking a 'progress check' based on pre-determined outcomes. The purpose of the progress check is to make 'best-fit judgements about whether a child is showing typical development for their age, may be at risk of delay or is ahead for their age' (DfE, 2014: 3).

Authors such as Rogoff (2003) and Burman (2008) argue that such practice 'privileges' a developmental psychological explanation of child development and is concerned with a universal measurement of expected outcomes based on a 'typical' child.

Think about the following questions for a moment and reflect on your experiences of working with children.

- Could you describe a 'typical' child?
- Which behaviours, attitudes or types of performance typify a young child?
- It would be helpful if you could make a note of your first thoughts and compare them with those of someone you work or study with.

Your image of a 'typical' child will be based on your own values and beliefs which have been shaped by your own culture and your own life experiences. Consequently, it is difficult – and probably not helpful – to try and come up with a universal definition because we have such different experiences, values and perspectives. Now let's take this idea a step further and think about the implications for practice. Is there a possibility that the child who has not met the expected outcomes is viewed as a 'problem'? Carr (2001) would argue that a model of assessment that highlights problems, or 'deficits' can result in practitioners adopting a mechanistic approach to trying to fill the gaps in development. This can be at the expense of seeing the other learning characteristics a child may bring to a learning situation. The case study later in this chapter illustrates this point.

Now let's return to the original DfE (2014) statement, and consider the two *other* elements practitioners are asked to observe: 'interests' and 'learning styles'. What happens when a child's interests and learning styles do not necessarily fit with what has been provided for in the setting? Or what happens when the observation does not provide the practitioner with relevant evidence that fits with a particular expected outcome? Luff (2012: 114) argues that the expectation to follow children's interests *and* ensure that every child makes progress towards the same prescribed outcomes becomes a contradiction for practitioners. This poses an interesting question – how possible is it to adopt a pedagogical approach that allows learning to be personalised, while at the same time ensuring that all children progress sufficiently to meet the same expected outcomes? This is an issue that became apparent for some of the practitioners who shared their accounts of assessment practice in their workplace settings.

All of this matters enormously when it comes to developing inclusive practice and it is worth pausing a while to summarise some of the issues and questions we should bear in mind. If asked, we would surely say that different areas of learning and development *all* matter. It matters that we can form and sustain friendships, talk to one another, be patient, enjoy singing and dancing. Just as it matters than in time we learn to read, write and develop an understanding of conservation, shape, space and measures. It is also likely that most of us show better skills and more enthusiasm for some activities over others – I might prefer to read, you might prefer to ride a bike. Much of the time our skills are improved by playing and sharing with others – in part, because so much learning is rooted in social and cultural patterns of behaviour. We learn not only to ride a bike, but when and where we can ride. We learn that there are different ways of talking and that how we talk in the playground sounds very different to the way we talk in the nursery. We learn all this information at different rates and at different times and places – in part, as a result of the richness and variety of social experiences available to us. As practitioners, we will say 'all children are different' – yet as practitioners we are encouraged to look at children as though they are essentially the same and on the same predictable path of learning and development.

The next section will provide you with an alternative perspective related to documenting and assessing learning. It builds on the ideas that were introduced earlier related to sociocultural perspectives. Applying a sociocultural lens to assessment values the power of a collaborative approach to learning, but more importantly it does not assume that any young child is 'typical'. Instead, a sociocultural approach to assessment provides an authentic opportunity for children's individual and unique characteristics to be valued.

An alternative perspective: sociocultural approaches to assessment

Assessment practice reflecting a sociocultural perspective has become predominant in a number of countries both in Europe and in the Southern Hemisphere. Most noteworthy is the New Zealand, Te Whāriki bi-cultural curriculum framework (Carr, 2001) and in Northern Italy, the Reggio Emilia approach (Edwards *et al.*, 1998). What is distinctive about these two approaches is that they adopt a 'consultative' approach (Soler and Miller, 2003: 66) to learning. This means that the learning goals are effectively negotiated and agreed through a shared approach involving the child (and his/her community) and practitioner, rather than being decided solely by the setting.

You will no doubt be familiar with the idea of Learning Journeys or Learning Stories in your own practice. This pedagogical practice originates from Margaret

Carr's work that has become the mainstay of the Te Whāriki approach. The intention of the Learning Story from Carr's perspective is to provide a document that situates learning as a process, and one that demonstrates how children's involvement with learning in a collaborative context can help to develop their working theories (Hedges, 2011) and demonstrate the complexity of their thinking. Such an approach also acknowledges that learning involves the development of a repertoire of dispositions, rather than just knowledge and skills (Carr, 2001). If you refer to the Development Matters (Early Education, 2012) document, and the work of Nancy Stewart (Early Education, 2012), it is clear how Carr's work has directly influenced the notion of 'characteristics of effective learning'.

The use of pedagogical documentation to make the learning process visible is also very evident in the Reggio Emilia approach. A significant principle of this pedagogic approach is the sense of collective responsibility for children's learning. It is based on the premise that no one person can verify knowledge about a child's learning, it is something that has to be negotiated between all parties – including the child and family (Forman and Fyfe, 1998). Documentation in this context is not a child observation tool that can be used to measure development. Instead, it is as Moss (2007: 15) states, a tool for 'resisting' the dominant discourses related to universality that seem to be apparent in English Early Years childhood policy. This sense of resistance means that decisions about children's learning take a more collaborative and democratic approach to practice. The notion of democracy is particularly important here, as it suggests that no one single person makes a decision about what is valued in the learning process – it is a negotiated process. This approach, which recognises the individual child and the many relationships she has – with children, family, carers and educators – stands in stark contrast to the English Early Years assessment process which tends to be linear and one way. (A single observer observes, judges and records without any necessary reference to the child or others who know the child.)

Several countries, particularly the USA, the United Kingdom and in parts of Scandinavia, have attempted to replicate the documentation process within their own curriculum practices. What seems to have emerged from studies that have explored the practice of 'transplanting' such culturally specific approaches (Soler and Miller, 2003) into a different cultural settings is that it is in fact problematic. The reasons for this seem to be three-fold. First; the desire to replicate an approach in its entirety in other cultural contexts is unrealistic due to the deeply embedded cultural values and principles that underpin the original phenomenon (Stremmel, 2012). Second; interpretations of the purpose and value of documenting learning can be contradictory (Luff, 2012). Third; political pressure related to accountability seems to have led to a technical and mechanistic approach to assessment and documentation and a loss of practitioner confidence in adopting a practice that fits with personal beliefs (Cottle and Alexander, 2012). Therefore, for many practitioners who wish to adopt an approach to assessment and documentation that reflects a more sociocultural perspective, it seems this is not necessarily straightforward.

The next section provides an insight into some of the personal challenges practitioners have encountered regarding how to reconcile their own values and beliefs with policy expectations. They illustrate how the expectation to adopt certain mechanistic approaches to assessment have led to missed opportunities to work with children in a manner that values their working theories, their learning dispositions and their individual interests. Consequently the voice of the child was sometimes not included in the assessment and documentation process.

Think about how you document and assess learning in your own setting:

■   What is the purpose of documentation in your setting?
■   Do you use it to document learning *outcomes*, or the learning *process*?
■   Who contributes to the assessment process in your setting?

Case study 2.1: Rebecca's story

This case study provides a useful context to illustrate assessment and documenting practices from two perspectives. Two significant events are captured in this case study, told by Rebecca, the practitioner. The first event provides an illustration of practice from a sociocultural perspective. This happened *outside* the nursery. The second event illustrates some of the tensions that practitioners are faced with when trying to reconcile their own values and beliefs with policy expectations. This event occurred *inside* the nursery.

During morning play today a group of children decided to pretend that the playground climbing frame was their rocket which could take them into space. The nursery theme of the month is space and the children had been drawing their very own rockets with wax crayons earlier that morning. The three children playing on the rocket appeared to really enjoy jumping on and off the rocket and tried to get the other children to join in their game.

Sarah (aged 4) was watching the three children play from the play house; she appeared to enjoy watching them. However, she rarely plays on the slide because it gets so busy. I encouraged her to go and join in and she eventually climbed up the slide holding on as the children pretended the rocket was flying through space. Sarah shouted, 'Bye, mummy, see you when we get back.' Sarah was smiling and screaming with her peers as they used the wheel on the climbing frame to steer the rocket. The children all cheered when they landed on 'the moon' and got off to explore what they could see. Sarah pretended she had

(Continued)

(Continued)

space boots on and walked around the playground slowly, while other children stayed on the rocket. Sarah picked up a bean bag and told me she had found some 'moon rock', saying, 'Wow, can you see what I've found?' as she put it in her pocket.

One of the practitioners on playground duty announced to the children that they had ten minutes left before they needed to tidy up and suggested they should get the rocket back home. Sarah ran towards the rocket ready to do their blast off countdown which they had practised every morning. She said: 'Quickly, guys, before it goes, we need to hurry!' as she held hands with another child running towards the rocket.

Before Sarah had reached the slide, her key person came to the door and shouted for Sarah to come inside, saying 'You need to come into the nursery now, Sarah, to draw a picture on the computer.' The key person told the practitioner on duty that she was lacking an observation of her 'computer skills' in her profile. She was concerned that the Reception teacher from her new school was coming to visit that week, and she needed to have 'evidence' in order to prove Sarah could use the computer efficiently. Sarah went straight inside when her name was called and sat at the computer for ten minutes. As she finished the drawing programme, her peers came in from playtime.

Outside the nursery

In this example the practitioners who were situated outside were endeavouring to make use of the different 'working theories' that the children had brought to their game. Hedges (2011) provides a useful explanation of working theories that can be applied to this situation. She defines working theories as 'creative links between existing and new experiences and thinking in children's knowledge building in areas of deep interest. These links [are] facilitated by opportunities for children to share, test or explore ideas' (ibid.: 273).

The working theories in this scenario were based on the children's developing knowledge that the moon is located beyond their immediate environment, and can only be reached by travelling on a space rocket. They knew that a rocket needed to be 'launched' and that once they arrived at their destination it could be an exciting place to explore the contrasting landscape. What was also significant in this case study was that the practitioners had tuned into the children's game, and their interactions with the children were orientated around the children's narratives. For example, the practitioner used the context of the game to remind the children it would soon be tidy-up time. She encouraged the children to return to their rocket in order to get home in time. The interactions between the children and practitioners in the first half of this example seem to suggest the practitioners were comfortable with adopting a sociocultural approach that values a more 'relational pedagogy' (Papatheodrou and Moyles, 2009: 4) than the interaction between Sarah and her key person later on in the case study. A relational pedagogy is concerned with the child and the practitioner embarking on a learning journey together, where the outcomes are not an endpoint – but a starting point for further discovery.

For these particular practitioners, becoming 'lost in the moment' of a learning situation was something they seemed to value. Further insight into this is provided by other practitioners' perspectives that were shared in a focus group discussion: 'Sometimes you are so engaged with the children that you don't write it down, or you have to stop the play so that you can write it down ... then you lose the momentum of the play.'

At this point it is useful to stop and reflect on the idea of evidencing and documenting the learning moment. How might Rebecca have documented the learning that was taking place? The event was clearly significant to her, as she was able to recall some key moments that illustrated her own values and beliefs. If her setting used Learning Stories in the way that Carr intended, then the 'story' may well have been captured by, not only Rebecca, but the other practitioner, Sarah and her peers, and her parents. By including the perspectives of others in the documentation process, there is a greater likelihood that the interpretation of the learning moment is one that is an authentic representation of the situation, as it involves a range of perspectives. By sharing the Learning Story with Sarah and a family member, Rebecca may have gained further insight into Sarah's interests, and the motivation behind the rocket ship narrative that had emerged from the outside game. It may have allowed Rebecca to understand that Sarah is not necessarily reluctant to play on the slide in the nursery because it is too 'busy', but actually because when at home, she prefers to play at the park with her older brother, as he is able to help her climb the steps to the top of the slide.

Let's now imagine how the practitioners might have used this event as evidence to document learning. Practitioners are required to make judgements about levels of development using the Early Years outcomes document (DfE, 2014). Look at Table 2.1 and consider where you would have located Sarah in relation to 'Making Relationships'. It would seem reasonable to suggest that due to the elaborate nature of the rocket ship narrative, Sarah was demonstrating the typical behaviour of a child in the 30–50 months age range. Taking into account Sarah's age, then this would suggest that she is developing at the rate that is expected.

Now let's consider an alternative perspective. It was noted by the practitioner at the beginning of the case study that Sarah was usually reticent to join in play. Imagine if the practitioners had not spent time endeavouring to understand the play they were observing, and had not joined in with the game. The judgements made about Sarah's development could well have been based on previous assumptions about her. Consequently the observation may have

TABLE 2.1 Early Years outcomes document

3. Personal, social and emotional development	Making relationships
Age	Typical behaviour
16–26 months	• Plays alongside others • Uses a familiar adult as a secure base from which to explore independently in new environments, e.g. ventures away to play and interact with others, but returns for a cuddle or reassurance if becomes anxious • Plays cooperatively with a familiar adult, e.g. rolling a ball back and forth
22–36 months	• Interested in others' play and starting to join in • Seeks out others to share experiences • Shows affection and concern for people who are special to them • May form a special friendship with another child
30–50 months	• Can play in a group, extending and elaborating play ideas, e.g. building up a role-play activity with other children • Initiates play, offering cues to peers to join them • Keeps play going by responding to what others are saying or doing • Demonstrates friendly behaviour, initiating conversations and forming good relationships with peers and familiar adults

Source: Adapted from DfE (2014).

placed her in an earlier developmental band. Here we see an example of Carr's 'deficit' model of assessment. Sarah would no longer be seen as the child who is imaginative and enjoys sustained play with her peers. The original perception of her as a shy, quiet child may well have been confirmed by the observation, and she would be described as a child who was not demonstrating the 'typical' social skills that were expected for her age.

To illustrate this point further, it is useful to refer to the experiences of two practitioners in the focus group who shared their experiences of what sort of evidence was perceived as valid in their own setting.

When we write a summative report, we have to have enough evidence to prove that the child is at a certain stage in Development Matters. If there is not sufficient evidence, then they are 'working towards'.

If you have evidence of a child that has done something in an 'older' box than their age, then you are challenged as to whether that is appropriate.

Such practices seem to fit with the mechanistic approach to assessment, which was discussed earlier, and fit with the idea of learning being a singular process, that occurs in isolation from the social and cultural context in which it is happening. There is a danger here that practitioners may be inclined to adopt an approach that involves 'watching and waiting' (Wood and Attfield, 2005) for significant moments that can be recorded in order to match children's learning behaviours to predetermined stages. There is also an inference that such practices do not allow for opportunities for pedagogic interactions that enable sustained shared thinking (the benefits of which were illustrated in Case study 2.1). How can a practitioner gain a sense of a child's interests and learning dispositions if they only wait for desired behaviours to occur? As Drummond (2012: 49) argues, adopting this approach means that there is a danger that adults look for what they expect to see, at the expense of picking up on the glimpses of unintentional learning that children may hint at in their play. This could well have been the situation if the practitioners in the case study had adopted a 'watch and wait' approach.

There is something significant here that needs to be considered, and that is the extent to which practitioners translate theory into their practice. Katz (1999) suggests that this may be due to a misinterpretation of relevant theory that forces practitioners to adopt a literal approach: 'Believing that children "construct their own knowledge," some adults do little more than set out a variety of activities that children enjoy, while studiously avoiding formal instruction in basic academic skills' (ibid.: 2).

An analysis of the events that took place inside the nursery builds on the notion of assessment as a mechanistic and technical procedure.

Inside the nursery

In the final part of the Case study, we see Sarah's key person calling her inside to complete an activity that has been pre-determined by the practitioner. There is a sense that the learning opportunity has been 'manufactured' in order to produce evidence for an aspect of learning that was missing in her profile. This situation suggests there is a different relationship between the child and practitioner inside the nursery, compared to outside. While Sarah was outside, there was a consensus between the children and practitioners regarding the purpose of the play. This suggests an equitable distribution of power between the child and the adult – Sarah's identity as a learner was seen as confident and competent. However, when Sarah came inside the nursery, the power quickly shifted to the adult, and Sarah effectively 'lost' her voice. The adult was now controlling the learning agenda and determined what was deemed a valuable learning experience. Canella and Viruru (2004: 91) would argue that the practice of making 'assumptions' about progress along a developmental continuum is a way of maintaining hierarchal levels between the adult and child and legitimising control over children. Therefore, the requirement to measure and judge progress potentially overrides any desire to authentically adopt a more sociocultural perspective in supporting children's learning that attempts to include the child's voice in the learning process.

It would be easy to pursue this discussion as a criticism of the practitioner, and question why she seemed to have no regard for the events that had just occurred outside. This is not the intention of this chapter. What I hope Case study 2.1 illustrates is the tensions that practitioners are experiencing when trying to adopt an approach to assessment that fits with two competing demands. I have previously referred to this as a 'game of two halves'. Practitioners are charged with findings ways of mediating and implementing policy expectations that seem to advocate two competing purposes to assessment practice. One is concerned with the assessment of children against a measurable set of outcomes at a set point in time to assure readiness for the next stage of their education. Yet, on the other hand, they are also trying to support children's learning and development as an on-going learning journey that is reflective of the culture and practice of the community in which the setting serves. Documenting learning from this perspective is seen as a joint endeavour in order to gain a reliable and valid picture of the child's learning characteristics – not just predetermined knowledge and skills. A fundamental feature of this approach is that it *includes* rather than *excludes* the child's voice.

So there appears to be a genuine tension for practitioners here between the valuing of a sociocultural perspective and a suggestion that when a curriculum framework commands a greater level of prescription, and subject knowledge, as identified in the EYFS framework (DfE, 2014), this may lead to an inappropriate pedagogy. Jordan (2009: 41) also cautions a subscription to 'school-type' programmes, where there is a 'mistaken belief' that an early introduction to formal activities is the best preparation for later success in school. In this case study, this seems to be happening. The practitioner seems concerned that she has insufficient evidence of Sarah's capabilities in using the mouse on a computer – a skill that is valued in a school setting. By setting up an activity for her to complete, the end product (a 'drawing') is evidence that she has accomplished the desired competence. This would also satisfy the teacher who was coming to visit the setting that Sarah is developing the necessary skills to be 'ready' for school.

Was there another way that such information could be gleaned? If we return to the original purpose of Learning Stories from the Te Whāriki approach, then the documentation of children's learning is not concerned with making an assessment of a fixed point in time, but is more accumulative. More importantly, parents are authentically involved in the creation of learning stories in order to gain an understanding of the funds of knowledge children bring with them to the setting. Such practice is based on the premise that effective joint involvement episodes require practitioners to understand a child's unique sociocultural and historical background. Hedges (2010: 39) exemplifies funds of knowledge as the informal learning that takes place in the home environment, which generates further informal learning opportunities in a formal setting. Research by Riojas-Cortez (2001) concluded that:

> Funds of knowledge tell teachers what children know and are capable of doing. This is important because it allows the teachers to become an observer of children, thus discovering what these youngsters know and their way of life.

Hedges (2010) discusses the importance of the practitioner endeavouring to build authentic relationships with parents as a vehicle for gaining such understanding. It is interesting to note that the statutory EYFS framework states: 'Practitioners must discuss with parents and/or carers how the summary of development can be used to support learning at home' (DfE, 2014: 11). In order to truly value a child's funds of knowledge, it would perhaps be equally as desirable to add a further statement that requires 'opportunities for parents to discuss how learning at home can be used to support learning in the setting should be available'. In a setting that adopts such an approach, there would be no need to manufacture a learning opportunity to gain 'evidence'. Information about a child's interests and capabilities at home would be shared. This would provide the starting point to build upon in the setting.

Implications for practice

What seems to be emerging from this case study is that practitioners feel they are required to work within the parameters of specific systems for evidencing learning. Dahlberg and Moss (2005) refer to such required knowledge and systems as technologies of 'normalization'. This then creates the image of the Early Years practitioner as a 'technician' (Moss, 2007: 35). Moss defines a technician's role as someone who applies a 'set of defined technologies through regulated processes to produce pre-specified and measurable outcomes'. Technicians use tools, and within this context, observation is the tool. But the lens through which the observation is viewed can determine what is seen as important (see Drummond, 2012).

As this case study illustrates, this can sometimes result in competing interpretations of a child's learning capabilities and developmental characteristics. For Sarah, this could mean that if a sociocultural perspective to the assessment and documentation process was adopted, she would be described as a confident and capable learner who demonstrated a range of learning dispositions that showed her as able to think creatively and engage in episodes of highly involved learning. Alternatively, by adopting an approach that situates learning along a developmental continuum where observed behaviours are matched against a hierarchy of skills, Sarah may well have been perceived as a child who possessed deficiencies in her development. Such deficiencies would serve as the basis for further intervention by the practitioners in order to successfully remedy problems.

It seems reasonable to suggest therefore, that the adoption of a sociocultural approach to assessment may provide greater opportunities for inclusive practice. A sociocultural approach to assessment places a greater emphasis on the process of learning, rather than development. So rather than our observations being used as a tool to help assess development, they become a tool that is used to help document learning. Now that you have reached the end of this chapter, I hope you will understand the fundamental differences in these two approaches.

Using observation as a tool to document learning means that an observation is used as a starting point, rather than an end point. An observation serves as a starting point for collaborative dialogue between the practitioner, the child and his or her parent/carer. Sharing the observation allows opportunities for all parties to share their insight and interpretation of the documented moment. A child or parent may provide a different reading of the moment. This is because they will be sharing with you the 'funds of knowledge' (Hedges, 2011) from their unique social and cultural background that you may not necessarily know about. You now have a richer and more authentic insight into the child's life outside your setting. Some of your original ideas about the child may well have be overturned as a result of this collaborative venture. However, the implications for your practice are now very significant, because when you plan learning experiences to support children's development, you have an informed base on which to establish a learning context that is inclusive of the child's voice.

In addition to this, there are also implications for the ways in which you interact with the child. Now when you play alongside the child in a joint endeavour, your understanding of the funds of knowledge he or she is bringing to the play venture will be very significant. You may have a better understanding as to why a child is reluctant to do something, or why he or she seems to be particularly fixated with a certain toy or narrative to a game. You will no longer see this as a 'deficit' to their learning, but you will understand why this type of play is happening, and how you can tune into it in order to support the learning journey. What was previously seen as problematic may now be seen as a unique learning characteristic.

Conclusion

The aim of this chapter was to explore three key questions in relation to assessment practice. It seems that the purpose of assessment and documentation in Early Years settings can be dualistic and not always complementary. A key reason for this is that the current curriculum frameworks that practitioners are required to adopt advocate competing purposes. Practitioners tell stories that imply that, on the one hand, they are required to use assessment as part of their technical duty to measure children's development. This approach sits within a developmental psychological tradition that assumes there is a 'typical' child. Such a view does not take account of the social, cultural and political factors that can influence development.

On the other hand, assessment is also seen as a key pedagogic strategy to celebrate the 'unique child'. By observing children in their self-directed play, and joining them in sustained episodes, the practitioner is able to gain an insight into the child's social, cultural and historical heritage. From this they can describe children's learning characteristics, such as their dispositions to learning and their working theories. These provide the basis for appropriate intervention that enables the child to participate in rich learning experiences that value their *potential*, rather what they can do in just one fixed point in time. The consequences for this are that not only is the child's voice included, but learning is seen as a collaborative venture that can enhance rather than hinder learning and development.

The process of trying to assess development, *and* document learning is not necessarily a straightforward endeavour. Yet in order for our assessment practice to include, rather than exclude a child's voice, it is an important element of practice that we should carefully consider.

References

Burman, E. (2008) *Deconstructing Developmental Psychology*, 2nd edn. Hove: Psychology Press.

Canella, G. and Viruru, R. (2004) *Childhood and Postcolonization: Power, Education and Contemporary Practice*. London: RoutledgeFalmer.

Carr, M. (2001) *Assessment in Early Childhood Settings: Learning Stories*. London: Sage.

Cottle, M. and Alexander, A. (2012) Quality in Early Years settings: government, research and practitioners' perspectives. *British Educational Research Journal*, 38(4): 635–54. http://dx.doi.org/10.1080/01411926.2011.571661.

Dahlberg, G. and Moss, P. (2005) *Ethics and Politics in Early Childhood Education*. London: RoutledgeFalmer. Retrieved from: eBook Collection (EBSCOhost).

DfE (2014) *Statutory Framework for the Early Years Foundation Stage*. Available at: www.gov.uk/government/uploads/system/uploads/attachment_data/file/299391/DFE-00337-2014.pdf (accessed 15 January 2015).

DfE/SCAA (1996) *Desirable Learning Outcomes for Children's Learning on Entering Compulsory Education*. London: DfE/SCAA.

Drummond, M. J. (2012) *Assessing Children's Learning*. Classic edn. London: Routledge.

Early Education (2012) *Development Matters in the Early Years Foundation Stage*. London: Early Education. Available at: www.education.gov.uk/publications/eOrderingDownload/Development-Matters.pdf (accessed 3 April 2013).

Edwards, C., Gandini, L. and Forman, G. (eds) (1998) *The Hundred Languages of Children: The Reggio Emilia Approach. Advanced Reflections*. Greenwich, CT: Ablex.

Forman, G. and Fyfe, B. (1998) Negotiated learning through design, documentation, and discourse. In C. Edwards, L. Gandini and G. Forman (eds) *The Hundred Languages of Children: The Reggio Emilia Approach. Advanced Reflections*. Greenwich, CT: Ablex, pp. 239–60.

Hedges, H. (2010) Whose goals and interests? The interface of children's play and teachers' pedagogical practices. In L. Brooker and S. Edwards (eds) *Engaging Play*. Maidenhead: Open University Press, pp. 25–38.

Hedges, H. (2011) Connecting 'snippets of knowledge': teachers' understandings of the concept of working theories. *Early Years: An International Journal of Research and Development*, 31(3): 271.

Jordan, B. (2009) Scaffolding learning and constructing understandings. In A. Anning, J. Cullen and M. Fleer (eds) *Early Childhood Education: Society and Culture*. London: Sage, pp. 39–52.

Katz, L.G. (1999) Curriculum disputes in early childhood education. *Eric Digest*, December. Available at: http://ecap.crc.illinois.edu/eecearchive/digests/1999/katz99b.pdf (accessed 24 March 2012).

Luff, P. (2012) Challenging assessment. In T. Papatheodrou and J. Moyles (eds) *Cross-Cultural Perspectives on Early Childhood*. London: Sage.

Moss, P. (2007) Bringing politics into the nursery: early childhood education as a democratic practice. *European Early Childhood Education Research Journal*, 15(1): 5–20. doi: 10.1080/13502930601046620.

Papatheodrou, T. and Moyles, J. (2009) *Learning Together in the Early Years: Exploring Relational Pedagogy*. London: Routledge.

Riojas-Cortez, M. (2001) Preschoolers' funds of knowledge displayed through sociodramatic play episodes in a bilingual classroom. *Early Childhood Education Journal*, 29(1). Available at: http://springerlink3.metapress.com/content/j7747917871554r8/fulltext.pdf (accessed 1 April 2012).

Rogoff, B. (2003) *The Cultural Nature of Human Development*. New York: Oxford University Press.

Siraj-Blatchford, I. and Manni, L. (2008) Would you like to tidy up now?: an analysis of adult questioning in the English Foundation Stage. *Early Years: An International Journal of Research and Development*, 28(1): 5–22.

Siraj-Blatchford, I., Sylva, K., Muttock, S., Gilden, R. and Bell, D. (2002) *Researching Effective Pedagogy in the Early Years*. Research report no. 356. London: DfES.

Siraj-Blatchford, I., Sylva, K., Taggart, B., Sammons, P., Melhuish, E. and Elliot, K. (2003) *The Effective Provision of Pre-School Education (EPPE) Project*. Technical Paper 10. *Intensive Case Studies of Practice across the Foundation Stage*. London. DfES and Institute of Education, University of London.

Soler, J. and Miller, L. (2003) The struggle for early childhood curricula: a comparison of the English Foundation Stage curriculum, Te Whäriki and Reggio Emilia. *International Journal of Early Years Education*, 11(1): 57–68. http://dx.doi.org/10.1080/0966976032000066091.

Stremmel, A. J. (2012) A situated framework: the Reggio experience. In N. File, J. J. Mueller and D. B Wisenski (eds) *Curriculum in Early Childhood Education: Re-Examined, Rediscovered, Renewed*. London: Routledge, pp. 133–45.

Wood, E. and Attfield, J. (2005) *Play, Learning and the Early Childhood Curriculum*. London: Sage.

3

Creating an inclusive environment for supporting children with English as an Additional Language

Sharron Galley

The aims of this chapter are:

- To explore inclusion and English as an Additional Language (EAL)
- To examine language acquisition
- To analyse some strategies for supporting children with EAL and their inclusion in school and Early Years settings.

Introduction

This chapter will draw upon established theories, research articles and my own primary research in two different primary school settings to consider strategies that practitioners and teachers can adopt to include and support children who are learning English as an Additional Language (EAL). Teaching children with EAL requires us to be reflective of our practice and to be knowledgeable of the pedagogies involved in order to implement the strategies well. Two case studies will be included in the chapter which are based upon two primary schools in the north-west of England. Advice and reflections from the Head Teacher (Teacher A) of one of the schools, a large multicultural setting, and the Special Educational Needs Co-ordinator (SENCO) and class teacher from the other school (Teacher B) which has predominantly white British children, will also be included. Murakami (2008: 266) describes a setting with few EAL children as a 'low incidence' context and explains that due to the low numbers of EAL children within these schools, the settings have difficulties responding effectively 'to their social, linguistic and academic needs'. When working as a class teacher in a primary school with predominantly white, British children, I saw the challenges that staff faced when a non-English-speaking child arrived in their class because inclusive practices were not firmly embedded within their everyday practice. Therefore, strategies to create an inclusive learning environment where all children's language skills can be developed will be explored in this chapter.

Neaum (2012) explores the idea of there being two different language needs for children who have EAL. The first is that the child should know that their home language is valued; the second that the child needs to learn English in order to access the curriculum. Both of these needs must be considered carefully by practitioners in order for them to produce careful planning that goes some way to meeting these needs. Settings need to build partnerships with the families of EAL children in order for children to achieve. How this can be achieved will also be discussed in greater depth.

Case study 3.1: Challenges of welcoming two new children with EAL into a Reception class

Teacher B is a Reception teacher in an inner-city school where 91 per cent of the children are from white British backgrounds. Although the number of children with EAL is small in comparison with most inner city primaries, the school numbers show that the percentage is growing steadily year on year.

In Teacher B's class, there are 30 children in total (21 of them are boys), 14 children in the class are on the SEN register for varying needs, including autism and behavioural problems and there are five children with EAL, two of whom joined the school recently speaking no English at all. These two children do not receive any external specific language support within the class.

Teacher B and the classroom support staff have employed various strategies to ensure that the two new children have settled into the school, and five months on, the children are able to speak basic English at a level where they can be understood when they are talking to their friends and staff and can understand most of the teaching that goes on in the class.

Initial aims for the two new children are:

- to settle into school life so they feel happy and secure enough to engage in learning;
- to understand the routines and expectations of the class.

Discussion

- What strategies could Teacher B and the classroom staff use to ensure a stable transition for these two children?
- What challenges might the staff in the class face during this process and how could they plan for these challenges?

In your career as an Early Years practitioner, you will, at some point, work with children who do not speak English as their first language. Depending on where you work, you may work with very few children learning EAL, or you may work with whole cohorts. Nevertheless, your setting needs to be prepared in such a way that all children's language skills can be developed in positive and creative ways through your inclusive practices and environments. I would argue that a 'model' setting that has effective, embedded practices to support children with EAL should not look very different from other effective settings that do not have children with EAL. All children's speaking and listening skills need to be developed in their settings, as Hartshorne (2009) reports that up to 80 per cent of children enter school at the age of 5 with impoverished speech and poor listening skills. A lack of speaking and listening skills leads to poor achievement in literacy and numeracy as the child gets older; therefore creating Early Years environments that promote good speaking and listening is vital. If we also consider that now more children who do not speak English are entering settings, then it becomes clear how important and necessary it is for practitioners to know how to create an inclusive environment that develops language skills within the early years.

Pim (2010: 6) defines children learning English as an Additional Language (EAL) as being 'individuals nurtured from birth in another language where English has been acquired subsequently'. In the UK, the number of school-aged children who are learning EAL has doubled since 1997, and 1 in 6 primary school-aged children (612,160) do not have English as their first language (NALDIC, 2013). Therefore, teachers and practitioners need to scrutinise their practice more than ever before to ensure that these children and their families are supported effectively in order for every child to succeed. The needs of children with EAL differ enormously due to their varying levels of second language acquisition and therefore settings need to be prepared to offer differentiated support. However, support can be expensive for schools to implement and the issues surrounding funding for children with EAL can be complicated and contentious.

The NASUWT teachers' union produced the *Ethnic Minority Achievement: Quality Matters* report in 2012. Their research showed that due to the UK Coalition Government's cuts in public spending, 65 per cent of school leaders stated that they could not sufficiently meet the demands of EAL children. With school leaders feeling the strain of government cuts on their budgets and specialised support being expensive to implement, it is important for teachers, practitioners and students to be aware of the practical measures that can be put into place within their setting to support EAL children to access and enjoy the curriculum. These strategies and discussion points to promote reflection will be explored later in this chapter.

Overview of first and second language acquisition theories

There are established and differing theories as to how children acquire their first language, with some theorists stating that children are born with a natural predisposition for learning speech and grammar (Chomsky's 1957 Nativist Theory), while others argue that language is something that children mimic and learn through positive reinforcement (Skinner, 1957). These theories, though often at odds with one another, add a great deal to our knowledge of children's first language acquisition and therefore it is important to reflect on how practitioners use these theories to practically support inclusive practice in speaking and listening.

- Consider a child you know who is beginning to speak their first language. How are they encouraged to talk by the adults around them? Which theories can you identify?
- What have you noticed about your speech when you are talking to a child who is beginning to learn their first language?
- How do you adapt your language and why do you think you do this?

Hall, Smith and Wicaksono (2011: 1) explain that there are two types of scholar who explore the ways in which children acquire their second language. The first type is concerned with contributing to 'our understanding of human language and human development' rather than resolving the challenges that face the bilingual child; whereas the second type of scholar takes a more 'problem-solving' approach and is concerned with finding practical solutions to help learners and their teachers. Due to the nature of this chapter being in essence a discussion of practical methods to aid the inclusion of EAL children, the second scholarly approach will be adopted here, though it will begin with an overview of the main second language acquisition (SLA) theories.

As with first language acquisition theories, Chomsky's theory of grammatical competence has had a strong influence on the way that we understand how children acquire a second or even third additional language. His 'Universal Grammar' theory explains how children learn phrases and new vocabulary relatively effortlessly due to the brain being wired specifically to accommodate grammar. Similarly, Dulay and Burt (1974, 1975, cited in Krashen 2009: 12) report from their research that children acquiring a second language (irrespective of their first language) show a 'natural order' for grammatical morphemes though the order of this acquisition differs from their first language.

Krashen (2009: 10), in his influential research on SLA, presents different hypotheses of SLA, the first being 'The Acquisition–Learning Distinction'. This hypothesis concerns itself with an adult's SLA, and he explains that there are two distinct ways of learning a second language: (1) language acquisition (a similar 'if not identical' way to how children learn their first language); and (2) language learning, where the 'rules' and grammar of a language are consciously learned.

Krashen (ibid.: 10) explains that children learn a second language the same way in which they learn their first – this is through the subconscious process of language acquisition where an individual is not aware that they are actually learning a language but are 'picking it up'. Currently, in Early Years settings and schools in this country, the ways in which practitioners will aid a child's second language acquisition will vary according to the needs of the children. However, it is usually the case that children entering an Early Years setting with little or no English will not receive formal instruction in English, but will be included in the play and learning opportunities within the setting in the hope that the child will indeed 'pick it up'. The Office for Standards in Education (OFSTED, 2009: 5) suggests that 'pupils learn more quickly when socialising and interacting with their peers who speak English fluently and can provide good language and learning role models'. This statement echoes the scaffolding theories of Vygotsky (1978) and Bruner (1978) who advocate that a more knowledgeable other is essential to children's learning.

Krashen's research also showed that a second language can be learned consciously through formal instruction. Research has shown varying degrees of success when children are taught language formally in additional classes either in school or in separate weekend/evening classes. Brière (1978) studied the effects of SLA formal language tuition on Mexican children and found that attendance at a village school to learn a second language (Spanish in this case) was the main predictor of successful language acquisition, due to there being few opportunities to speak meaningful Spanish outside of the village school. Interestingly, the other predictors were the father's level of Spanish and the parents' need to speak Spanish. Clark (n.d.: 184) also discusses the actual need to speak a language as being significant in SLA and explains: 'Young children will become bilingual when there is a real need to communicate in two languages and will just as quickly revert to monolingualism when there is no longer a need.' This highlights one of the reasons that children may seem to acquire a second language so effortlessly; they need to speak a particular language in order to communicate with friends, and have their needs met by those around them. This is further supported by Tabors (1997: 81) who reports that a child needs to be 'sufficiently motivated' in order to learn a new language.

In SLA research there are many models that describe the stages through which children learn a second language (Tabors, 1997; Pim, 2010). These models, though often worded differently, will usually refer to similar stages. One stage that the theorists seem to agree on is that there is always a 'silent stage' though there is disagreement as to whether this is always the first stage. Teachers in both the schools where the research for this chapter was carried out have noticed that children who enter the setting with no (or very little) English may be silent for many weeks – months in some cases. Krashen (2009) acknowledged that in formal language classes, adults and children are not allowed a 'silent period' which could add support for a second language to be learned through an 'acquisition' method rather than through formal learning. Haynes'

(2005) model will be discussed here as this is one that could be used practically as a means of assessment when working within an educational setting.

When learning a second language, Haynes (2005) explains that children pass through five different stages, though she acknowledges that the time spent at each stage will differ greatly. Each stage is clearly defined and it is a useful exercise to use observations of the child and conversations with adults who know the child well to decipher which stage a child is at in order to plan support and next steps.

Haynes' five stages of second language acquisition are:

1. Pre-production: the silent period.
2. Early production: one or two word phrases.
3. Speech emergence: simple phrases and sentences.
4. Intermediate fluency: beginning to use more complex sentences and questions.
5. Advanced fluency: the child will be near-native at this stage.

While it is believed that children may learn conversational levels of English that are on a par with their English classmates within two years, Cummins (1981) argues that an academic level of English will only be attained after four to nine years of learning a language. However, current government additional funding for children with EAL is only available to them for the first three years of their compulsory education (DfE, 2012a) regardless of whether they have caught up with their English-speaking peers or not. Therefore, as funds are only available for the first three years of a child's school-life, teachers have a huge responsibility to ensure that these children have gained a sufficient amount of academic English in order to achieve and access the curriculum alongside their native English-speaking peers.

- Consider a child you know who is learning to speak English as an additional language. How are they learning to speak English?
- Is this through formal English instruction or through play-based learning opportunities in the setting?
- What are the benefits of the child learning English in this way and what do you consider to be the limitations?
- What examples of language acquisition theories do you see happening in practice? For example, do you notice children passing through certain stages of development?

Main challenges and strategies

The rising numbers of children with EAL entering mainstream settings mean that all staff and senior leaders must reflect upon their provision in order to meet the needs of the children in their care. Reflective practice is a key driver behind educational change and undoubtedly teachers are the agents who are 'indispensable' in making these changes happen (Fullan and Hargreaves, 1992: 635). In order to gain insights into some of the challenges and opportunities that teaching staff face when welcoming a child with EAL into their setting, two experienced senior leaders from mainstream primary schools in the north-west of England were consulted and many of the following discussions reflect their advice for positive inclusion of EAL children.

There are a few settings, particularly in rural areas, who do not have children with EAL in their care. However, the number of children with EAL in a setting can vary greatly from having very few – sometimes just one or two – to upwards of 95 per cent of children on the roll. This obviously has an impact on what support is available and provided, however, even if children with EAL are not enrolled in a setting, procedures should be in place for when EAL children do enrol in order to facilitate a smooth transition.

Induction into a setting

Teacher A, who is a Head Teacher of an urban primary school where most of the children have (or are learning) EAL, asserts that a vital element of ensuring good inclusive practice is maintaining consistency of procedures. This not only means that the staff are fully aware of their responsibilities, but the children who are entering the setting (and their families) feel confident that the school will support them. One area of practice where consistency is particularly necessary is when a new child enters the setting. This can be an unsettling time for a child who may recently have arrived in the country and, therefore, they need to be treated as sensitively as possible. Consequently, most local education authorities produce guidance for maintained settings to inform staff of the induction period and how best to manage this important transition for the child and their family. The Bradford Metropolitan Borough Council (2014: 3) is experienced in managing schools with a high migrant population and advise that new arrivals (this could mean to the setting and/ or the country) must be valued for the richness of the diversity, experience and expertise that they bring to their new setting and therefore their needs should be met through 'different forms of representation of their language, culture and identity'.

The practitioners consulted for this chapter have provided their insights into managing the induction of children who speak little or no English into their settings. The flow chart (Figure 3.1) reflects the strategies of Bradford District Borough Council, and the consulted practitioners, to show a detailed and practical guide on possible strategies that settings can adopt when inducting a child.

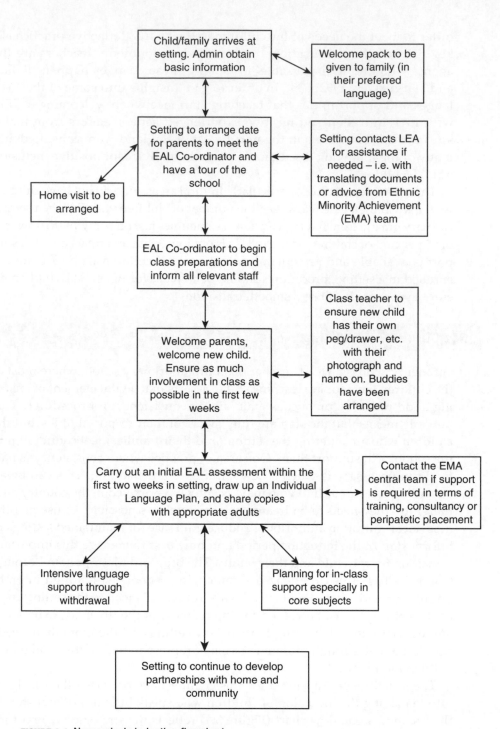

FIGURE 3.1 New arrivals induction flowchart.

Consider your own setting or a setting you know well. Drawing on your professional experiences, consider how you prioritise and manage the induction process and develop your own flow chart with colleagues to ensure a consistent approach.

Assessment

'Learners of EAL have, on average, lower levels of attainment than pupils whose first language is English' (Overington, 2012: 1). Therefore, assessment, early intervention and target setting are crucial in supporting a child to learn English and access the curriculum.

After the initial induction and settling-in period, and as soon as it is reasonable to do so, it is essential (and a statutory requirement) that the child is assessed in order to establish their current levels and to plan next steps in their learning. Within the Early Years, when assessing children with EAL, observational assessments are the most effective form to take (DfE, 2012b) and in these early observations it is important to note that the children may likely be going through their 'silent period' of language acquisition when they first enter the setting. Teacher B explained that it is vital that staff give the children time to settle in (for them to observe the class, their new classmates and the routines) and to be prepared for a child to be silent for several weeks – up to six weeks and longer in some cases. This teacher had noticed that older children, particularly in Key Stage 1 and Key Stage 2 often feel embarrassed that they cannot communicate in English and therefore strategies must be in place to encourage their language development, such as a 'buddying' system to support the child through this period.

The *Early Years Foundation Stage Profile Handbook* (EYFSP) (DfE, 2013) provides specific guidance for practitioners assessing children who are learning English as an additional language and it describes the three aspects that are specific to these children as:

1. development in their home language;
2. development across areas of learning (assessed in their home language);
3. development of English.

It is important for practitioners to note that all Early Learning Goals, with the exception of 'Communication and Language' and 'Literacy' may be assessed in the child's home language. The EYFSP acknowledges that this has implications for practice but does not suggest how settings can carry out these observations if there is not a member of staff available who speaks the child's home language. Added to this challenge is the fact that in some settings, particularly in the inner cities and coastal towns, pupil mobility is high and teachers find themselves continuously carrying out baseline assessments of children arriving at the setting. High mobility has been found to affect academic performance (Mott, 2002; Demie and Strand, 2004, cited in Demie *et al.*, 2005) and Teacher A confirms this by explaining that admitting pupils into the school on a weekly basis and carrying out baseline assessments within the first two weeks of the child's arrival is one of her school's biggest challenges. However, these challenges are met by maintaining thorough and rigorous assessment procedures that ensure the staff have a good understanding of the child's needs, their likes, dislikes and potential next steps.

The teachers consulted for this chapter advocate using bilingual staff whenever possible, to assess a child's competency in their home language, particularly when the child is new to the setting. However, this is obviously not a long-term solution but settings could enlist the help of staff from other settings or from within their cluster (if applicable) for help with the assessment of new children.

Many schools use Hester's (1990) Stages of English as a basis for assessing English learning (a brief overview is listed below) or their LEA will provide guidance of the stages:

Stage One: new to English.
Stage Two: becoming familiar with English.
Stage Three: becoming confident as a user of English.
Stage Four: a very fluent user of English in most social and learning contexts.

In his research on 'Good Practice' for pupils with EAL, Read (2012) encouraged a group of student teachers to consider a child in their class and then to use Hester's Stages of English to describe the child's stage of English, what targets they would set for the child and what strategies the student teacher would use to support the child's progress in English. For the purposes of his research, Read encouraged the students to work alone. However, to ensure a consistent 'whole setting' approach to assessing children with EAL (and to promote a consistent and collaborative approach to assessment and planning), this exercise would be most effective if carried out within a setting's teaching team.

Mistry and Sood (2011: 289) argue that children with EAL need to be monitored more closely than other children 'to assess the small-step changes in their progress through different contexts, which may be missed otherwise' and they cite Ofsted (2009) that reports that close monitoring and tracking need to be developed further in schools with high numbers of pupils who have EAL. Practitioners, particularly those who have an entire cohort of children with EAL, may find this an overwhelming prospect; however, it is worth bearing in mind that not all observations and assessments need to be formalised and recorded, it may be that practitioners informally discuss children's progress within the teaching team in order to plan progression and next steps in the child's learning.

- How does your setting track children's progress?
- Do you monitor children with EAL more closely than children who are native English speakers?
- Are you satisfied that your tracking procedures are effective?

Both teachers consulted for this chapter strongly endorsed the need for practitioners to have high expectations of the children who are learning English as an Additional Language. Teacher B stated that otherwise there is the potential danger of assuming a child has a special educational need solely on the basis that they cannot understand or speak English. She explained that a child may be highly literate and articulate in their home language and, therefore, there is no reason why, with appropriate and targeted support, they cannot gain these skills in English. She noted:

> There is a danger that the children with special educational needs and the children with EAL are ability-grouped together, even if the child with EAL does not have a special educational need. This is often due to staffing issues and where support needs to be targeted in class.

This echoes Blaire and Bourne (1998, cited in Mistry and Sood, 2011: 288) who explain that where there are high expectations and effective teaching: 'The attainment of pupils who have EAL is raised.' Cummins (1981) expressed his ideas on second language learning as a simple matrix that teachers could consider when planning learning activities for EAL children (Figure 3.2).

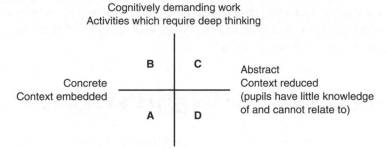

FIGURE 3.2 Second language acquisition matrix.

Cummins described someone who has conversational fluency in a language as having Basic Interpersonal Communicative Skills (BICS) and he believed that it would take a child between five and seven years to achieve this level on a par with their peers who speak English as their first language. Furthermore, Cummins described a child gaining proficiency in using academic English as having Cognitive Academic Language Proficiency (CALP).

The Milton Keynes Ethnic Minority Achievement Support Service (2004) advise that though it may be tempting to give a child who is not confident in speaking English undemanding activities in the D quadrant (such as copying, colouring in work sheets, etc.), this should be avoided. However, children with EAL should be provided with appropriate support to access activities in quadrant C and, following this, should be exposed to learning activities within quadrant B to develop their CALP.

When observing a Reception teacher in school A teaching facts about ants (in their topic of 'life cycles'), it was noticeable to see her high expectations of the children. She was not giving the children work from Cummins's quadrant D which might have involved 'look and say' only type of activities, but was extending their understanding through open questions (supported by Makaton signs), using pictures for the children to see and discuss alongside each fact, speaking clearly and using simple sentence structures. The children were instructed to explain what they knew about ants to a partner, which all children were able to do to some extent – some using the challenging new vocabulary they had just learned (such as 'antennae' and 'communicate') while some were using gestures, signs and were pointing to pictures to show what they knew.

Discussion

Peer observations are an informal and effective way of scrutinising your practice. Discuss the possibility of taking part in non-graded peer observations with your colleagues to instigate discussion of whether children with EAL are being suitably challenged within your setting.

Teaching strategies and the learning environment

Case study 3.2: One Early Years class, 14 languages ...

Class R1 is a reception class within a multicultural area of a city in the North of England. There are 30 children in the class. All of them are learning English as an additional language.

You have been employed as a practitioner within this classroom and you are one of the members of staff responsible for setting up the learning environment and planning for the learning opportunities that will happen within the class and in the outdoor areas.

- How would you plan the physical features of this classroom? Consider the resources you would include and the use of the indoor and outdoor space.
- How will you encourage speaking and listening inside and outside the classroom?
- What strategies would you use to communicate with the children?
- How would you encourage friendships and collaboration between the children?
- Would the behaviour management strategies you use with children who do not speak English be different from those for children who do speak English?
- Many of the children's parents do not speak English. How will you build partnerships with them?

Teaching strategies need to be carefully considered when planning for inclusive learning opportunities. The strategies that will be discussed here are by no means exhaustive and practised practitioners will obviously have their own established methods. However, these have proved to be effective and are endorsed by the two teachers consulted for this chapter.

Play-based learning

Both teachers advocate that children with little or no English learn best through play, whether the child is in an Early Years or a Primary setting. Due to curriculum requirements, planning for play within the Early Years is standard practice, however, within the National Curriculum it is not, though role-play is included in the KS2 English curriculum. The EYFS (DCSF, 2008a) states that role-play encourages children to practise new vocabulary and 'language items gained through first-hand experience'. However, Harrison *et al.* (2005: 18, cited in Grant and Mistry 2010: 157) claim that role-play, despite its usefulness in taught sessions, is often seen as a 'time-filler'. This is despite research claims that play-based learning can often enhance and extend children's learning within KS1 and beyond, whether they are learning EAL or not. Free play and role-play are still often absent from primary classrooms, despite research highlighting their benefits; according to Grant and Mistry (2010: 155): 'Results showed effective role-play activities can be beneficial to EAL pupils, allowing them to practise words and phrases in a relaxed atmosphere supported by their peers.' Cast (2007: 22) also advocates learning through role-play in Key Stage 2 as she believes it 'opens up opportunities to use speaking and listening skills'. She further explains that 'role-play gives the teacher a further opportunity to observe the range of speaking and listening skills used by the children'.

Teacher A promotes the use of construction and block toys within the Early Years classrooms to encourage children to play collaboratively and to prompt discussions with each another. She explained that the purchase of wooden blocks for each room was a conscious decision, as staff in the setting had noticed how motivated the children were to talk to one another when building a structure together. There is evidence from research studies to support the views of Teacher A and supporters of block play as a means of developing children's learning, social skills and language, which can be traced back as far as the 1830s when Friedrich Froebel used block play to promote mathematical and scientific development in his kindergartens. 'Blocks seem to provide a forum which gently promotes group play situations while still allowing the socially immature child the opportunity to acquire appropriate social skills through observation and imitation' (Rogers, 1985: 255).

Any form of play or role-play that promotes collaborative discussions is a positive inclusion in a setting and it is the practitioner's responsibility to audit their teaching spaces to ensure that appropriate play and role-play opportunities are provided.

The learning environment

The 'Every Child a Talker' (ECAT) (DCSF, 2008b) three-year programme was developed to support practitioners in creating a learning environment that would encourage language learning for children in the Early Years. Although the initiative is no longer funded, the resources and training materials may still be used as they provide useful guidance on how to encourage speaking and listening.

The following activity is a training exercise adapted from the ECAT programme resources which encourages practitioners to evaluate their learning spaces (Figure 3.3).

When considering the learning environment, it is important to consider the kind of stimuli such as displays and posters and the type of resources (including furniture) that are included in the setting, as striking the right balance for the children in a setting is crucial. Teacher A ensures that the learning environment supports children's language development. The furniture has been chosen carefully to encourage speaking and listening, such as using 'communicator' dining room tables that are oval in shape to promote sociable behaviours during meal times. In this school's classrooms, the furniture is made from natural materials and the absence of cluttered and overly bright resources is noticeable. There are areas in the classrooms for the children to climb into, such as tents, which are known to promote speaking and listening due to the privacy they provide, 'being able to access somewhere small, perhaps contained and private, somewhere to observe from, can be very important for children' (Jarman, 2014: 1). Elizabeth Jarman is an advocate of

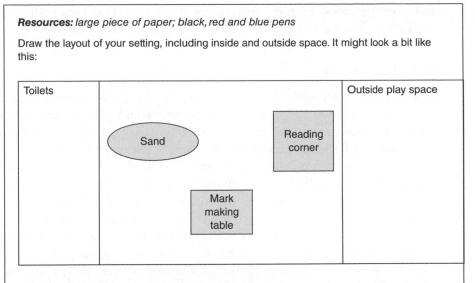

Resources: *large piece of paper; black, red and blue pens*

Draw the layout of your setting, including inside and outside space. It might look a bit like this:

Toilets		Outside play space
	Sand Reading corner Mark making table	

Think about places in the setting where talking takes place (this may be places where children initiate talk or where lots of talking takes place by children). Take a red pen and mark with a cross where the talking 'hot-spots' are: places where adults and children engage in conversation or where children talk to each other. Add one cross if talking takes place there sometimes, and more crosses if it takes place there a lot.

Take a blue pen and mark with a circle the places where you think talking could take place but does not at the moment. This could be due to the fact that this area lends itself to solitary play or there could be a lot of environmental noise that distracts the children from talking.

FIGURE 3.3 Exercise for evaluating learning spaces.

Source: Adapted from ECaT (2008: 15).

creating 'Communication Friendly Spaces' and believes that 'light, noise, colour and clutter can affect behaviour, communication, emotional well-being and general engagement' (ibid.: 1). Many Early Years pioneers state that children learn best when the environment is prepared and calm. Maria Montessori, who believed that children respond positively to an uncluttered and orderly environment, was working and researching children's behaviours in the early twentieth century, and many supporters of her work consider that 'her systematic approach can be replicated and sustained in almost any situation' (Seldin, 2007: 13).

These strategies are worth reflecting upon. Children with EAL may already be anxious and confused by their arrival in a new setting; many may have recently arrived from a country that is very different from the UK, culturally and linguistically, and could display their anxiety in different ways such as being withdrawn and shy or by showing aggression due to the frustrations they feel. Creating a calm, orderly and welcoming environment is one way of reducing their stress, as is creating ways for the children to effectively communicate with you.

Visual strategies

In a well-considered Early Years setting there are many ways of including a child with EAL to develop their language and learn through play without having to change practice or resources to any great extent. Any resources that promote questioning, collaboration and provide sensory experiences will all go some way to develop the child's language alongside extending their understanding. Alongside preparing the learning environment, practitioners working with children with EAL need to consider the resources and strategies that they use. Visual strategies such as picture books, posters, environmental labelling, emotions signs, visual dictionaries, visual timetables, PCS (Picture Communication System) and in some cases PECS (Picture Exchange Communication System) are considered useful resources, particularly when the children have very little or no English. Many settings, including the two schools consulted for the chapter, use a variety of these strategies as part of their everyday practice.

Picture books are an essential resource in the Early Years classroom to support early literacy. They aid discussion, extend vocabulary, can portray a range of genres and cultures and teach children the skills of book reading such as how to hold a book correctly, how to turn the pages and to know that pictures convey meaning. For children learning English, the merits of sharing picture books with an English speaker are obvious, however, Mendoza and Reece (2001: 7) explain in their US-based research that there are 'common pitfalls' that practitioners fall into when choosing 'multicultural' picture books with children, which should be considered before purchasing books for a setting. Some aspects to be considered are whether the characters within the book are portrayed realistically and not in a tokenistic way. They argue that just because a book is popular does not necessarily mean that the multicultural characters are portrayed sensitively or accurately. The writers also discuss whether 'a single book about a group can adequately portray that group's experience' (ibid.: 10), highlighting again the need to avoid tokenism. Their final discussion point is that practitioners should not assume that there is an abundance of high-quality multicultural picture books available to purchase; they acknowledge that this situation is improving, but this should highlight to practitioners the importance of critically analysing picture books before sharing them with children.

Examine the books found in your setting. How do they reflect a multicultural society? Are the characters portrayed sensitively and not in a tokenistic way?

Whether a setting has high numbers of EAL children or not, a poster displaying 'welcome' or 'hello' in a variety of languages is a common sight. This not only provides the sight of a familiar word to EAL children and families but highlights to the other children that many languages are spoken in their community. Using posters or signs that are written in many languages can be used in a discussion with children to explore what languages are spoken in their classroom alongside the teaching of some key words such as 'hello' and 'thank you' in those languages. Environmental bilingual labels are another frequent sight in settings and can be a useful way for children and adults to communicate with one another. The staff in Teacher A's school have learnt some key words and phrases in Arabic, due to the high number of children who speak this language in the school and have found this simple measure to be an effective way of building relationships with the children and their families.

Case study 3.3: Renat's story

Renat is 5 years old and joined his Primary School class three weeks ago. He speaks very few words of English and frequently becomes frustrated when he cannot communicate with the adults and children in the class. The teacher and teaching assistant often use visual timetables and picture cards to communicate with the children learning EAL in this school.

Observation

Renat is on the carpet listening to a story with the rest of the class. The TA sits next to Renat and uses Makaton signs to communicate the main points of the story to him which he responds to by copying the signs, pointing at the picture book or smiling. Eventually, he loses interest in the story and begins to crawl around the carpet and won't look at the book. He frequently points to the door and seems to be asking a question. The TA gently brings Renat to her and puts the small visual timetable on his lap; she puts his finger on the picture of the book and then shows him that lunch and playtime are next. He visibly relaxes and listens to the rest of the story with the TA while he holds the timetable on his lap, knowing that he doesn't have long to wait.

Without the use of a visual resource (and as she does not speak Renat's home language), the TA would have struggled to engage with him and to explain the sequence of the rest of the morning. However, as this information could be portrayed quickly, Renat was able to understand that he would soon be able to go for lunch – which obviously settled him.

Practitioners in many settings use visual timetables so that children can understand the structure of the school day and in which order the events/lessons of the day will happen. Initially these timetables were used primarily for children with autism, due to many children with autism being visual learners and needing structure (Blamires, 2004). However, they are now becoming a common resource in mainstream classrooms due to the inclusive nature of the resource. Lepkowska (2011: 3) reported on 'The Communication Project' carried out in a Kidderminster primary school that involved a whole school approach to using visual clues and timetables to support children's language development. A teacher involved in the project explained that though the timetables are initially time-consuming to create, the impact of the resources on children's behaviour has been 'tremendous'.

Another visual system that can be effective for initially communicating with children with no or little English is a picture communication system (PCS). Using pictures or photographs to communicate can mean that a child may not feel so frustrated or isolated, and (as with visual timetables), they are easily created through specific software or are downloadable from websites. Children may use a variety of pictures to convey their physical needs, such as wanting to go to the toilet, that they are too warm or cold or that they need a drink, which without a picture system, they may find very difficult to do. Using pictures to communicate alongside simple verbal communication and gesture, can also support a child's language acquisition; however, Donnelly and Kirkaldy (cited in Wilson, 2003) warn that a system of using pictures or symbols to communicate should be slowly built in to the setting's practice to allow both the adults and children to become familiar with the symbols/pictures and their meanings, particularly if some of the pictures seem quite abstract. It is also important to consider that children may become over-reliant on a picture communication system; therefore, it is crucial that spoken language is encouraged alongside the use of pictures.

Modelling correct speech

Alongside using a PCS, adults need to model correct language and ensure that they speak clearly. Adults may adopt 'caretaker speech' which is where speech is modified and simplified to aid comprehension rather than a conscious attempt to teach language (Krashen, 2009: 22). Krashen (ibid.: 65) does not suggest that making modifications to our speech such as 'slowing down, using more common vocabulary, using shorter sentences, less complex syntax with less embedding' is something that adults do consciously, rather it is an automatic process that we adopt.

Continuing this theme of 'caretaker speech', it is helpful to consider all of the different places within a setting where discussions between adults and children take place. The classroom and outdoor play areas are the two most obvious; however, Teacher A highlighted the importance of adults considering their language use in the dining room and during assemblies. She explained that many children who are not only learning EAL but are experiencing an educational setting for the first time may feel confused by large, noisy rooms and attending an assembly and may not understand basic 'rules' of being in an assembly, such as sitting down without speaking for a sustained period of time and walking in and out of a hall in lines with their classmates. It is worth reflecting on these daily events and adapting practice if necessary by keeping assemblies as short as possible, keeping to simple themes and using clear language so that this experience can be less confusing for newly arrived children.

Buddying

When a child arrives in the setting, they need to feel secure within the attachments they have within the setting, particularly if they have little or no English. The key person will be responsible for establishing a good relationship with the child to get to know their needs but he/she will also need to encourage friendships between the child and other children in the class. One established method is through 'buddying' the new arrival with a child who speaks the same home language and who is familiar with the routines of the setting. Conteh (2012: 65) explains that buddies can play different roles in helping a child to settle in and rather than there being one buddy, different children could fulfil different buddy roles for the new child. She suggests that a child may have a 'language buddy' who shares the same language and can take on the role of translator (this may have to be a child from another class or a sibling if there is no one to take on this role in the class). Then there could be a 'learning buddy' to help with curriculum tasks and a 'school buddy' to help with routines.

Conteh's work is obviously primary school-based, however, many of the suggestions can be adapted for some children in the early years. Teacher A explains that children in the Foundation Stage are provided with buddies; however, she was quick to state that practitioners should not assume that children will be friends just because they speak the same language! Also, it is worth bearing in mind that if children have left their home country due to a conflict or civil war, the children's families could have been on opposing sides of the conflict, and therefore, practitioners must be sensitive to these issues.

According to Conteh (2012: 65), the kinds of things buddies can do include:

- help familiarise the new arrival with things such as where the toilets, cloakrooms, dining hall, assemblies;
- explain who's who in the school and what they do, e.g. secretaries, dinner ladies, TAs;
- support the new arrival in making friends;
- introduce the new arrival to other members of the school.

Valuing home language and building partnerships with parents

While it is essential to help children with EAL to develop their understanding of English in order for them to access and enjoy the full curriculum, it is also vital to ensure that the child's home language is valued and maintained due to the many benefits of being bilingual.

Practitioners can bring different languages into their everyday practice, such as greeting the children or taking the register in different languages, reading stories that are set in the countries of origin of the children, providing dual-language books and singing songs in different languages. By celebrating the children's home language and culture, their self-esteem will be raised and the children will know that their language is valued as being an important part of their identity. Teacher B discussed the topic of 'traditional tales' and advised that practitioners should try to use traditional tales from a range of different countries and cultures in order to highlight to children the similarities and differences between the stories. Many settings welcome visitors and helpers from the community to help with certain topics and inviting family members to share their favourite traditional tales with the children would be a very positive experience if planned well.

When children share a common home language and choose to use this language together in their work and play (particularly in the Early Years setting), practitioners should encourage and promote the use of their home language. The Intercultural Development Research Association (IDRA, 2013) explains that if children who are not fluent English speakers try to speak only in English, then they will be functioning at an intellectual level that is lower than their age, therefore interrupting their academic development. Whereas, when a child continues to develop their home language alongside English, they achieve higher academic attainment than those who learn English to the detriment of their home language.

From the primary research it is evident that some parents from ethnic minority groups may be reluctant to be involved in their children's education for a variety of reasons, including their own lack of confidence in speaking English, having low self-esteem or having a different cultural expectation of an educational setting. It is worth noting here, however, that just because someone does not speak English does not mean necessarily that they are from a different culture; similarly a person with a different cultural or ethnic heritage may very well speak English as their first language. Nevertheless, parents and families are the child's first educators and should be encouraged to take a full part in their children's education, however difficult and challenging this quite often is for the settings and practitioners involved.

The notion of parents being 'partners' with the setting is not a new one. All practitioners know that when parents are consistently involved with their children's education, there are better outcomes for the child. However, when parents do not speak English, there are obviously barriers to communication that must be overcome. Teacher B pointed out that the amount of English that the parents speak is often an indication of how quickly a child's English learning will progress. Therefore, as some parents will not

speak (or be learning) English, it is important to build up effective procedures so that parents can still be involved in their child's education
regardless of their levels of English proficiency. The reflective practice box
includes ideas for settings to consider when planning their family partnership strategies.

- Ensure that induction procedures are provided to parents in the language of their choice.
- Appoint a member of staff to be a 'parent co-ordinator' who can liaise between the family, the school and appropriate services if necessary.
- Keep written communications clear. Letters and emails should be free of jargon and in plain English.
- Let the parents know when their children are doing well so that achievements can be celebrated at home.
- Be available, whenever possible, before and after the school/nursery day starts. An informal chat in the playground can often be more productive than talking in the office.
- Deal with complaints and problems quickly and keep the parents informed of any outcomes.
- Be proactive in engaging the parents. For example, set up a parent group where parents and staff can informally discuss issues surrounding the chil-dren and their learning. Consider being involved with intervention programmes such as FAST (Families and Schools Together) developed by Save the Children.
- Ask some parents to become 'parent buddies' who can assist new parents with the routines and expectations of the setting, preferably in a shared language.

Conclusion

Creating and maintaining an inclusive environment in order to support and
welcome children and their families is a vitally important part of your practice. Regularly reflecting upon your current provision and planning changes
to areas of practice that need updating or improving will ensure that positive
practices can take place. Whether you work in a culturally diverse area where
many of the children have EAL or whether there are very few, your setting
should be prepared in terms of procedures, staff training and the learning
environment. Then a child entering the setting for the first time will feel
valued and will be able to communicate their needs, either verbally or through
other means.

References

Blamires, M. (2004) Supporting the inclusion and achievement of learners with autistic spectrum disorders (ASD). In S. Soan (ed.) *Additional Educational Needs: Inclusive Approaches to Teaching. Teaching Assistants Foundation Degree.* London: David Fulton, pp. 139–56.

Bradford MDC (2014) *Support for Newly Arrived Pupils with English as an Additional Language,* Induction Pack for Schools. Bradford: City of Bradford MDC.

Brière, E. J. (1978) Variables affecting native Mexican children's learning Spanish as a second language. *Language Learning,* 28: 159–74. doi: 10.1111/j.1467-1770.1978.tb00312.x.

Bruner, J. S. (1978) The role of dialogue in language acquisition. In A. Sinclair, R. Jarvella and W. J. M. Levelt (eds) *The Child's Conception of Language.* New York: Springer-Verlag.

Cast, J. (2007) Role-play in Key Stage 2. *English 4–11,* 29: 22.

Chomsky, N. (1957) *Syntactic Structures.* Cambridge, MA: MIT Press.

Clark, B. (n.d.) *First and Second Language Acquisition in Early Childhood.* Available at: http://ecap.crc.illinois.edu/pubs/Katzsym/clark-b.pdf (accessed 20 June 2014).

Conteh, J. (2012) *Teaching Bilingual and EAL Learners in Primary Schools: Transforming Primary QTS.* London: Sage.

Cummins, J. (1981) Age on arrival and immigrant second language learning in Canada: a reassessment. *Applied Linguistics,* 2: 132–49.

DCSF (Department for Children, Schools and Families) (2008a) *Practice Guidance for the Early Years Foundation Stage.* Nottingham: DCSF Publications.

DCSF (Department for Children, Schools and Families) (2008b) *Every Child a Talker: Guidance for Early Language Lead Practitioners.* Nottingham: DCSF Publications.

DCSF (Department of Children, Schools and Families) (2009) *Your Child, Your Schools, our Families: Building A 21st Century Schools System,* White Paper. Available at: http://webarchive.nationalarchives.gov.uk/20130401151715/http://www.education.gov.uk/publications/eOrderingDownload/21st_Century_Schools.pdf (accessed 15 January 2015).

Demie, F., Lewis, K. and Taplin, A. (2005) Pupil mobility in schools and implications for raising achievement. *Educational Studies,* 31(2): 131–47.

DfE (Department for Education) (2012a) *School Funding Reform: Next Steps Towards a Fairer System.* Available at: https://www.gov.uk/government/uploads/system/uploads/attachment_data/file/179138/school_funding_reform_-_next_steps_towards_a_fairer_system.pdf (accessed 15 January 2015).

DfE (Department for Education) (2012b) *Statutory Framework for the Early Years Foundation Stage.* Available at: http://media.education.gov.uk/assets/files/pdf/eyfs%20statutory%20framework%20march%202012.pdf (accessed 20 June 2014).

DfE (Department for Education) (DfE) (2013) *Early Years Foundation Stage Profile 2013.* Available at: https://www.gov.uk/government/uploads/system/uploads/attachment_data/file/252766/eyfsp_2013_guide_v1_0.pdf (accessed 20 June 2014).

Fullan, M. and Hargreaves, A. (eds) (1992) *Teacher Development and Educational Change.* London: Falmer Press.

Grant, K. and Mistry, M. (2010) How does the use of role-play affect the learning of Year 4 children in a predominately EAL class? *Education 3–13: International Journal of Primary, Elementary and Early Years Education,* 38(2): 155–64.

Hall, C., Smith, P. and Wicaksono, R. (2011) *Mapping Applied Linguistics.* London: Routledge.

Hartshorne, M. (2009) *The Cost to the Nation of Children's Poor Communication.* London: ICAN.

Haynes, J. (2005) *Stages of Second Language Acquisition.* Available at: www.everythingesl.net/inservices/language_stages.php (accessed 20 June 2014).

Hester, H. (1990) The stages of English. In *Patterns of Learning.* London: CLPE.

Intercultural Development Research Association (2013) Newsletter. Available at: www.idra.org/IDRA_Newsletter/January_2000_Bilingual_Education/Why_is_it_Important_to_Maintain_the_Native_Language?/ (accessed 20 June 2014).

Jarman, E. (2014) *Why Lighting Matters*. Available at: www.elizabethjarmantraining. co.uk/downloads/CFS%20Lighting%20Paper.pdf (accessed 20 June 2014).

Krashen, S. (2009) *Principles and Practice in Second Language Acquisition*. Available at: www. sdkrashen.com/content/books/principles_and_practice.pdf (accessed 20 June 2014).

Lepkowska, D. (2011) *Believe in the Reach of Speech: Talk, Listen, Take Part*. Available at: http://europe.nxtbook.com/nxteu/tescreative/communicationstrust/index.php#/8 (accessed 15 January 2015).

Mendoza, J. and Reece, D. (2001) Examining multicultural picture books for the early childhood classroom: possibilities and pitfalls. *Early Childhood Research and Practice*, 3(2).

Milton Keynes Ethnic Minority Achievement Service (2004) *Supporting Children with English as an Additional Language*. Milton Keynes: Milton Keynes Council.

Mistry, M. and Sood, K. (2011) Raising standards for pupils who have English as an Additional Language (EAL) through monitoring and evaluation of provision in primary schools. *Education 3–13: International Journal of Primary, Elementary and Early Years Education*, 40(3): 281–93.

Murakami, C. (2008) 'Everybody is just fumbling along': an investigation of views regarding EAL training and support provisions in a rural area. *Language and Education*, 22(4): 265–82.

NALDIC (2013) *The Latest Statistics about EAL Learners in our Schools*. Available at: www.naldic. org.uk/research-and-information/eal-statistics/eal-pupils (accessed 30 June 2014).

NASUWT (2012) *Ethnic Minority Achievement: Equality Matters*. Available at: www.naldic. org.uk/Resources/NALDIC/Research%20and%20Information/Documents/ EMAG_Survey_Report.pdf (accessed 19 May 2014).

Neaum, S. (2012) *Language and Literacy for the Early Years*. London: Sage.

Ofsted (Office for Standards in Education) (2009) *English as an Additional Language. Schools and Inspection: Information and Guidance for Inspectors of Maintained Schools, Independent Schools and Teacher Education Providers*. London: OFSTED.

Overington, A. (2012) *A Brief Summary of Government Policy in Relation to EAL Learners*. Available at: www.naldic.org.uk/Resources/NALDIC/Research%20and%20 Information/Documents/Brief_summary_of_Government_policy_for_EAL_ Learners.pdf (accessed 20 June 2014).

Pim, C. (2010) *How to Support Children Learning English as an Additional Language*. Cheshire: LDA.

Seldin, T. (2007) *How to Raise an Amazing Child: The Montessori Way to Bring Up Caring, Confident Children*. London: Dorling Kindersley.

Skinner, B. F. (1957) *Verbal Behavior*. Cambridge, MA: Harvard University Press.

Read, A. (2012) 'Good practice' for pupils with English as an additional language: patterns in student teachers' thinking. *Research in Teacher Education*, 2(2): 24–30.

Rogers, D. (1985) Relationships between block play and the social development of young children. *Early Child Development and Care*, 20(4): 245–61.

Tabors, P. (1997) *One Child, Two Languages*. Baltimore, MD: Paul H. Brookes.

Wilson, A. (ed.) (2003) *Communicating with Pictures and Symbols: Collected Papers from Augmentative Communication in Practice: Scotland's Thirteen Annual Study Day*, Edinburgh: CALL Centre, University of Edinburgh.

Vygotsky, L. (1978) *Mind in Society*. Cambridge, MA: Harvard University Press.

Web resource

Every Child a Talker materials (2008) Available at: www.foundationyears.org. uk/2011/10/every-child-a-talker-guidance-for-early-language-lead-practitioners/ (accessed 4 July 2014).

4

Accent, dialect and phonics

Encouraging inclusion

Sue Aitken and Kate Beardmore

The aims of this chapter are:

- To explore the relationship between early years training, the Early Years Foundation Stage, the National Curriculum and dominant child development theory
- To offer alternative understandings of child development that go beyond traditional developmental psychology
- To consider how using sociopolitical theory, specifically post-colonial theory, may provide practitioners with a greater understanding of how teaching phonics awareness may lead to the loss of the *unique child* in favour of the *universal child*
- To examine how inclusion may be viewed in these perspectives
- To offer practical approaches that enable children to access and engage with the printed text without loss of identity or cultural inheritance.

Introduction

What might be the cultural, political and moral implications for understanding the child outside the usual bounded spaces that circumscribe childhood including those of developmental psychology?

(Barron and Jones, 2012: 1)

Childhood and education are both complex and interrelated subjects that require a rigorous and robust approach. Any attempt to understand children's development in depth requires criticality, in order to question powerful dominant discourses and ideologies that continue to inform existing Early Years practice. However, it is the impact of practitioners' benign 'acceptance' of current practice that may impact upon inclusion and inclusive practice.

This chapter will look at how practitioners and students engage with mainstream and alternative theories of child development using the acquisition of early reading skills and using synthetic phonics as a platform to analyse practice and regulatory guidance. It will explore how implicit cultural exclusion may result from the delivery of a singular approach to language, accent and dialect. We will look at both the Early Years Foundation Stage (EYFS) and the National Curriculum (NC) in terms of content, assessment and standards, and explore the training of the Early Years workforce. In so doing we intend that practitioners consider and reflect upon their own experiences in terms of cultural and language inclusion or exclusion in order to identify what is, or what should be considered as inclusive practice.

This chapter is divided into three themes: (1) curricular content; (2) workforce training; and (3) the application of theory into practice. Our aim is to provide current and future practitioners with approaches to use within their own settings and communities. Consequently, this chapter is both theoretical and practical. We use case studies, first-hand experiences and reader reflection, to explain and discuss potential dilemmas. This offers different ways of working with, and understanding how, children's early language and literacy may be encouraged and enhanced.

Curricular content: the Early Years Foundation Stage and the National Curriculum

Case study 4.1: Sarah's story

Sarah is a lively, talkative 4-year-old in a Reception class. She has been at school for two terms and has appeared confident and eager to learn but recently has been quiet and reticent to engage with phonics sessions.

Her family originate from and live in Stoke-on-Trent. They have recently been told that Sarah is in need additional support with her language development due to her strong 'Potteries' accent and dialect. The school is concerned that Sarah is struggling with her awareness of phonics. Both parents are feeling concerned about their daughter's academic achievement. They have never considered that there was anything wrong with her speech or her language development.

In terms of language and literacy, the EYFS (DfE, 2014) describes communication and language as 'giving children opportunities to experience a rich language environment; to develop their confidence and skills in expressing themselves; and to speak and listen in a range of situations' (ibid.: 8). Literacy is referred to as 'encouraging children to link sounds and letters and to begin to read and write. Children must be given access to a wide range of reading materials (books, poems, and other written materials) to ignite their interest' (ibid.: 8), while recommending that 'Practitioners must consider the individual needs, interests, and stage of development of each child in their care' (ibid.: 8).

Given the curriculum guidance above, consider:

- To what extent are Sarah's unique cultural and domestic experiences being acknowledged and celebrated?
- Is Sarah's accent, a fundamental part of her identity, seen as being disadvantageous in the development of her speaking, reading and spelling abilities?

Sarah would be taught to read by sounding out individual letters and blends of sounds using synthetic phonics. The use of synthetic phonics became the dominant strategy for the teaching of reading, following the publication of the Rose Report (2006). In his report, Rose stated: 'Having considered a wide range of evidence, the review has concluded that the case for systematic phonic work is overwhelming and much strengthened by a synthetic approach' (ibid.: 2). However, even without accent and dialectic variance, reading and spelling in English are complex activities, requiring the early reader to negotiate the differing pronunciations but similar spelling of 'most' and 'cost'; 'river' and 'driver'. As Honeybone and Watson state, when referring to teaching phonics to children with Liverpool English accents: '[D]ifferences mean that the sets of correspondences between sounds and letters (that is, between "phonemes" and "graphemes") that have been developed for other varieties do not fit Liverpool English perfectly' (2006: 1).

Honeybone and Watson clearly identify that irregular applications of phonics, when added to a distinctive accent, can present challenges. However, the teaching and assessment of phonics, by its very nature, must work on the basis of 'shared understanding' as to how words should be pronounced.

Honeybone and Watson go on to say:

In England, most phonics schemes are designed on the basis of the phoneme to grapheme correspondences that work for the closest thing that there is to a neutral, 'standard' accent. There isn't really a standard accent in England, but the closest thing is the accent often called 'RP' (or 'Received Pronunciation).

(ibid.: 1)

Logically, therefore, there is a need to privilege a universality of pronunciation. Sarah's pronunciation of 'bus', as 'buze', may not be acceptable. Therefore, Sarah will need to acquire the acceptable accent, often close to but not quite what has become known as Received Pronunciation (RP). It is the acquisition of the acceptable 'voice' that is seen as the natural precursor to successful reading, spelling and writing; and implicitly, future learning, social and economic success. As McMahon *et al.* (2011) suggest, we draw both 'geographical and social' conclusions from accent and dialect, leading to subconscious stereotyping and allocation of traits such as personality and intelligence. McMahon *et al.* also refer to the earlier research undertaken by Giles and Powesland (1975) where a university lecturer gave two identical lectures to two different groups of A-level students, one using Received Pronunciation (RP), the other using a Birmingham accent. The students' assessment of the content and the lecturer's intelligence gave greater academic credibility to the lecture delivered in RP. Luke (1986: 401) also states that children from backgrounds that are perceived as 'disadvantaged' suffer 'linguistic deficit', but he goes on to declare that this deficit may be 'an imposition of schools and teachers' rather than an inevitable consequence of inherent traits and poor acquisition of language at home.

Returning to the EYFS, the document (DfE, 2014: 6) states that its overarching principles are:

- Every child is a unique child, who is constantly learning and can be resilient, capable, confident and self-assured.
- Children learn to be strong and independent through positive relationships.
- Children learn and develop well in enabling environments, in which their experiences respond to their individual needs and there is a strong partnership between practitioners and parents and/or carers.
- Children develop and learn in different ways and at different rates. The framework covers the education and care of all children in early years provision, including children with special educational needs and disabilities.

Applying these principles to Sarah:

- Do you think Sarah is seen as a unique child or a child that is in danger of not meeting universal and centrally prescribed benchmarks for phonics assessment?

Sarah may be the only child in the setting with a Potteries accent but she may be one of a small group or she may be in the majority:

- How would you define inclusivity in each of these scenarios?
- How would you embrace and include cultural identity for the one, the few and the many?

(Continued)

(Continued)

- If Sarah is being categorised as 'linguistically deficient', what effect may this have on her relationship with education and her parents' relationship with the setting?
- Is she empowered to learn at her own pace and in her own way?
- How far does the rhetoric of the EYFS' overarching principles stretch to meet Sarah's needs?

Case study 4.2: Update on Sarah

Sarah is now 6 years old and coming to the end of Year 1. Her parents notice that when she reads to them, she does so in a different accent. When they ask her why she does this, she explains that she needs two voices, a voice to read in and a voice to use at home.

As a 6-year-old in Year 1, Sarah would be following the National Curriculum at Key Stage 1. Since June 2012, children such as Sarah have been subject to statutory phonics screening (Standards and Testing Agency, 2012). Consequently, by the end of Year 1, Sarah should be able to do the following:

- Apply phonic knowledge and skill as the prime approach to reading unfamiliar words that are not completely decodable.
- Read many frequently encountered words automatically.
- Read phonically decodable three-syllable words.
- Read a range of age-appropriate texts fluently.
- Demonstrate understanding of age-appropriate texts.

(ibid.: 8)

The Standards and Testing Agency (STA) goes on to advise that: 'A child's accent should be taken into account when deciding whether a response is acceptable. There should be no bias in favour of children with a particular accent' (ibid.: 21). However, as shown in the Case study update, by the time of the Year 1 screening, some children will have self-regulated their accent or dialect in order to 'fit in'. In essence, Sarah has accommodated the requirements of the phonics to the reading process. She has renegotiated her accent and in part, her identity, to fulfil the institutional expectations of how reading is accomplished. She has, in effect, facilitated her own inclusion. In her autobiographical essay, Maylor (1995: 45) refers to the language used in her Jamaican home where she was told to 'speak English at home and reject patois. Father spoke patois at home, English outside … He associated patois with underachievement.'

It would seem therefore that while both the EYFS and National Curriculum allow for uniqueness, accent and dialect, in practice there is little space for individuality if it cannot deliver phoneme-to-grapheme understanding.

Having discussed the statutory and regulatory guidance, we will now examine how the training of the workforce may reinforce singular approaches to phonic awareness and how this may lead to unintended exclusion rather than inclusion in your setting.

Early Years training and education

Colley (2006) has carried out research into level three qualifications in childcare. Her research suggests that there are frequent discussions about 'good' and 'bad' ways to care, which reinforces a need for trainees (later practitioners) to demonstrate their suitability in terms of moral propriety. Skeggs (1997: 68) adds: 'The curriculum is organized in such a way that certain dispositions are invalidated and denied, while others are valorized, advised and legitimated.' While training, students are taught the 'correct' way to work with children and later as practitioners they will often use this knowledge to inform and develop their own 'good' practice. It would appear that there is little scope for criticality in such programmes of study, as the teaching suggests a 'singular truth' with regard to the correct way for children to learn and develop, consequently this affects the workforce and, most importantly, the child. However, when the trainee becomes the practitioner, that singularity becomes fragmented and unstable as practical experiences of working with children highlight the difficulty of applying universal measurements to individual children.

At level 3 in Child Care and Education programmes, inclusion is often dealt with in the UN Convention on the Rights of the Child (1989), which makes reference to both participation and 'voice' – the right to be heard. The irony here perhaps is that in Sarah's case the 'voice', which includes her accent or dialect, quite literally becomes not the right to speak but the right to speak in an *acceptable way*. Foucault (2002), Lippi Green (1997) and Fairclough (2001) discuss the relationship between language and power in the context of phonics. This presents the practitioner with a dilemma: how to include the child within the framework of the curriculum while respecting her culture and identity. Lippi Green (1997) questions whether children's language rights, the individual right to an accent or dialect is overridden by the interests and needs of a wider society.

It is vital at this point to consider the ethics of assessing children against what could be considered an artificial set of beliefs. Children such as Sarah may be classed as 'non-able' children or 'failing', because their skills are not covered or do not match universal benchmarks.

Unpacking theory and putting it into practice

We begin our exploration of theory by looking at how practitioners might understand developmental psychology. In essence, we want to start with the familiar (the known) and move towards the unfamiliar (the unknown). The dominance of developmental psychology has provided practitioners with a useful but potentially one-dimensional way of understanding the development of children. Developmental psychology and its influence, however, has increasingly been the focus of criticism from sociological (Qvortrup, 1987; Corsaro, 1997; James and Prout, 1997; James *et al.*, 1998) and psychological perspectives (Bradley, 1989; Morss, 1996; Burman, 2001). However, the emergence of alternative perspectives of child development, such as feminism, postmodernism, sociocultural and sociopolitical approaches have enabled practitioners to develop multiple narratives, different ways of understanding how children learn and develop. It is not our aim to discuss developmental psychology *per se*, more to read Sarah's story using alternative perspectives alongside notions contained with developmental psychology. In this context we are articulating Bronfenbrenner's (1979) ecological model, where the radiation circles impact on the child, from personal engagement to institutional and political directives.

Developmental psychology represents the scientific explanation of how babies and children change and learn over time. Conditions of learning are seen as sequential and predictable, phased and staged. Its key premise is that the more the mind's sequence of development can be mapped, the more effective and appropriate programmes of teaching and learning can become. While primarily but not exclusively associated with Piaget, developmental psychology has become a powerful influence on curricula and practice. As Yelland and Kilderry (2005: 10) suggest: 'Developmental psychologies, and the structuralist approach inherent in it, have privileged theories such as that of Piaget.' So much so, that Piaget's developmental stages can be identifies in both the EYFS and National Curriculum Key Stages. However, while a prescription of the sequence and nature of the curriculum may be in essence Piagetian, ironically it may lose the Piagetian sense of self-initiated learning and original thinking. Consequently, it may provide practitioners with an understanding of child development that may ignore the need to understand children within a social, political and cultural context. Equally, while Piaget's theory states that the directions of travel, in terms of child development, will always be the same, he recognised that the speed of travel would be different for every child. Thus, curriculum models such as the EYFS and the National Curriculum may be seen as both inclusive and exclusive at the same time. Inclusive, in that every child is assessed against the same criteria (the direction of travel), but exclusive in that some children will be negatively assessed if their speed of travel is different from the norm. Therefore, using Piagetian theory in this way must inevitably break one of the basic rules of delivering inclusivity – the equality of learning outcomes. Equality of outcome is not based on treating all children the same, it is treating all children as individuals in order to meet their needs.

While there are many sociological explorations of the intersection of class, accent and identity, our decision to employ post-colonialism, was taken in the belief that it operates as a useful paradigm for unsettling the accepted landscape. This allows us the space to use the unfamiliar, in order to reassess the familiar. The aim is not to create the consummate practitioner, who becomes the definitive expert and has a complete set of resources to understand the way children learn and develop, but rather to facilitate other ways of 'seeing', in order that practitioners may recognise the potential connection between a range of perspectives and the lived lives of children. The aim is not to provide absolutes, but merely to provide the approaches to see the connections between theory and the experiences of children, the better to engage and facilitate a child's holistic growth. The process is not designed to arrive at a definitive answer to questions that may arise on child development, but to raise potential answers that practitioners may consider.

The range of readings we intend to apply to Sarah's situation include post-colonial, post-modern and political theories. The decision to use post-colonial theory (Fanon, 1967; Spivak, 1990; Said, 1993) was made as it breaks with traditional linear 'readings' and instead applies a sociopolitical lens, since one of the underlying concepts of the theory is to make visible 'diverse ways of viewing and living in the world' (Viruru, 2005: 7). Viewing the world from other perspectives is perhaps the first step in understanding how difference can lead to exclusion. From an understanding of exclusion, you can start to ensure inclusive practice.

Post-colonial theory

Using post-colonial theory, according to Young (2001), is to address the legacy of colonialism imposed by Western attempts to dominate the globe, and its attempts to universalise society. Cannella and Viruru (2004) observed first-hand experiences of oppressive regimes that underpinned their own children's education at school, and thus developed a critique of the power relationships exercised within the education system. They used the post-colonial lens to challenge the notion of limiting and colonising those who are 'younger': 'Beliefs about children serve as violence against children, a kind of epistemic violence that limits human possibilities, freedom and actions' (ibid.: 2).

Both Derrida (1974) and Spivak (1988) refer to 'catachresis'. Spivak uses the term as part of her examination of the colonial and post-colonial legacy where language is misused, misappropriated and abused. She refers to a cultural continuum where the coloniser and colonised 'share' a language that serves both to underpin and validate a discourse of supremacy. The language of the oppressor becomes the language of the oppressed, seamlessly and without question.

This presentation of shared rather than imposed beliefs holds fast as the decolonised seeks to resurrect their pre-colonial language and culture, only to find it no longer has currency, and instead is regarded as a curiosity and has little value in the globalised and largely capitalised world (Ashcroft *et al.*, 2002), just as Sarah quickly learns her home speech may have very little value in the learning of phonemes-to-graphemes techniques.

Using post-colonial theory to explore notions of child development presents two issues. The first is to disengage perceptions of colonialism and post-colonialism from its traditional and Eurocentric reading as a discourse that encompasses and articulates political and military imperialism, usually contained within a distant geography. The second issue is to realign the theory so that practitioners may, while recognising that there remains a political imperative, acknowledge that military power has been replaced by economic dominance and imperatives. Additionally, recognising that there is the need to reconstitute post-colonial theory as less defined and binary and more nebulous, and therefore as relevant to 'here' as to 'there'. Post-colonialists thus endeavour to challenge the notion of 'universalism' and explore the 'oppressive regimes and practices that they delineate' (Young, 2001: 58). In this context, we can begin to tease out how post-colonial theory may be applied to childhood and education, and subsequently to Sarah and her family.

Childhood and education have been greatly influenced by dominant Western discourses about young children, and these dominant discourses rely heavily on the work of theorists such Piaget and Vygotsky. At the core of public policy are ideas based on notions that linear progress and measurable outcomes lead to meaningful development. This can be seen to be profoundly reflected in documents, such as the EYFS and the National Curriculum, which directly affect Sarah's personal and academic experiences.

Linguistic inclusion

In the context of Case study 4.1, if it is perceived that Sarah does not 'fit in' with the dominant cultural norm of 'using appropriate language', and she slips into the deficit model, this in turn could lead to marginalisation, isolation and exclusion. The dominance of the Westernised perception of 'correct English' and Sarah's perceived lack of it result in reduced levels of power and status for Sarah and for her family. Frantz Fanon's *Black Skin, White Masks* (1967) places great emphasis on language being at the heart of marginalisation, in his own context, as a black person, in a perceived 'white' society. 'A man who has a language,' Fanon suggests, 'consequently possesses the world expressed and implied by that language' (ibid.: 14). Fanon argues that language becomes an index of social/cultural difference and the power imbalance. His work, though based on the black/white dichotomy, can also be applied to Sarah's situation in the sense that one's culture and status specify a particular code of speech, and if this speech is not classed as 'correct' by more powerful groups in society, she and her family will become a subordinate group. Fanon states: 'What we are getting at becomes plain: Mastery of language affords remarkable power' (ibid.: 18).

Consequently, linguistic inclusion in the Early Years can mean mastery, not of language itself but mastery of *the* language, in the belief that there exists a shared and good way of speaking and, as referred to earlier, the curriculum 'is organised in such a way that certain dispositions are invalidated and denied' (Skeggs, 1997: 68).

In a developmental sense, the school has the power to decide Sarah's language competency. To avoid being assessed as incompetent, Sarah must accept that she falls short of speaking in the correct way and must change her way of speaking. That becomes the 'undeniable truth'. However, it is important at this point to consider the notion of 'truth', especially the post-modern notion that there is no single and absolute truth merely perceptions of truth (MacNaughton, 2005). However, it appears that current ideology and practice are premised on the idea that there *is* a singular 'truth', a shared understanding. However, what is 'true' for some individuals and groups can be very different for others; truth, for that reason, could be seen as culturally determined. Consequently, the 'truth' of government educational policy, informed by biological, scientific research, such as Piaget's ages and stages theory, is only one truth among many. If, arguably, every child is unique, what is the value of a one-size-fits-all education system, where culture has little or no part to play, save for tokenistic acknowledgement? Perhaps the trick is to see inclusion not as gaining 'membership' of an established order by being the same, but to continuously reinvent the learning environment so to acknowledge and work with individuals to achieve the same goals – but just in a different manner.

Walkerdine (1988), using a feminist sociocultural perspective, also questions these developmental 'truths' using another lens. Her work examined the perceived unquestionable 'truths' of child development and pedagogical practices in the early years. She argued that the child-centred pedagogies constitute a 'regime of truth' based 'on fantasies rather than facts of who the child is' (Walkerdine, 1988, cited in McNaughton, 2005: 38). Work such as that of Walkerdine demonstrates that child development is far more complex than linear approaches might suggest. However, where policy guidance reinforces a single approach, that approach becomes highly regarded, regulated and implemented, establishing its own validity and truth. By implication, inclusion itself may become another indisputable 'truth' where complexities are not discussed and therefore not dealt with.

Education policy is largely driven by a Piagetian model of learning, as evidenced in the EYFS and the National Curriculum, stating what a child should have learnt and achieved during and by a prescribed stage. Equally as concerning is the prescription as to how these skills ought to be taught and subsequently learnt. It would appear that the product of learning is easier to measure than the process. Assessment and accountability play a huge part in the education system. Children's attainment is measured in order to identify past and future progress, but arguably it is also to measure school performance. While the Year 1 phonics screening does not feed into published performance tables, it is recorded and made available to Ofsted. It is used as part of the inspection process, and national and local authority results are fed back to schools in order that they can benchmark the performance of their children. Sarah, by the age of 6, has become part of that assessment, both of herself and of the school. However, is encouraging Sarah to 'speak properly' and engage with phonics done for her benefit, or for the benefit of the school, which will be monitored against her performance?

Staff at Sarah's school may encourage her to speak 'properly' in order to meet politically inspired 'norms' as well as statutory regulations, guidance and documents. The impact that this may have on Sarah and her family could be negative, suggesting that Sarah's cultural understanding and surroundings are not good enough. However, by the age of 6, she has reconciled herself to the fact that success in reading means adopting the language and pronunciation of 'the system'. Sarah has become, as Goffman (1959) would describe, one of 'life's actors', playing a part, in order to succeed at school and in later life.

Inclusion, culture and language

The impact of language use in society and culture is something that requires careful consideration. Language plays a key role in shaping the people we are, and the society that we are part of, but also on the way that others view us. The 'correctness' of a child's speech is therefore determined by culture, which will vary from place to place, and from time to time. Sarah's parents did not consider Sarah's accent was problematic, which may be due to their own social and cultural location. Therefore, absence of a 'correct way' to speak initially presents Sarah and her family with what Bourdieu and Passeron (1977) would describe as poor 'cultural capital'. Bourdieu would advocate that Sarah will either have to *earn* additional cultural capital or be demonised by its lack. Society will categorise or pigeon-hole Sarah, according to Payne (2000). He contends that: 'Social divisions result in social inequalities. Those in the "better" categories have more control over their own lives, usually more money, and can be generally seen to have happier lives' (ibid.: 4). Certain forms of speech are therefore favoured, but at the expense of others and those other speakers become a less powerful group. From this perspective, schools and policy-makers set the level of acceptable cultural capital usually on par with the standards and morals of the middle class. Employed in a classroom situation, it can divide the children into groups, those who share the same cultural capital and those who do not, and set the latter apart. Bourdieu's concept of the cultural arbitrary states that the cultural values taught in schools are not intrinsically better than any other set of values, but are simply the dominant ones. What is selected and taught in the curriculum, including how to 'talk', is merely one selection of knowledge among many (Lambirth, 2007). Sarah has had to earn additional cultural capital. This she has achieved by modifying her accent, in order to make herself fit into an imposed model of attainment. However, in gaining inclusion in the classroom, she has had to exclude (or deny) her domestic voice, the voice she uses at home and with friends. Thus inclusion can be both partial and fragmented across her life experiences.

What could be taken from this is that policy-makers and subsequently practitioners and teachers are teaching and building children how to increase their 'cultural capital' by correcting a child's unwanted speech, in an attempt to meet arbitrary norms and measurements. What they fail to address, however, is the effect that this may have on a child and their family and this can effectively exclude them from the perceived norm. They are ultimately being told that their language is not good enough, and in order to achieve success they will need to speak differently. Wood (1988: 150) stated: 'No one dialect of English, in any linguistic sense, is superior as a means of communication to another.' Drawing on Bourdieu and Passeron's (1977) theory, O'Connor (2011) suggests that teachers unknowingly reaffirm the cultural power of one social group over another: 'Children's home life and parental attitudes, beliefs and traditions, if not fully integrated into the pedagogic and social practises of the setting, can disadvantage a child and lead to a failure to learn' (ibid.: 120). To extend O'Connor's ideas may also mean that children like Sarah may 'learn to fail'.

Specifically looking at linguistics and language use, Fairclough (1989) used sociocultural perspectives to understand language use in an attempt to formulate what he called 'critical language awareness'. He suggested: 'Linguistic phenomena are social in the sense that whenever people speak or listen or read or write, they do so in ways which are determined socially and have social effects' (ibid.: 56). In the same way as Vygotsky viewed language use, or discourse, as socially determined, Fairclough was aware of how culture and discourse worked mutually upon one another. As much as language affected the culture of society, culture also shapes language. He also discusses discourse and power in detail: 'We can say that power in discourse is to do with powerful participants controlling and constraining the contributions of non-powerful participants' (ibid.: 46). There is potentially a subordinate relationship between Sarah and her family and her teacher. Sarah's teacher has the power to control and regulate Sarah's behaviour and speech within her classroom, while Sarah, the non-powerful participant, is required to conform to her teacher's demands.

If certain language practices are deemed to be 'correct', then by implication some language practices are deemed 'incorrect'. For Sarah and her family, there is an imbalance of power that has been created by their perceived lack of 'appropriate' language. These implications can be seen in Marxist theories of children and their social status within society. Wyness (2006: 41) argues that children are 'positioned within the school primarily as future members of the class system'. Children from different class backgrounds, according to Bowles and Gintis

(1976), have differing degrees of control and autonomy in school, which reflect the class positions of their parents. Thus, children's economic and cultural background determines their experiences in school and beyond.

Stoke Speaks Out (a partnership approach to tackle the causes of language delay within the geographic area of Stoke-on-Trent) and the EYFS both state, as if it were unquestionably true, that language acquisition, if not gained by the time the child starts school, means the child will have 'failed' or will substantially struggle in their later language development. Stoke Speaks Out says: 'Language underpins all learning. Without language, children are unable to make friends, socialise and learn. The consequences of growing up with language delay include low educational attainment, poor job prospects and often, anti-social behaviour' (Stoke Speaks Out, 2008: 1).

Another theoretical position, which endeavours to challenge the model of universalised state education, is that of 'de-schooling'. This position is thoughtfully articulated in great depth by Illich (1971), who maintained that it is not education that is problematic, but the 'institutionalisation of education'. Similar to the institutionalisation of other social functions in society, it has created state dependency on such organisations, where to be included means to be the same: 'The pupil is thereby "schooled"' to confuse teaching with learning, grade advancement with education, a diploma with competence, and fluency with the ability to say something new' (ibid.: 9). In this context, the state 'has become a "schooled society", obsessed with certification, selection, social control and the "ritualisation of progress"' (Suissa, 2010: 111). The notion of social control is particularly disconcerting in any society where 'freedom' is celebrated as an intrinsic right. In the United Nations Convention on the Rights of a Child, it states: 'You have a right to learn and use the language and customs of your family whether or not these are shared by the majority of the people in the country where you live' (UNICEF, 1989: Article 30). However, it would seem that for Sarah and her family, the fundamental right to speak in a way that reflects their cultural values is somewhat difficult when 'state institutions' demand otherwise. Illich (1971) powerfully advocates that this institutionalisation is particularly damning for the poor. He claims that the increasing reliance on institutions such as the school 'adds a new dimension to their helplessness: psychological impotence, the inability to fend for themselves' (ibid.: 11).

Inclusion in the classroom

It would seem that in a bid to facilitate ways to enrich appropriate speech in the classroom, some academics and teachers have often failed to take into account a number of key cultural, ideological and political issues that affect a child's ability to 'succeed' in school. Currently the education system seems to present a deficit model of working-class children and concentrates on repairing those deficiencies in the children using the EYFS as guide, instead of choosing the alternative, of restructuring the curriculum and setting other criteria for success. Government documents, as referred to earlier, seem to illustrate a confidence in a 'universal truth', when in reality there can be multiple truths translated from multiple experiences. Understandings of inclusion therefore have to be revisited in order to replace the perspective of a fixed state which you must join in order to be successful, with a willingness to be flexible and accommodating of individuals' identities, backgrounds and needs, to embrace richness and difference.

When considering Sarah's experiences, we have highlighted the relationship between Sarah's identity, the assessment of her competency and school accountability in terms of phonic awareness.

1. How would you approach Sarah aged 4? She is described as: (a) lively, talkative, confident and eager to learn; and (b) with a 'Potteries' accent.
2. How would you celebrate her identity while subscribing to the inevitable regulatory need for her to be measurably phonically competent?
3. What can you learn from her?
4. How can you provide Sarah with the tools to understand reading from both a standard phonics approach as well as alternatives that recognise what she can do rather than what is perceived as what she cannot do?

Case study 4.3: Pronunciation dictionary

Sarah is a competent speaker and listener; she has already proven this in her ability to converse confidently.

In her third term in Reception she is asked by the teaching assistant (TA) to help her create a shared audio dictionary. Sarah and the TA enlist the help of Sarah's parents and grandparents. Together they create a dual pronunciation dictionary, as the TA explains to Sarah so that they can both hear where words sound the same and when the sound is different. At the end of the year Sarah takes part in a multicultural event staged by the school. She recites a poem about sounds, mixing standard and non-standard words.

Making use of theory

Rich (1979: 6) suggests that literacy in its many forms can become a tool of control. 'My daily life as a teacher confronts me with young men and women who have had language and literature *used against* them, to keep them in their place, to mystify, to bully, to make them feel powerless.'

Case study 4.4: Joanne's story

Joanne is a recently graduated PGCE student with a First Class degree in Early Childhood Studies. She was born and brought up in the North Midlands where the local accent and dialect are quite marked. However, her mother, a primary school teacher insisted that much of her local accent was 'ironed out' before she got to school.

Her first teaching role is in a Reception/Year 1 class in a school in a multicultural school in the Midlands. When planning for her first literacy session, she reflects upon her own attitude to accent and phonics teaching.

■ How will she achieve her dual aim of successful phonic awareness and preservation of cultural linguistic heritage?
■ How will she prevent one overpowering the other?
■ How will accent and dialect be celebrated and not berated, in the classroom and beyond?

The coupling of knowledge, language and power so famously articulated by Michel Foucault (1971) and Fairclough (2001) was in many ways pre-empted by Fanon (1967). Fanon argued that language becomes an index of social/cultural difference and power imbalance. Obviously, it could be argued that much has changed in the half century since Fanon was writing. Overt colonialism and its links to subjection may have receded. However, have they been replaced by a more subtle yet still persuasive imperative? Do children have to adapt their behaviour, including their speech, in order to 'fit' into the universalised schooling system? Many would argue that underlying structures of oppression and injustice remain prominent in today's society. Dominant Westernised discourses of 'favoured' behaviour or language can be seen to perpetuate social differences: 'Dominant ideologies of how children grow and develop have become another of colonialism's truths that permit no questioning, and that is imposed unhesitatingly upon people around the world for their own good' (Viruru, 2005: 16).

Educational policy-makers, both now and in the past, appear to be informed by biological and scientific truth, such as Piaget's ages and stages theory, which has become translated into both the structure and content of curricula, where assessment is set against preformed and generic 'norms', yet the wording of the revised Statutory Framework for Early Years Foundation Stage (2014) is 'every child is a unique child'. However, if every child is unique and no two children are the same, there cannot be a one-size-fits-all education system. Culture and language play a huge part in who we are and how we develop, and cannot be assessed uniformly.

Conclusion

This chapter has demonstrated that adopting an alternative way of seeing the world can challenge the dominant authority of developmental psychology, potentially revealing other ways of seeing children. We used Sarah's case study to look specifically at post-colonial theory (Fanon, 1967; Spivak, 1990; Said, 1993) and the dominant strategies currently used to develop reading in young children.

We have explored how a dominant theory may be translated and grounded within the practitioner's consciousness. Using notions of dominant discourses and hierarchical positioning, we have examined how colonising constructions may permeate students' understanding of child development. Our aim was to disturb ideas of 'norms' and acceptability, especially with regard to language. By focusing on accent and dialect, we have tried to demonstrate how these may be perceived as a hindrance, due to their deviation from the 'mother tongue'. We considered the concept of singular and 'correct English' and how deviation may be represented as inferior and a less worthy attribute. Much of our discussion was based on the teaching of reading via phonics, specifically synthetic phonics, where all too easily success at reading is seen as a requirement to adopt one language culture at the expense of a more personal culture and identity.

In using post-colonialism to explore how facets of children's learning might be perceived by practitioners, we have identified how practitioners may become, unwittingly, instruments of an implicit but powerful cultural dominance. This has provided an alternative to conventional, traditional and dominant ideas, which are prevalent in much Early Years training and which dictates the practice of many practitioners. These ideas help to create social notions of what is acceptable and normal, potentially at the expense of originality and individuality. Consequently, our aim was to provide some approaches that may allow practitioners and students to take up the challenge of engaging in different ways of seeing children's learning and development. This allows practitioners to question and challenge their own thinking with regard to the 'unique child', the privileging of Received Pronunciation and the status of non-standard language.

For practitioners, it provides an opportunity to explore their own experiences and the experiences of children with strong regional accents or who use local dialects. The reflective questions highlight the potential for conflict between the concepts of the 'unique child', 'school readiness,' and phonic screening. This could, in turn, affect identity and identity migration.

Fanon (1967) suggests that the powerless may achieve a modicum of acceptance and a promise of self-determination only by replicating the cultural nuances and characteristics of the powerful. In linguistic terms, this could result in the removal and/or suppression of those dialects (languages), which might be seen as a hindrance to social mobility and social acceptance. As Fanon (ibid.:17) notes: 'A man who has a language consequently possesses the world expressed and implied by that language.' However, what of the child who has yet to acquire that singular and preferred language of the dominant culture? If words and accent can become a social passport, then who becomes the border guards? Who are the judges who can regulate or deny entry? How can language reinforce notions of acceptability, notions that implicitly suggest that not possessing the *lingua franca* may become a barrier to inclusion or, in the post-colonial sense, assimilation? Thus the dominant colonial power directs the dominant discourse. Speaking English in its colonies was the personification of the acceptable and assimilated aboriginal.

References

Ashcroft, B., Griffiths, G. and Tiffin, H. (2002) *The Empire Writes Back: Theory and Practice in Post-Colonial Literatures*. London: Routledge.

Barron, I. and Jones, L. (2012) Performing child(hood). *Children & Society*. Wiley Online publishing.

Bourdieu, P. and Passeron, J. C. (1977) *Reproduction in Education, Society and Culture*. London: Sage.

Bowles, S. and Gintis, H. (1976) *Schooling in Capitalist America*. London: RoutledgeFalmer.

Bradley, B. (1989) *Visions of Infancy*. Cambridge: Polity Press.

Bronfenbrenner, U. (1979) *The Ecology of Human Development: Experiments by Nature and Design*. Cambridge, MA: Harvard University Press.

Burman, E. (2001) Beyond the baby and the bath water: post-dualistic developmental psychologies for diverse childhoods. *European Early Childhood Education Research Journal*, 9(1): 5–22.

Cannella, G. and Viruru, R. (2004) *Childhood and Postcolonization: Power, Education, and Contemporary Practice*. London: Routledge Falmer.

Colley, H. (2006) Learning to labour with feeling: class, gender and emotion in childcare education and training. *Contemporary Issues in Early Childhood* , 7(1): 15–29.

Corsaro, W. A. (1997) *The Sociology of Childhood*. Thousand Oaks, CA: Pine Forge Press.

Derrida, J. (1975) White mythology: metaphor in the text of philosophy, trans. F.C.T. Moore. *New Literary History*, 6(1): 5–74.

DfE (Department for Education) (2013) *More Great Childcare: Raising Quality and Giving Parents More Choice*. London: Department for Education.

DfE (Department for Education) (2014) *Statutory Framework for the Early Years Foundation Stage*. London: Department for Education.

Fairclough, N. (1989) *Language and Power*. London: Longman.

Fairclough, N. (2001) *Language and Power*, 2nd edn. London: Routledge.

Fanon, F. (1967) *Black Skin, White Masks*. Sidmouth: Pluto Press.

Foucault, M. (1971) The discourse on language, trans. Rupert Swyer. In H. Adams and L. Searle (eds) (1986) *Critical Theory Since 1965*. Tallahassee, FL: University Press of Florida, pp. 148–62.

Foucault, M. (2002) *Power: Essential Works of Michel Foucault, 1954–1984*, Vol. 3. Harmondsworth: Penguin.

Giles, H. and Powesland, P. F. (1975) *Speech Style and Social Evaluation*. London: Academic Press.

Goffman, E. (1959) *The Presentation of Self in Everyday Life*. Harmondsworth: Penguin.

Honeybone, P. and Watson, K. (2006) *Phonemes, Graphemes and Phonics for Liverpool English*. London: Education Committee of the Linguistics Association of Great Britain.

Illich, I. (1971) *De-Schooling Society*. Harmondsworth: Penguin.

James, A., and Prout, A. (eds) (1997) *Constructing and Reconstructing Childhood*. London: Falmer.

James, A., Jenks, C., and Prout, A. (1998) *Theorising Childhood*. Cambridge: Polity.

Lambirth, A. (2007) Challenging the laws of talk: ground rules, social reproduction and the curriculum. *Curriculum Journal*, 17(1): 59–71.

Lippi-Green, R. (1997) *English with an Accent: Language, Ideology and Discrimination in the United States*. London: Routledge.

Luke, A. (1986) Linguistic stereotypes, the divergent speaker and the teaching of literacy. *Journal of Curriculum Studies*, 18(4): 397–408.

McMahon, A., Barras, W., Clark, L., Knooihuizen, L., Patten, R. and Sullivan, A. (2011) Language Matters 1: Linguistics. In J. Bates (ed.) *The Public Value of Humanities*. London: Bloomsbury Press.

MacNaughton, G. (2005) *Doing Foucault in Early Childhood Studies: Applying Poststructural Ideas*. London: Routledge.

Maylor, U. (1995) Identity, migration and education. In M. Blair, J. Holland and S. Sheldon (eds) *Identity and Diversity: Gender and the Experience of Education*. Maidenhead: Open University Press.

Morss, J. R. (1996) *Growing Critical*. London: Routledge.

O'Connor, J. (2011) Applying Bourdieu's concepts of social and cultural capital and habitus to Early Years research. In T. Waller, J. Whitmarsh and K. Clarke (eds) *Making Sense of Theory and Practice in Early Childhood: The Power of Ideas*. Maidenhead: Open University Press.

Payne, G. (2000) *Social Divisions*. Basingstoke: Macmillan.

Qvortrup, J. (1987) The sociology of childhood. Special Issue of *International Journal of Sociology*, 17(3): 3–37.

Rich, A. (1979) *On Lies, Secrets and Silence*. New York: Norton.

Rose, J. (2006) *Independent Review of the Teaching of Early Reading*. London: Department of Education and Skills.

Said, E. (1993) *Culture and Imperialism*. London: Vintage.

Skeggs, B. (1997) *Formations of Class and Gender*. London: Sage.

Spivak, G. C. (1988) Subaltern studies: deconstructing historiography in other worlds. In G. C. Spivak, *Essays in Cultural Politics*. London: Routledge.

Spivak, G. C. (1990) *The Postcolonial Critic*. London: Routledge.

Standards and Testing Agency (2012) *Assessment Framework for the Development of the Year 1 Phonics Screening Check*. London: Department of Education.

Stoke Speaks Out (2008) The challenge. Available at: www.stokespeaksout.org/home/About%20Us (accessed 25 April 2012).

Suissa, J. (2010) Should the state control education? In R. Bailey (ed.) *The Philosophy of Education*. London: Continuum.

UNICEF (1989) *The United Nations Convention on the Rights of the Child*. New York: UNICEF.

Viruru, R. (2005) The impact of postcolonial theory on early childhood education. *Journal of Education*, 35: 7–29.

Walkerdine, V. (1988) *The Mastery of Reason: Cognitive Development and the Production of Rationality*. London: Routledge.

Wood, D. (1988) *How Children Think and Learn*. Oxford: Blackwell.

Wyness, M. (2006) *Childhood and Society: An Introduction to the Sociology of Childhood*. Basingstoke: Palgrave Macmillan.

Yelland, N. and Kilderry, A. (2005) Against the tide: new ways in early childhood education. In N. Yelland (ed.) *Critical Issues in Early Childhood Education*. Maidenhead: Open University Press.

Young, R. (2001) *Postcolonialism: An Historical Introduction*. Oxford: Blackwell.

5

A family's perspective on Special Educational Needs and inclusion

Gill Pritchard and Kathy Brodie

The aims of this chapter are:

■ To consider children with Special Educational Needs (SEN) and their inclusion in a setting
■ To examine one family's perspective on inclusion and their child with SEN
■ To analyse the questions that this may raise in your setting and with your practice.

Introduction

More often than not, when 'inclusion' and Early Years practice are mentioned, there is an assumption that it is about Special Educational Needs (SEN). A statement such as 'We have a child who wears glasses and he gets involved in everything' may follow this. However, the inclusion of children with SEN is much more complicated than this. In this chapter, the inclusion and integration of children with SEN are discussed, but from the perspective of a single family with a child who has SEN and who has attended an Early Years setting. The family's perspective was recorded in a series of interviews with different family members, each telling their unique story. These insights will help you to make respectful and thoughtful choices about how you support and challenge the children in your care.

Note on the language used

The language and terminology change more rapidly and more significantly in the Special Educational Needs arena than in any other area of Early Years provision. We have tried to use the most up-to-date terms possible, but you should be aware they might change over time. Where there is any query over the term to be used, we have simply tried to be respectful of the child.

The Children and Families Act (2014: 19) defines a child with Special Educational Needs thus: 'a child or young person has special educational needs if he or she has a learning difficulty or disability which calls for special educational provision to be made for him or her'. In addition, for those children under compulsory school age, SENs defined as a child

> [who] has a learning difficulty or disability if he or she is likely to [have a disability which prevents or hinders him or her from making use of facilities] when of compulsory school age (or would be likely, if no special educational provision were made).

Having English as an Additional Language (EAL) is defined as 'the language (or form of language) in which he or she is or will be taught is different from a language (or form of language) which is or has been spoken at home' (The Children and Families Act, 2014: 19). Note that this is not automatically an SEN. There may well be children who have EAL, but who have no additional requirements at all.

Over the years Special Educational Needs and the inclusion of young children has changed beyond recognition. Until 1970, the responsibility for educating 'handicapped' children laid with the Health Authority, not the Local Education Authority (LEA). Then came the ground-breaking Warnock Report in 1978, which moved children from segregated 'Special Schools' into mainstream education, wherever possible. Since then, Baroness Warnock has suggested that the pendulum has swung too far in this direction and that some issues need to be redressed (Warnock, 2005; Warnock and Norwich, 2010). Her worries include that there is still a need for smaller, specialist schools which is going unfulfilled; that children with SEN are now susceptible to bullying in mainstream schools; 'Statements' (now Education, Health and Care plans) should only be used to access special schools and not be used merely to procure resources and that, most crucially, any child who is included in the mainstream school should have a sense of belonging and well-being within their school.

The UK Government's Education and Skills Committee reported, in 2006, that the Warnock SEN framework was 'struggling to remain fit for purpose' (Education and Skills Committee, 2006: 12). Although a lot of the educational and aspirational ideology was the same, for example, joined-up services, tailored support and meeting the needs of the children, it was felt that radical changes to the framework and legislation were needed in order to make these ideas a reality.

This really started the momentum for change in how we think about inclusion, Special Educational Needs and education. Most recently it has been the Children and Families Act (2014) that has updated the Code of Practice (COP) for Special Educational Needs for children in the UK. This has updated some of the terminology, for example, Special Educational Needs and Disability (SEND) replaces SEN. In addition, the age range has been extended from birth to 25 years of age and some of the paperwork has been replaced, though the process of a graduated approach is still recommended. 'Statements', those documents which state the unique, individual and sometimes complex needs of the child, have been replaced by Education, Health and Care (EHC) plans. However, the main heart of SEN and inclusion is still the same, with the aim of integration between the various agencies involved, an ethos of co-operation between agencies and the vital support requirements for families.

In practice, this has meant that in the past few decades, many Early Years settings have welcomed more and more children with a wide range of SEN, including reasonably complex needs. These may be referrals from specialist or outside agencies, or be simply the parents' or carers' choice. Parents, carers and families now, more than ever, have the choice of which Early Years setting their child may attend. In general, in the sector, it is no longer assumed that a child with SEN will attend a special school, but they have the choice of settings just as any other child would.

For settings and practitioners, this means that they now have to become proficient in including children who may have additional needs that practitioners have not previously encountered. As local authority services and support are cut in the current economic climate, this may have to be done with reduced resources, both in terms of money, and people with expertise to support practitioners.

Integrated, co-operative and collaborative working between parents, carers and families has always been critical to the success of inclusion. With parents and carers having more choice and a louder voice, there is the possibility of more conflict between the multi-agency and the families. Both parties will certainly have the child's best interests at heart, but how this may be best served could be viewed differently.

Case study 5.1: A new child in the setting

A family has been recommended to come to your setting, because you have an excellent reputation for your inclusive practice. The family's little boy, Alex, who is 3 years old, has speech and language difficulties.

When Dad phoned up to make an appointment to come to visit the setting, the practitioner who answered the phone asked some questions about Alex, including:

- Will he be able to take part in circle time?
- How much time have I got to spend doing his therapy each day?
- Can he go to the toilet without bothering a member of staff?
- Does he play well with other children?

(Continued)

(Continued)

When Mum and Dad came for their visit, they were welcomed at the door and shown in. During the look around the setting, the practitioner showing them around engaged in conversation with Mum, but didn't really talk to Dad at all. Several times she referred to Alex's inability to talk or communicate.

When the setting manager and SENCO met with the family later on in the day, to discuss the arrangements needed before Alex started, it transpired that Dad was a speech and language therapist. He also explained that he was the main carer, along with his parents, while his wife, a GP, was working. Although Alex had some speech and language difficulties, he could communicate proficiently with sign language and was a very independent little boy.

Dad had felt that Alex would not be made welcome in the setting or be included in the other social activities that they wanted him to experience. He was also concerned that the practitioners did not understand the speech and language programme that had been designed for Alex, and would not bother doing it.

The SENCO was able to reassure Dad and explained how many other children had had very successful speech and language support at the setting.

Afterwards, at a staff meeting, the situation was discussed with all the practitioners.

Looking at Case study 5.1, consider the following questions:

1. Were the questions asked by the practitioner who answered the phone relevant?
2. How could the language used by this practitioner be changed to make it more positive?
3. What could the practitioner, who did the show around, do to further include the family?
4. How would this have improved the outcomes for Alex?
5. Who else could be involved in the process?
6. How would you deliver the resultant staff meeting?

If you are going to work in an effective partnership with parents, it is essential to appreciate a family's point of view. They will know and understand their child better than anyone else and have a unique awareness of how inclusion will affect the whole family.

As a practitioner, it can sometimes be difficult to truly understand what it is like to be a parent of a child with Special Educational Needs. In order to give an insight into this, one family, who has a child with SEN, talked about their experiences and views on inclusion. This gives us one perspective on the things that are important to a family and the kinds of frustrations that may occur. These may be similar to the experiences that families in your setting may have, but they may also be very different. The reason for sharing these perspectives with you is to demonstrate how a family may view inclusion differently to that of the SENCO or other multi-professionals and to raise some reflective questions about this.

Members of the family were asked a range of semi-structured questions on their experiences of inclusion with Lily, who has attended a private Early Years setting and is now in school. Lily is a vibrant, very sociable and charming girl, with a diagnosed SEN. The interview narratives are analysed under four broad themes of interest: (1) inclusion; (2) inclusive practice; (3) wider family concerns; and (4) the multi-professional team. These were the four themes that appeared the most prevalent during the interviews. Each theme is introduced with some theoretical background and concluded with some reflective questions.

Interview narrative: inclusion of a child who has Special Educational Needs

Many people have explored the concept of inclusion and Special Educational Needs in Early Years education and care. The discourse used by Professor Cathy Nutbrown is one that encapsulates our personal approach to inclusion: 'Respectful educators will strive to afford every child equality of opportunity. Not just children who are easy to work with, obliging, endearing, clean, pretty, articulate, capable, but *every* child – respecting them for who they are' (Nutbrown, 1996: 54). This highlights children as individuals, as unique beings, who should be included as a moral and ethical right. However, this may be much easier said than done.

As a practitioner you may hear the word integration being used as well as inclusion. Integration suggests that the child needs to change to be able to fit into the system that already exists. Inclusion, on the other hand, implies that the setting, practitioners, policies and procedures must adapt to meet the children's individual needs, to 'enable the child to participate as fully as possible' (Drifte, 2013: 16). This is true for any child, whether they have Special Educational Needs or not. From a family's perspective the two approaches could feel very different and for the family who have a child with SEN, it may mean the difference between joining the setting or not. For example, an inclusive setting would ensure that there is a visual timetable for the children, but a setting with integration-style policies would expect children to 'get to know' the routine with no support.

In terms of observation, assessment and planning, including a child who has SEN may be simple because the types of observations are already defined. For example, a child who may be stammering will need lots of observations on their speech. There may also be parameters defined by other professionals that have to be observed and recorded, such as how far a child can walk unaided. The information is then used to update the play plans or therapy programmes, forming the planning. However, occasionally this complicates observations because practitioners may need to learn new skills in order to make accurate observations. For example, a speech disorder may require observations to be recorded of the exact nature of the speech pattern – is the front of the word missing, the end or is there no pattern?

Although inclusion may be desirable from the practitioner's perspective, as well as a legal perspective, the reality can be difficult to achieve for some practitioners. There may be anxiety about learning new skills for observations or having to modify systems to ensure inclusion. There may not be sufficient support from the setting manager or the local authorities.

A family's perspective

From a family's perspective, it is acknowledged that full inclusion is the ideal situation, but that it may not always be perfect in reality. There will always be times when either the system is unable to cope or there is a lack of sufficient funds or time to meet an individual's needs. However, it is desirable that practitioners should strive for full inclusion and not settle for 'good enough' or use excuses for not improving inclusion. Inclusion and inclusive practices need to be reviewed and reflected upon frequently, to ensure that practice is as good as it can possibly be.

One very important aspect of inclusion for the family is that it is available to every child, regardless of background. The family members interviewed for the research for this chapter have good knowledge of the local authority's systems, as well as the theory of inclusion. They felt this facilitated them in asking the right questions and making sure that things, like school applications, were followed up. This could be a very different experience for families who either do not understand the systems in place for their child, or who are less confident in asking 'the experts' about the next steps for their child.

The family's experience shows that there is a massive range of inclusive practice and inclusion. This varies from setting to setting and even room to room within a larger setting. It may depend on a single practitioner who has encouraged and enabled inclusion in the setting or the support available at that specific time from the local authority. The family's assessment of this situation is that it is natural to have different levels of inclusion, especially when it is beyond the setting's control, such as being reliant on local authority funding. However, the critical aspect was that the practitioners were responsive and kept the family informed when there were changes.

> ■ You will be reflecting constantly on your practice. How do you evidence or record this? Do you get an opportunity to discuss this with other professionals?

- How do families who have children with SEN in your setting know that you are constantly reflecting on your practice with their child? How do you share your reflective practice with them?
- How would you classify your practice – is it inclusion or integration? Do the children have to fit into your systems, or do you adapt, modify and adjust your practice to include the children?
- Where is your setting on the continuum of inclusion and inclusive practice? Does this vary with your personal practice? Is there anything you can do to improve inclusion across the whole setting?

Interview narrative: what is effective inclusive practice to a family?

Background

Any relationship between practitioners, the family and the multi-professional team will take time and dedication. As Wall comments, '[We] should never presume to have empathy with, or understand, all parents. At best we can respect, listen and use the systems in place to support parents' (2011: 59). Every family will consider effective, inclusive practice to be something different, because every family has different life experiences, children and family structures. Some parents may be very keen to have support and to involve professionals. Others may be protective of their children, possibly to the point of being over-protective and not allowing anyone else to help them. You should also remember that circumstances will almost certainly vary over time as things change, maybe with the arrival of a new sibling or altered childcare arrangements due to work commitments.

A family's perspective

The family's examples of good, effective inclusive practice often hinged on preparation and the family being kept informed. These included the Child Development Centre (CDC) being ready for Lily to attend assessment sessions as well as other, suitable classes being arranged, such as physiotherapy and aqua-therapy. This made it very easy for parents, and grandparents, as well as extended family members, to get involved. Lily benefitted greatly both from attending classes, but also from having the whole family getting involved with her therapy.

Interestingly, the language that was used by practitioners and multi-professionals came up several times during the interviews. The choice of words or phrases can help or hinder a situation. It was felt that the way language was used illuminates the practitioner's or multi-professional's thinking. For example, it may be as simple as placing the child before the SEN, e.g. saying 'a boy with autism' rather than 'an autistic boy'. By putting the child first, you are demonstrating that it is the child who is important, not their disability or SEN.

When inclusive practice works well, Lily's views were represented and noted. When Lily was younger, this was through observations of her body language and actions. This was seen as desirable, and the family felt that they could also be advocates for Lily. As she gets older, the hope is that Lily will be able to express her own views. The social experiences of school are as important, or possibly more important, than academic achievement for the family. Lily is fully included in all social dimensions of the school, including being invited to parties, going on school trips and doing school performances, which is obviously extremely important for the family.

One very important relationship is that between the inclusion worker and Lily, both in the Early Years setting and, in later years, in her school. The inclusion worker at school, a Teaching Assistant (TA), has been a good advocate on Lily's behalf, representing her views to multi agencies, but also cascading information back to the family about the latest information, courses, and so on. While Lily is at school, her inclusion worker will move through the school with her. This is viewed by the family as hugely positive experience for Lily and the family as a whole, because mutual trust and respect have already been built up. She has experience of working with Lily, is well informed about Lily's SEN, and understands the family. The inclusion worker and the class teacher evidently have a good relationship, and communicate well between themselves. They are clear on their individual roles and who will interact with the family and how this will be done. For example, the inclusion worker always does the morning and evening handover. This makes it much easier for the family to know who to go to in different circumstances and to understand the internal lines of communication.

In brief, Lily has been *enabled* to do everything. She has been fully included and the small considerations and support that have been necessary have made a massive difference to her experiences and to the family.

- How does the language that you use to families demonstrate your thinking?
- Do you have information about specialist classes or groups that the children could attend? How could you find out about more groups?
- Are the families you work with aware of who to go to and when? For example, who would they ask about their child's Individual Education Plan (IEP) or play plan? Is it a different person who does their speech and language programme? How do you make this clear to families in a positive and helpful way?
- How can you ensure the relationship between the inclusion worker and the family is effective and enabling?

Interview narrative: including the wider family circle

Background

Children with SEN, especially those with complex medical histories, may have complicated lives outside of your Early Years setting. Depending on the type of SEN or medical interventions needed, there may be doctors or hospital appointments and visits to the child development centre (or unit). This may affect the rest of the family, as siblings have to be picked up from the setting by other family members or friends. For this reason, including the wider family circle for a child with SEN is a much more important consideration than with other families. It is useful to get to know who will be going to the appointments, so you can liaise more effectively. You should also be aware that there might be a lot of other things going on at home that could disrupt the family life, such as alterations to the home, or even having to move house. This will affect the whole family, including siblings, grandparents, aunts and uncles, and support that you can give to the whole family at this time could be invaluable.

It could be that childcare needs to be more specialised, due to things like feeding buttons, so other members of the family are unable to come to babysit as easily. This can make parents and carers feel isolated and create tensions. Respite care may be available, but this can be expensive and infrequent. These problems can be compounded if there are other considerations, such as not having transport to get to hospital or specialist appointments; not being able to understand or speak English; mental health issues within the family; domestic violence – to name a few. You should be conscious of these additional pressures on families and how this could affect a child's attendance at your setting, their mood and the interactions between parents and practitioners.

Most children will have SEN that are simpler, such as speech and language difficulties. However, these will still have implications for the wider family, as parents, grandparents and carers help with therapy programmes, attend meetings and arrange for childcare for siblings.

A family's perspective

For the family interviewed, it was particularly important to have the wider family circle included, because the grandparents take a very active role in the childcare, especially as Lily has a younger sibling, who is not at school yet. He is very loving and caring, thinking and talking about Lily when she is at school.

This also means that the grandparents and other family members need to be apprised of the SEN, attend meetings and understand choices that are being made, because it will affect their care routines. During the interviews, it became obvious that family members could see the choices from different perspectives. This does not mean to say that there was right and wrong, but that some family members are more practical, because they have greater knowledge and practical experience. Other family members need to keep the balance of views in order to make choices about Individual Education Plans (IEPs), therapies or treatments.

Both the school and the Early Years setting liaised with all family members equally, because they understand the childcare situation and the involvement of grandparents in this role. This made the family feel valued and able to collaborate more readily with practitioners, sharing experiences and stories of Lily's adventures outside of the setting. This may be a natural part of parent partnership for the vast majority of practitioners. However, practitioners may not realise the very significant difference this makes to the family.

- How have you been able to involve other members of the family?
- What do you do to support siblings?
- How could facilitate therapy programmes for families?
- How do you support families who may be experiencing additional difficulties, such as low levels of literacy or mental health?
- What sort of positive difference do you think you could make to a family's experience of collaboration with your setting?

Interview narrative: the multi-professional team

Background

In an Early Years setting, it is every practitioner's responsibility to be aware of children with SEN and to have an overview of the therapies or programmes in place to support the children. The Special Educational Needs Co-ordinator (SENCO) co-ordinates, facilitates and manages the SEN for the setting. The SENCO may also have some key children with SEN who will require specific support. However, it is not good practice to simply leave all the children with SEN in the SENCO's care; the education and care of children with SEN must be a whole team issue. This is because other practitioners will be caring and supporting children with SEN, so they need to be conscious of their key children's additional needs. Other practitioners will observe children with SEN in the setting and may see something that the SENCO has missed. Similarly, it could be more effective to have the key person liaise with other professionals, such as the speech and language therapist, because they know the child best.

You may have a range of multi-professionals come to the setting, some from the local authority, and some from the health services and, possibly, some from specialist services such as the cochlear implant team, for example.

The variety of roles and what is available to settings, especially private, voluntary and independent settings, differs massively from local authority to local authority. For example, some local authorities may have a Portage team, whilst others do not; some teams may charge to visit the setting, while others provide a service free of charge. This may limit the therapy that families can access, or may mean that they have to pay or travel to visit the professionals, rather than attend at the setting. It is useful to be aware of what is available, bearing in mind that this may change as local authorities change over time.

It is very easy to use jargon with families, especially as you become more familiar with the systems for children with SEN. You should always check that the family understand both what the acronym stands for and what this actually means. For example, telling the family that TAC stands for Team Around the Child does not fully explain that this is a multi-professional meeting or what happens during the meeting. Similarly, the implications of completing a Common Assessment Framework (CAF) form or an Education, Health and Care plan (EHC plan) need to be explained, as well as the phrases.

Working with families and multi-professionals is most effective when it is collaborative working, with a full two-way communication. This does take more time and effort but can make the difference between a child making good progress or not.

A family's perspective

When asked about their experiences with multi-professionals, the family were very positive, stating that there had only been a couple of instances when they felt that the system had not worked. In the first example, a chair had been provided for Lily, which she had to be strapped into. This meant that Lily could not socialise independently with her friends and highlighted her differences. In fact, Lily was very able to sit in a regular chair and did not need anything extra. The second example was fitting Lily with hearing aids, even though there was not clear evidence that she needed them. In both cases the parents queried the decisions of the professionals and Lily was reassessed, reversing these two decisions. It was noted by the family that less well-informed or less confident parents might not be as self-assured to ask the questions or challenge the multi-professional team.

The family also commented that, though the general experience has been of caring professionals, the professionals are still under pressure to provide a service with restricted time and budgets. This means they may only have limited knowledge of Lily and her abilities. On occasions they found the professional could be single-minded about their own discipline, to the exclusion of others.

The best experiences were when the professionals worked with the family, as a two-way process, with mutual respect and active listening. This was the most successful when done over a longer time period, such as with the physiotherapist, who has seen Lily grow and progress. The family felt that being able to trust the professionals improves both the process and the quality of the outcomes for Lily.

- If you were a parent, would you understand this sentence: 'You need to meet the SENCO and SALT at the TAC to discuss the CAF and capture it on an EHC'? Reflect on how often you may use jargon or words that may not be familiar to parents and carers. How could you make your setting more family friendly with respect to jargon?
- How could you work more closely with the multi-professional team in your area? What pressures do you understand that they are under?
- How could you find out about the teams in neighbouring areas?
- How do you know if all the practitioners in your setting are up to date on SEN issues?

Implications for practice

The family's personal knowledge/ experience/attitudes matter

It is worth remembering that every family is different and has different experiences, knowledge and attitudes. Some parents may be very confident and able to question professionals. Others may be finding the whole situation difficult to comprehend. You will need to gauge every family's strengths and the areas where they may need additional support from you.

- *Knowledge*: What is the family's current knowledge of the system? What may be available from other support services and how do you access support and help? Depending on the type of SEN and diagnosis, it could be that the family are already experts on their child's SEN and can support you with knowledge and practical help.
- *Experience:* What kind of previous experiences have they had of professionals? It could be that they have had negative experiences, so are unwilling to engage with the system. You may need to give extra time to this type of family, for reassurance. It could be that the family feel their current experience is not as good as previously. This occasionally happens when their child moves from an Early Years setting into compulsory schooling, because there may be less flexibility in the timetable and the multi-professional team may not be as accessible.

■ *Attitudes:* You can sometimes find that a family's attitudes vary over time. For example, initially they may resist a diagnosis or any external help, but once a diagnosis is confirmed, then they want every form of help available. You should make yourself aware of the difficulties that families might be experiencing, in order to understand some of the mixed attitudes that you might encounter.

It could be that parents or carers may not have direct experience of their child's SEN, but extended family, for example, grandparents may have. This presents an ideal opportunity to involve the wider family in both the setting and the multi-professional team, while benefitting from their knowledge. It is sensible to ask parents if there are other family members who would like be invited into the setting for just this sort of reason. Of course, it could be that other family members would prefer not to be directly involved, but might want to advise and help the parents away from the setting.

Conversely, it could be that other family members have had bad experiences with health or educational professionals, so are more hesitant to let the family get involved. Sometimes it is as simple as family members making assumptions, with no real knowledge. For example, that being given a diagnosis of an SEN means that their child *must* leave your setting to go to a 'special school', which may not be the case at all.

Be aware of how family members may want to be viewed. For example, grandparents may have a lot of the caring responsibilities outside of the setting and are viewed as equal partners during decision-making processes. Other families may see the parents as the only people to make choices, even if other family members have expert knowledge or information. It is sensible to discuss who will be involved with decision-making with the family, so they feel comfortable either bringing someone else along for the decisions or not.

Parents and carers come from a wide range of backgrounds. It could be that you have families who are very highly qualified, but are not familiar with childcare or children's education. This can sometimes make the family feel bewildered or defensive, purely because it is outside of their expertise and they are normally in control. Conversely, you may have families who need additional support themselves while you support their child. As with the children in your care, you should treat each family as unique and not make any assumptions about their background, knowledge or attitudes.

■ What roles do the different multi-agency members have? How does this fit with the SENCO role? What are the parents' roles?

■ Is the key person clear on their role and their position with the SENCO, managers and multi-agency professionals?

(Continued)

(Continued)

- How do you communicate with parents and families when there may be additional complicating factors, such as parents with EAL or SEN themselves?
- When working with blended and split families, how do you know who to communicate with and the most effective way to communicate with everyone?

Supporting families with inclusion: what's important to families?

One of the main messages that came from the family interviewed was that they valued enabling strategies. These go beyond simple support, they are the extra things that are done to empower the children with SEN to be more independent, more social and to reach their potential. For example, having an environment where all children can access resources independently and not making assumptions about what children cannot do. These are the things that help children to reach their full potential and do not restrict or limit children simply because they have additional needs.

Another common message was that the family appreciated practitioners who valued and demonstrated their understanding of parents and carers as the children's first and most enduring educators. This could be as simple as a word of encouragement about something done at home or it could be more elaborate, such as collaborating with parents on the setting's planning.

Having individualised provision already prepared in advance is a positive action for families. It shows that the setting is welcoming of their child and that some thought has been given to the relationship. If you do have problems with the environment or resources, keep these as your problems; don't make them the family's concern. Similarly, make sure you have briefed all the team on how you will be including children and that they have an understanding of the situation. This stops parents having to keep repeating their story to every practitioner.

It is good practice to explain your reasoning to the family. If you have moved the inclusion worker, or there is a change in staff, for example, then explain why this is in advance and be ready to talk through the implications of this. It could be really obvious to you, but it may not be for the family. This can alienate them if it is not handled sensitively and appropriately. It is an easy thing to include the family with a quick verbal update and this will help your collaboration at the same time.

Although it may seem like a minor part of your role, do listen carefully to everything that the family would like to share with you. To you, it may seem like a small problem, but it will have taken some thought on behalf of the family to overcome their misgivings to talk to you, meaning it is of importance to them. By building the small trusts, when it comes to the big decisions, it will be much easier for you both.

Do be aware of what is best for the child. Keeping the same inclusion worker throughout their time with you could produce over-reliance on one person and may make transition more difficult, but it could equally be that one person needs to know all about the situation to provide continuity. This is a situation that will need to be constantly reviewed and will vary from family to family, child to child.

The needs of each child are unique. Having options open for things such as therapies makes life much easier for families. They may not want to, or be able to, access everything, but giving families the options really helps.

Give some careful thought to how multi-professionals meetings may be a different experience for you and for families. This may be the hundredth meeting you have attended, with familiar people, but the very first meeting for the family, in a room full of strangers. It is beneficial if you can talk parents through the meeting schedule, with explanations of who everyone is (even better if you can get pictures) and their role. Explain jargon that may be used and provide an abbreviations list for them to refer to. Explain where and how the meeting fits into the larger picture, especially if there are many different meetings. Often thinking through this explanation will also clarify ideas for you as well. If you are nervous about doing this with the family, do a test run with a knowledgeable colleague first.

Many professionals have lots of experience and expertise. They can usually make decisions quickly, and in many cases they have to, because they only have limited time allocated to each child in their care. To families, this can feel like professionals are making 'snap judgements' about their child, in a very short time. This should be discussed with families and you should explain how decisions have been made (it is useful for you to know how they were made too!). There could be situations where additional information from the family or more time for observations may have resulted in a different choice. As a bare minimum, it often helps families if you can discuss the therapy programme or decision with them, so there is shared understanding of what will be happening in the future and the benefits of this.

Children are unique, so are their families, so flexibility is key when providing support for families. There will be times when you have to take the lead, setting up meetings, for example. There will be other times when your role will be to provide a listening ear or sounding board. You are likely to become more confident as you gain more experience in a range of circumstances and use different strategies. Be prepared to have new situations present themselves, and when they do, work with the family.

Transition is very stressful for families, and you can expect a bit of a backwards step at this point. For example, the family may be hesitant to give full collaboration, until they trust the practitioners at the new setting and understand their systems. It is sensible to allow some extra time to work with families during transition periods.

Language that we use

Very often, when we are used to having children with SEN, we can sometimes forget that for families this may be a whole new world to them. This can manifest itself in the language that we use with families. The language that we use should be respectful and accurate. For example, always ensure the child comes before the SEN so we have a boy with autism, not an autistic boy. Of course the language we use to describe additional needs will change over time as new phrases are coined. For example, children used to be referred to as 'educationally subnormal' if they had additional needs. We would now consider this to be disrespectful and even offensive. It is not unusual to find that as language changes, it can sometimes be considered to be disrespectful to use the wrong term. This may be entirely unintentional on the part of the practitioner, but it is well worthwhile keeping practitioners up to date on both the newest terms and when it is appropriate to use them. Similarly, it is important to keep up to date on things like the multi-professionals' job titles and the way that the local authority teams are organised, so you know who to go to in each circumstance.

It is necessary to describe children's SEN for a number of reasons, including shared understanding between professionals and access to funding. The negative side to this use of language is 'labelling', which can be misleading, and prompt biases or stereotypes. For example, labelling a child with 'dyslexia' means to some people that she will not be able to read or write, which is clearly not the case in most circumstances. You should be aware that sometimes using SEN terms might be reinforcing negative stereotypes, which is not helpful for the family or the child.

You should not use an SEN term until an official diagnosis has been given to the family and they have shared this with you. The way that you can describe a child's additional needs before diagnosis does vary from SEN to SEN. For example, a child with suspected autism might be described as a child who has 'social and communication difficulties'. There is a wide spectrum of children who may be described as having 'speech and language' problems and issues, from mild dysfluency to selective mutism, but you should not guess at a diagnosis.

Sometimes it is not the language of the SEN at all where extra thought is needed. The language that we use is indicative of the feelings that we have. For example, rather than 'your child is able to join our setting' it is much more positive to say 'we would welcome your child to our setting'. This is true for all children, of course, but for families who have a child with a SEN this could be a very significant difference that they may notice.

Finally, your language should be inclusive and empowering for children and their families.

Look back at Case study 5.1.

- What could have been done differently so the practitioners were more aware of the family's experience and knowledge?
- What would have made it easier to listen to the parents' concerns?
- How could you change the language to be more inclusive and empowering for the child?
- Identify and list some SEN terms that have negative connotations and some that have positive connotations.

Conclusion

Inclusion and inclusive practice are closely related to children with SEN and have a long history in the UK. However, it is still a complex and changing landscape. As a practitioner, you may encounter many children with a wide variety of SEN, or you may only have the occasional child with speech and language difficulties. It could be that you have children in your setting now who have an undiagnosed SEN. In all cases, it is important to be fully inclusive, interested and engaged with your children and their families. Good inclusive practice is very often thought about from the setting's perspective. There tends to be a focus on the paperwork, liaison with multi-professionals and ensuring all the legal policies and procedures are followed. However, we know that families are the first and most enduring educators of children. The collaboration with, and co-operation of, parents and carers are a vital part of effective inclusive practice.

Although this chapter is based on one family's experiences with one child, there are several common features that run through it. Enabling and empowering children with SEN are a fundamental part of their inclusion. The language that you use should be positive. It may only be a small consideration for you, but it may be a significant difference for the family. Finally, for effective and successful inclusion of children with SEN, it is especially important to have mindfulness. You *have* to be in the here and now to support both the family and their child.

Further reading

Italy/Holland trip, available from: www.our-kids.org/Archives/Holland.html

This narrative illustrates how some families may feel about finding out that their child has a Special Educational Need.

www.gov.uk/childrens-services/special-educational-needs

This is a good reference site from the Department for Education for the implications of the SEND Act, word definitions, access to support and various statistics.

References

Children and Families Act (2014) *Part 3: Children and Young People in England with Special Educational Needs or Disabilities*. Norwich: The Stationery Office. Available at: www. legislation.gov.uk/ukpga/2014/6/schedule/2/enacted (accessed 5 June 2014).

Drifte, C. (2013) *The Manual for the Early Years SENCO*, 2nd edn. London: Sage.

Education and Skills Committee (2006) *Special Educational Needs: Third Report of Session 2005–06*. Vol. I. London: House of Commons.

Nutbrown, C. (1996) Wide eyes and open minds. In C. Nutbrown, *Respectful Educators – Capable Learners*. London: Paul Chapman.

Wall, K. (2011) *Special Needs and Early Years: A Practitioner's Guide*. London: Sage.

Warnock, M. (2005) *Special Educational Needs: A New Look*. London: Philosophy of Education Society of Great Britain. Available at: www.philosophy-of-education.org/impact/impact_details.asp?id=11.

Warnock, M. and Norwich, B. (2010) *Special Educational Needs: A New Look (Key Debates in Educational Policy)*. London: Continuum.

6

Re-thinking children's well-being and inclusion in practice

Zoe Nangah and Gill Mills

The aims of this chapter are:

- To encourage practitioners to reflect critically on the concepts of well-being and inclusion from a variety of perspectives
- To consider the multifactorial influences underlying children's well-being and how these may impact on inclusive practice
- To assess the effectiveness of strategies which can support well-being and promote inclusion.

Introduction

This chapter will explore the concepts of well-being and inclusion. Initially, consideration of key terminology and definitions concerning well-being and inclusion will be encouraged. The clarification of these terms in relation to your practice will aim to aid reflections, while we seek to encourage exploration and discussion of practices concerning supporting inclusion and well-being and to highlight possible ethical dilemmas that may occur when aiming towards being inclusive of all well-being arenas. Furthermore, definitions will be accompanied by specific models and views of health/well-being with the consideration of how these models/views may affect the terminology, support and factors perceived as being influential in well-being and inclusion topic areas.

The chapter will seek to facilitate reflections on the practices, policies and theories related to well-being and hope to extend criticality regarding how these approaches can achieve inclusion. Alongside definitions, specific models (medical, social constructivist and holistic) to support well-being and to probe considerations regarding how some approaches may be more inclusive than others will be discussed. Recognition of the range of strategies used within the Early Years setting to promote well-being will be suggested. Furthermore, the justification for the focus on inclusion will centre on its crucial contribution to children's well-being in the broadest sense. The research detailed in the research boxes was mainly gleaned from interviews and focus group discussions with practitioners.

Ultimately, we wish to encourage critical reflection on the complexities and dilemmas that may occur in practice (via key reflection points that inspire deeper thinking in relation to well-being and inclusion) and then conclude with some suggested strategies, practices and reflection opportunities for embedding inclusive practices regarding well-being.

What are inclusion and inclusive practices?

Inclusion is a concept; it cannot easily be defined. Booth and Ainscow (2011) provide a description of what inclusion in education is and outline key elements for consideration. Further information regarding inclusion can be gathered from the Centre for Studies on Inclusive Education (CSIE). Booth and Ainscow (2011) highlight that all children should be viewed as equal; the support offered to children in settings should be equal and seek to be anti-discriminatory and anti-oppressive while simultaneously valuing and respecting diversity to celebrate the differences that appear in each child 'individually'. These differences could be along race, class, gender, personality, disability, religious, dietary and numerous other themes and therefore inclusion does not solely refer to specific children, but to *all children*. This ideology of inclusion referring to all children is essential; it is a common mistake to assume that inclusion refers to only specific children and thereby this could lead to exclusion and marginalisation of some children.

The term inclusion overlaps with other key terms such as respecting diversity, valuing diversity, anti-oppressive practice, anti-discriminatory practice and many other related concepts and terms. It is important in your practice that these terms are understood and considered to ensure that planning, teaching, learning and assessment include all children and are applied equally. It is suggested that the concept of inclusion is clarified on a personal and professional level and that you critically consider this terminology and how you are seeking to be inclusive in your practice.

Further exploration of these terms is required to ensure inclusive practices and therefore we would encourage you to consider your use of terminology. The terminology reflection task provides an opportunity to reflect on the terminology used regarding inclusion.

Consider the terminology used regarding inclusion, here are the key terms:

- anti-discriminatory practice
- anti-oppressive practice
- equality and diversity
- inclusion
- inclusive practice
- integration
- respecting and valuing diversity.

Now answer these questions:

- What do you understand by the above terms?
- How does your setting define these terms related to inclusion?
- How does your setting ensure that these principles are transmitted within your practice?
- What are the key policies stating regarding inclusive practice in your Early Years setting?
- Are you an inclusive practitioner? If yes, then how do you achieve inclusion? What does this look like in practice?
- Which policies do you follow?
- Are you inclusive for all children? If yes, then how do you ensure this?
- Is your view of inclusion and diversity influenced by your own experiences, values, attitudes and does it differ or is it the same as the views of colleagues?
- Are any of your practices excluding (unintentionally)?
- What might cause practice to be oppressive or marginalising? How would you seek to challenge these practices and to become more inclusive?

Research results

The findings from the research focus group and the interviews yielded responses to specific questions and it was found that the practitioners' responses to 'What is inclusion?' highlighted equality, valuing all and including all, respecting differences and diversity arenas.

Progressing on from your reflections, it is a legal requirement that your practice is inclusive, for example, within the Equality Act 2010, the United Nations Convention on the Rights of the Child and other legislation, and these inform current policies in your settings and therefore acknowledgement of guidelines, legislation and policies is essential.

- Are you aware of the relevant legislation and policies on inclusion?
- Identify examples of policy and legislation that address the issue of inclusion in the Early Years settings.
- Write a brief summary of the content of the policy and legislation, and interpret how these documents might be used to achieve inclusion.

Legislation ⟶ Policies + Theory ⟶ Practice

Law informs policies. These policies and key theories inform your practice

Why does inclusion matter?

The assumption in this chapter is that inclusion is a vital part of supporting well-being in children. It is acknowledged that if we do not sufficiently understand well-being in general, but especially in children, then how can we, as practitioners, facilitate effective support? In other words, if we are not completely aware of what the major influencing factors are or what inclusion or well-being concepts include, then how can we be confident that our efforts to support inclusion and maximise well-being will be effective? There is not yet enough research into children's well-being to give us a definitive answer (Public Health England, 2013). Inclusion can be seen as one approach to pre-empting potential problems later in life, such as mental ill health. This suggests an overlap between numerous theoretical perspectives, in that it emphasises the importance and perceived effectiveness of early proactive or interventionist approaches. It merely adds to the conviction that inclusion in Early Years practice is not just beneficial for children's well-being, but that it can pay dividends later on.

How do practitioners define health and well-being?

Research results

The findings from the interviews and focus group regarding 'What is "being healthy"?' gave some interesting replies. Practitioners referred to 'dietary elements', 'exercise as healthiness' and the physical elements of health in some cases, while other responses referred to 'feeling good about yourself' and the psychological elements of health.

The psychological, emotional and physical health areas appeared to be represented in the replies provided and these highlight the different perceptions regarding 'being healthy'. Overall, health has many definitions and this chapter cannot cover all of these, but we hope to encourage your reflections in acquiring and refining terminologies used when discussing specific terms. Health and well-being are subjective concepts and can be defined depending on one's own values regarding what it means to be healthy and to have good well-being. For example, if you think that being healthy involves being outdoors in the fresh air, then you may seek to support health in others by providing outdoor opportunities. You may consider that this provision will in turn create greater well-being.

- What definitions do you use for health and well-being?
- Are health and well-being related within your perception and usage of the terms?
- How do resilience, emotional contentment, distress and key emotional terms relate to your definition?
- Do you perceive that well-being affects all children? If yes, then how? If no, then justify why not.
- Are there key influences that may affect well-being more than others?
- How do self-esteem, identity, locus of control, choice and autonomy relate to your well-being definitions?
- If settings and practitioners use different definitions, then can inclusion be achieved?
- Is inclusion easy to observe?
- Will inclusion appear differently for children depending on their well-being needs?
- Are there any ethical dilemmas that emerge from your discussions? If there are, can you resolve them?

Discuss your responses to these questions.

It is clear that health is a complicated concept and can be defined in numerous ways, according to your personal and professional beliefs. Possibly the professional career role that you hold may emphasise particular facets of health and views of what is deemed as healthy/unhealthy. Well-being may be perceived as separate or as connected with the health concept that you hold. One definition of well-being is:

> Well-being is more than the absence of illness and goes beyond life satisfaction. It is linked with an individual's physical health, health behaviours and resilience (the ability to cope with adverse circumstances).
>
> (Public Health England, 2013: 5)

Well-being co-exists with health in some sources. Not only is well-being closely allied to the concept of health here; it is so entwined in the arguments that the two cannot exist independently of each other. Well-being is used 'to refer to the quality of people's lives' (Rees *et al.*, 2010: 2), but what can be interpreted by 'quality' could vary according to context, profession and opinion, culture and individuality as highlighted in the reflection exercises.

A range of perceptions of health and well-being exists in relation to mental health and this positions mental health and well-being along a continuum (see the dual factor model of mental health proposed by Greenspoon and Saklofske, 2001, in The Scottish Government, 2009). This diagrammatic model is a very useful tool for envisioning health and well-being concepts as it indicates that poor mental health does not equate to minimal well-being – this is a crucial consideration for all practitioners and reinforces that well-being is pertinent to all.

The terminology and definitions vary regarding well-being and therefore it is advisable and useful for specific terms to be further clarified. You have been directed to consider terminology related to inclusion and therefore well-being terminology and perceptions could be explored too. Some policies use terms such as 'subjective well-being' (or personal well-being) referring to life satisfaction, positive emotions and whether life is meaningful. Conversely, 'objective well-being' refers to rights and needs such as food, education, mortality rates and life expectancy (Department of Health, 2014). These specific views of well-being present different aspects of well-being and may lead to critical consideration of the wider ecological system. For example, objective well-being may differ in different geographical locations or there may be influences on rights dependent on government policy.

The concepts of inclusion and well-being are vast, therefore the definitions used may differ depending on settings, practitioners' values, approaches and other influences. These terms are ever changing and not fixed. They require on-going reflection to ensure that they are embedded in your practice. The NICE Guidelines on social and emotional well-being in the Early Years uses the term 'vulnerable children' (NICE, 2012b), which effectively suggests that 'well-being needs' may be peculiar to this particular group, rather than all children. This is a divisive assumption. We would argue that practitioners should consider *all children* to have 'well-being needs' and that each child should be considered on their own merit, rather than approaching inclusion from the perspective of a collection of specifically identified needs, which may or may not be assessed as relevant to particular children.

Your choice of definition will show a particular emphasis on specific perspectives; this chapter will support your growing awareness of this, while encouraging your reviewing of this area and appropriateness of specific views. The key areas in the definitions are emphasised.

Perspectives on health and well-being

The psychological perspective

Well-being can be perceived as 'A positive state of mind and body, feeling safe and able to cope, with a sense of connection with people, communities and the wider environment' (National CAMHS Support Service, 2011: 4). Interestingly, this definition highlights the psychological areas, the self-concept, the aspect of safety and the importance of a sense of belonging for well-being. It acknowledges aspects of well-being that have been highlighted in a range of theories historically, for example, Bowlby (1969), indicating attachment, safety and the importance of predictability in relation to emotional well-being. Other theories have emphasised the self-concept, for example, Rogers (1961). There are psychodynamic, humanistic, behaviourist and other sub-perspectives within this approach.

If practitioners take this definition of well-being, then inclusion would involve elements of seeking to ensure a positive state of mind and body. Would a positive state of mind involve positive emotions such as happiness, contentment, etc., or is an Early Years child's emotional development reflected in all emotions being expressed depending on the context or situation? Or do all emotions need to be expressed, as argued by some psychoanalytic perspectives, for appropriate well-being to be achieved?

The safety aspect has been echoed in many theories. Attachment theory (Bowlby, 1969) often centres on concepts such as the 'safe base' and other aspects of emotional security. Does this safety lie within the child's resilience factors or within the context and setting? Safety may involve locked gates and secure environments, key persons and external variables or it could be within the child and be an internal sense of safety gained from earlier relationships.

Internal safety is often neglected and you could consider whether the internal sense of safety comes from within the child (psychoanalytic perspective), or is it linked to the parents/caregivers (psychoanalytic and systemic perspectives)? Is it learnt from the role models (social learning perspectives) or is internal safety associated with neurology and early *in utero* and in non-verbal experiences (Gerhardt, 2004)? Or is it associated with reinforcements and behaviourist perspectives? The social areas and relational elements should be considered, i.e. the 'sense of connection' with people. Is this emphasised in your approach to well-being support and do you consider it a factor in well-being? Psychoanalytic thought may locate earlier templates and experiences as being crucial to later well-being needs, and some authors would agree that earlier emotional and cognitive experiences may affect personality and well-being throughout life (Crittenden, 1997).

Some of these influences on well-being will be discussed later in the chapter. First of all the three specific models – medical, social constructivist and holistic – will be explored.

The medical perspective

Other definitions of well-being highlight the medical and physical elements. The medical views highlight the 'negative' aspect of health and tend to focus on the absence of illness, disease and impairment equating with being healthy. The (now infamous) WHO (1948) definition focuses on well-being as part of a more positive definition of health, but stops short of defining well-being fully in itself. It has been criticised as being more about 'happiness' than health.

Most purist physical health definitions present a more medical angle and emphasise physical health domains regarding well-being arenas, i.e. the presence of ill-health or disease. This medical view is sometimes linked with other social definitions, such as that supplied by CAMHS regarding 'a positive state of mind and body'. This echoes the dualism approach in health and well-being spheres, i.e. the fact that mind and body are connected. Therefore, supporting well-being would involve outdoor play opportunities, healthy eating and dietary requirements alongside psychological and social elements. Primary care approaches to mental health and well-being seem to acknowledge the interconnectedness between mind and body (NHS, 2012).

Consider the medical and physical aspects of health within your practice:

- Does your setting cater for all dietary requirements?
- How are outdoor play opportunities made accessible for all children?
- How do you know if there are equal health interventions and support for all of the children and families in your setting?
- How do you support healthy eating for families? Do you ensure that your healthy eating guidance encompasses all children's (irrespective of culture) dietary preferences, e.g. vegan and considers health needs such as lactose intolerance?
- How is medical support provided? Can all staff administer all medications? Do certain medications require monitoring? Are you qualified to monitor the impact of medications, e.g. Ritalin? How do you ensure that all children are included when they have medical needs?
- Is integrated working part of the provision and is communication effective between these services/practitioners?

Medical views may seek to assign labels, and this may appear to be linked to well-being support, for example, the label may be deemed to signify greater well-being needs and support is required. However, this may not be the case if you consider that some commentators may perceive health and well-being separately.

Do children require a label to have health needs or well-being needs? Defining well-being along 'deficiency' lines creates problems, i.e. it is usually understood in relation to children with some level of additional need. The idea that all children have a range of needs and that these vary along a continuum is often overlooked. Inclusive practice therefore needs first to place the child at the centre, rather than identifying a range of needs or deficiencies which are then 'allocated' to the child in order to inform our approach to supporting children's well-being.

The social constructivist perspective

Rather than being static, well-being emerges from how people interact with the world around them at different points in their lives. It incorporates emotions, thoughts and behaviours, but is a concept influenced by many factors and these may lie within the society and a social construction of terminology.

A range of views can define and shape a rounded sense of what we understand by 'well-being' and it is necessary that we keep such a sense in mind for meaningful inclusion to occur. Additionally, integrated working will be aided by practitioners having an awareness of these different definitions within their discussions and the support that they offer for well-being. Integrated approaches would then seek to ensure that all professionals support children's needs.

In summary, there are many views of health and well-being, including medical, social constructivist and psychological views. These views can be synthesised and considered within a dynamic interconnected way via the holistic perspective. This is the preferred way for well-being support and reflects the areas that can be supported via an integrated approach.

The holistic perspective

The holistic perspective considers the 'whole person' and the dimensionality of health (Ewles and Simnett, 2003) (Figure 6.1). It is another useful resource for identifying well-being and health and these facets show the many aspects to a person's well-being. Practitioners may hold personal values that influence the way that they define and support well-being.

There are numerous well-being and holistic health models available. Some models do not include sexual health, but this is a relevant area (see Chapter 8 by Rooney and Taylor in this volume). All of these aspects will interact and are interconnected (Ewles and Simnett, 2003). This means that if one area of health is promoted or adversely affected, then the whole system will be improved or will decline. If this holistic view of health is taken, then a child's spiritual aspect of health can be promoted and will interact with and influence the other aspects, which will consequently result in an improvement throughout the whole system – hence the holistic model. Therefore, you may support a child's health/well-being by promoting one dimension and this will raise the whole system. Conversely, an impact on one area may suppress the whole system.

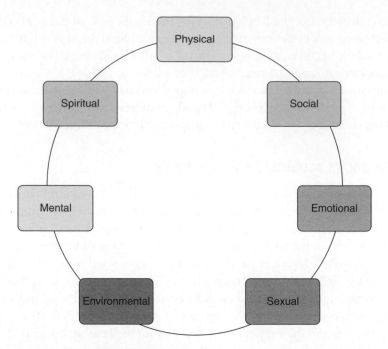

FIGURE 6.1 Aspects of the holistic perspective.

Consider these questions regarding the holistic model in action:

■ How do you perceive sexual, environmental, physical, psychological, social health?
■ Why might some children have an area of health that needs to be promoted more than others?
■ Is a child's well-being affected by this influence or is it natural for children to have set learning goals for specific areas?
■ Where is the family located within this model?
■ How is holistic health influenced by family members/caregivers via role modelling?
■ How does your setting acknowledge these differing well-being elements?
■ When and how does your team have discussions regarding well-being and how you are supporting and promoting well-being across all areas?
■ How, by recognising and considering all of these well-being areas, are you developing inclusive practice?
■ Every child is an individual, so do you accept each child's emotional, spiritual, social, physical and mental well-being?
■ How would inclusive practice involve catering for and providing opportunities to develop/to support all of these well-being elements?

Consider the holistic model and practitioner approaches shown in Figure 6.2.

Considering the holistic perspective, which areas of health and well-being would be emphasised by each practitioner?
Are there other practitioners that could be included in an integrated approach?

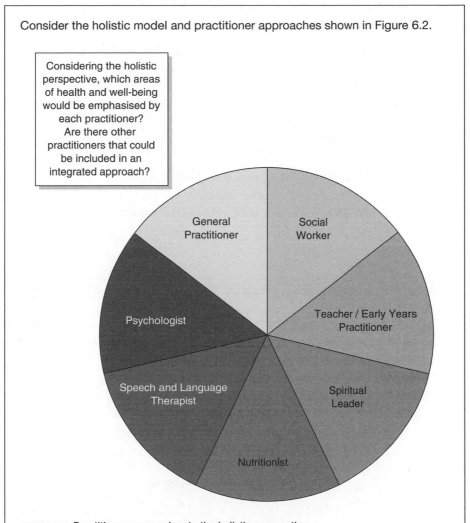

FIGURE 6.2 Practitioner approaches to the holistic perspective.

- Is well-being fluid or fixed?
- Do you consider that well-being is a fixed concept or does well-being change from day to day?
- If well-being is a changing concept, then how will this affect health promotion and how children's well-being is supported within settings?
- How will the perspective regarding well-being and the dynamic nature of the term affect inclusive considerations?

Research results

Research findings indicated that practitioners might tend to view well-being as emotional contentment, or occasionally, the view of 'well-being' may be perceived to centre on those with additional needs, those who have SEN labels or where there are safeguarding issues/external influences. Consequently, this view can exclude many children.

All children have well-being needs and while you have explored the necessity to be inclusive, you have simultaneously been acknowledging the challenges of being inclusive with regard to supporting the well-being of all children.

The continuum model of health and well-being

As we have already explored, health and well-being can be approached from a medical, social constructivist and/or holistic angle. These are not the only approaches. Another very interesting construct is the continuum ideology of health and well-being. This could be useful and can be created pictorially for your setting. The continuum separates the elements of health and well-being, so they can be analysed independently.

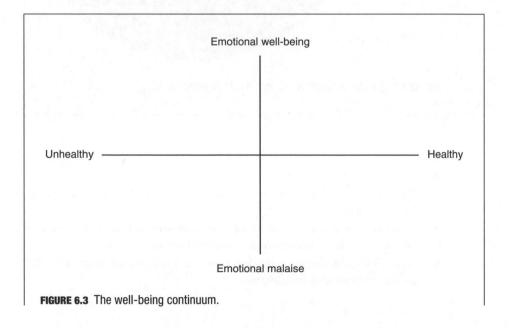

FIGURE 6.3 The well-being continuum.

- How would you position children on this diagrammatic model (Figure 6.3)? Could you position them?
- Considering children: would they remain in the same position on a daily basis? Do you remain on the same position all day?
- What indicators would be present for emotional well-being or emotional malaise?
- What would indicate 'healthy' or 'unhealthy'?
- You can be unhealthy, yet have emotional contentment and therefore these may relate to medical and psychological health domains. Does this adhere to your perception of health and well-being for children?

Case study 6.1: Joshua's story

Joshua is 3 years old and has just started attending nursery. Joshua is dual heritage and has a sister who is 8 years old. His parents work full-time and he will be attending the provision for 2½ days per week. Joshua has not attended an Early Years provision previously, as he has spent time being cared for within the family. He enjoys playing outdoors, painting and reading books. He is the youngest member of his family and has visited the setting on two occasions prior to commencing his nursery attendance.

- How would you support Joshua's holistic health and well-being?
- What factors would you consider as important influences on his well-being?
- What would indicate his:

  ❑ emotional well-being?
  ❑ spiritual well-being?
  ❑ physical well-being?
  ❑ social well-being?
  ❑ psychological well-being?

- Would any of these areas be more important or emphasised in the setting (or by you personally due to your own values) compared to others?
- Do you consider the words and terminology used to collate information in readiness for the transition to nursery?
- How would self-identity relate to well-being? Would inclusive practices support dual heritage, family forms, transitions, play opportunities, self-esteem, choice, safety, social relationships? If yes, then how would the setting do this?
- How would you relate the EYFS themes and principles to supporting Joshua's well-being?

  ❑ 'A unique child': how would you support and develop Joshua along the 'unique child' theme? What resilience-building strategies would you use? How would you support and promote his capability, confidence and self-assuredness?

(Continued)

(Continued)

    ❑ 'Positive relationships': how would you create, maintain and promote positive relationships with Joshua?

    ❑ 'Enabling environments' and 'Learning and Development' areas would need to be considered and you may reflect on the current curricular policies to enable this to be conducted.

The factors affecting all children's well-being

Consider the influences on well-being shown in Figure 6.4.

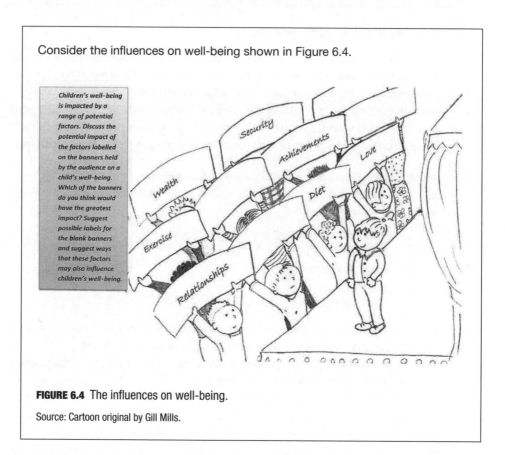

Children's well-being is impacted by a range of potential factors. Discuss the potential impact of the factors labelled on the banners held by the audience on a child's well-being. Which of the banners do you think would have the greatest impact? Suggest possible labels for the blank banners and suggest ways that these factors may also influence children's well-being.

FIGURE 6.4 The influences on well-being.

Source: Cartoon original by Gill Mills.

Influences on health and well-being

Systemic influences and findings

Well-being could be understood as something that is 'enhanced when people can fulfil their personal and social goals' (Statham and Chase, 2010: 2). Supporting well-being could therefore be understood in terms of the strategies adopted to enable individuals to fulfil these goals. Given that well-being is a diverse concept, which is potentially influenced by many factors, any attempt at inclusive practice must account for the diversity of influencing factors, coupled with the complexity of interactions between these factors and the individuals we aim to include.

The impact of families and the process of socialisation is a contentious debate – children who grow up with only one biological parent are disadvantaged, relative to other children, across a wide range of outcomes in childhood as well as adulthood (Amato and Keith, 1991a, 1991b; Amato, 1993; McLanahan, 2002, cited in Sigle-Rushton and McLanahan, 2002: 3). This focus on the makeup of the family is contested by Statham and Chase (2010) who cite evidence to show that the quality of the relationships within families are more key to a child's well-being than coming from a 'broken family'. This could be interpreted in a broader sense, to include the relationships between children and those whom they encounter in the settings where they spend some of their time, the relationships with their peers, and also the relationships that they enjoy with others. 'The well-being of children – especially young children – is closely tied to their lives within their family' (Wollny *et al.*, 2010: 6). Theorists such as Melanie Klein and Donald Winnicott, echo this view. However, the biopsychoscial model (Bronfenbrenner, 1979) documents the interconnectedness of biological, psychological and social influences on well-being and signifies the multiplicity of influencing factors from external and internal sources. The ecological context relevant to well-being is extremely important and situates the child within the systemic layers and therein highlights the uniqueness of each individual child, the related influences on well-being and considerations for practitioners within their inclusive approaches.

There is a need to effectively 'operationalise' well-being, if we are to successfully develop effective policy and practical strategies for supporting and improving it. The impression given by some authors is that despite the concept itself being poorly understood, there is a recognised need to address some of the issues around it, such as the fact that there is a range of influential factors, which has implications for how it will be supported and optimised (Statham and Chase, 2010).

Rather than being static, well-being emerges from how people interact with the world around them at different points in their lives. This is a significant consideration in terms of supporting and optimising well-being, as it will inevitably influence the approach adopted. We have to accept that, as well-being can neither be easily defined nor understood on a simplistic level, our approach to inclusion must be tailored to account for the potential variations in the interactions and perceptions of the influences driving the status of individual well-being. Not insignificant is the possibility that well-being is poorly understood because there is more work to be done on understanding the complex relationships between the individual, their psychology and their environment.

Peer pressure, commercialism and corporate bullying

The impact of commercialisation can be damaging to children's well-being. Supermarkets have been accused of 'interfering in education' by encouraging parents to participate in promotions by collecting vouchers in exchange for equipment for schools. These promotions often result in a hugely disproportionate exchange in terms of investment versus outcome (Compass, 2007).

Children are thought to respond well to 'cool' images; hence this is a concept that is often exploited when trying to sell to children. An executive from an advertising agency in Los Angeles has been cited as having said that advertising which makes people feel like 'losers' if they do not have the product in the advert is 'at its best' (Shalek, cited in Compass, 2007). Children are seen as 'easier' targets in this respect because they are more likely to get the impression that they are less than their peers, if they do not buy the product. In this respect they are more vulnerable to advertising than adults.

The recommendation has been made that we should err on the side of caution where potential harm to children is concerned when considering whether changes should be made to current practice, rather than hesitating in the hope that absolute proof will show us whether or not any 'real harm' exists in terms of the threat from the pressures of commercialisation (Department for Education, 2011).

The *Bye, Buy Childhood* report from the Mother's Union (2010) claimed that the advertising industry deliberately targets children on the basis of 'pester power' as this section of the market can be extremely lucrative to the tune of millions of pounds per year. This encourages materialism, which is detrimental to children's health and well-being. Materialism has also been shown to be negatively associated with school performance.

The study, *The Commercialisation of Childhood* (Compass, 2007) argues that the pressure to buy or wear 'the right thing' can have a dramatic impact on the way that children interact with each other, creating peer pressure. Recent research has suggested that self-esteem and materialism are negatively correlated; children who are highly materialistic are more likely to have lower self-esteem, and vice versa (Kasser *et al.*, 2014).

Research has shown higher levels of depression and lower levels of happiness in children who are highly materialistic (Hurst *et al.*, 2013). The point is that commercialism feeds on this 'need' to have the latest clothes, shoes, gadgets, etc. This is a form of corporate bullying. Self-esteem undergoes a 'dip' in puberty, in any case (Tiggemann, 2005). Could this be exacerbated by unmet materialistic needs? This suggests that early intervention is important from this perspective too.

What is the solution to this particular aspect of challenges to positive well-being in children? Banning advertising and commercialisation in schools and Early Years settings might be a start. Making it illegal for commercial organisations to gain access to educational settings would support this. In Sweden, it has been illegal to aim advertising on TV at children under the age of 12 since 1991 (*The Economist*, 2001).

■　How could we as practitioners deal with commercialisation in practice?

■　What might be some of the challenges to safeguarding children from influences such as commercialism, which we often see as damaging?

You should be able to appreciate the links to the environmental aspects of health and well-being from the holistic perspective.

Gender issues

Sexualised content used in advertising is singled out for particularly strong criticism. The premature sexualisation of children has featured large in the media in recent years. Rush and La Nauze (2006) introduced the term 'corporate paedophilia', arguing that the current advertising strategies employed by the media are an affront to public morality and are equivalent to child abuse. They claimed this is more magnified when examined in relation to girls than boys in educational settings.

Could it be that girls' voices are being 'drowned out' by their male counterparts? Boys tend to take up more time and gain more of the teacher's time than girls, and it has been theorised that gender inequality early in life can be linked to later occupational inequality (Bousted, 2013).

Dietary: junk food advertising

The government advises healthy eating while allowing (and apparently failing to discourage) the promotion of consumption of food that has been shown by research to lead to poorer health and well-being outcomes. Childhood obesity is becoming a major health issue. McDonald's and other fast food outlets have been criticised for their part in this. At the same time, pre-school children are more likely to recognise the 'golden arches' of McDonald's than to know their own surname (Compass, 2007).

■　Consider how you as a practitioner would promote healthier choices to support the health and well-being of the children in your setting. Account for a range of needs in your ideas.

■　Concerns over children's mental ill-health, behaviour and conduct disorders are becoming increasingly common (Compass, 2007). There are gender differences in the nature of the concern here. Suggest reasons for this.

Consider how you would deal with emotional intelligence and the management of emotions. It has been suggested that when a child is repeatedly expressing anger, frustration and other negative emotions, that they may be having emotional difficulties.

■ How would you recognise this?
■ What strategies would you suggest in order to support a child in this situation?

Health and well-being needs

Palmer (2010) argues that the approaches to meeting children's 'real needs' have changed in modern practice, for example, the need for conversation and interaction in the real world has been met by alternative means of interaction via technology such as social network sites on the internet.

■ How is information technology used in your setting?
■ How do you feel about the role of technology in children's development?
■ What do you think about the benefits/drawbacks of children having access to technology?

Health promotion and prevention strategies for supporting well-being

WHO claims that that status of health in childhood determines health status in later life, so issues addressed early may reduce potential ill-effects and the resulting financial burden for society later (WHO, 2005).

A number of issues need to be considered before any change can be contemplated in policy and practice. Some strategies are detailed here:

1. *Being inclusive*: Palmer (2010) argues that children's 'real needs' are simple, can be counted on the fingers of one hand and are free. It could be argued that provided each child's needs are 'assessed' on a case-by-case basis, then meeting the needs of each child should be relatively straightforward. Is this view rather naïve, given that children are required to navigate an increasingly

complex social landscape which is arguably made more complex by the technology-driven ever-increasing availability of information and potentially influential material?

2. *Adoption of holistic approaches* to childcare and education that focus on addressing individual needs, rather than assuming there are different 'types' of needs which may be expressed (i.e. universal needs vs. special needs).

3. *Valuing diversity*: activities across a whole range should be designed and implemented which are aimed at practitioners, parents and the children in the setting (allowing children to explore issues that are meaningful to them).

4. *Communication and information-sharing*: through inter-agency information-sharing, review, action-planning.

5. *Minimising risk:* safeguarding, exclusion of potentially harmful influences, exclusion of commercial interests in Early Years settings, including advertising. Encouraging and building resilience for every child.

Ways of enhancing inclusion and supporting well-being

The provision of boundaries, trust, significant others, key persons, routine, predictability and associated neurological connections may aid well-being from a psychological and holistic approach. Parents are central to effective well-being support in early relationships. Other key issues and strategies may acknowledge the role of brain development, relationships, language development and early interventions.

> Significant reductions in chronic disease could be achieved across the life course by decreasing the number and severity of adverse experiences that threaten the well-being of young children and by strengthening the protective relationships that help mitigate the harmful effects of toxic stress.
>
> (Centre on the Developing Child, 2011)

Nurture groups were first introduced by Boxall, an educational psychologist in London in 1969, as a means of reinstating early learning experiences from the first few years of life, which had been omitted due to impoverished early nurturing. The main focus is on developing attachments and re-establishing interactions, which may have been missing from the child's early experience (Boxall, 2002). The basic underpinning principles centre on consistency, reliability, firm boundaries, behaviour as communication, importance of language, nurture, learning and self-esteem.

- Which perspectives or models will you apply to well-being and inclusion?
- What are the issues with the above strategies? For example, do society and media influence self-esteem?
- If the unconscious aspect of well-being cannot be seen, then how can it be easily supported?
- What are the challenges and benefits of integrated approaches for effective well-being support?
- Are nurture groups and attachments present within your setting to target psychological/emotional/social areas of health? If they are present, do they seek to reduce specific influences on health and well-being areas?
- If these areas of health are targeted, will they create emotional well-being or do you believe that there are other specific ways to improve well-being?

Conclusion

We would highlight that the *relationship* is crucial to creating effective well-being support for all, irrespective of your particular perception of health cause, definition or strategy preference. This highlights child-centred provision and the centrality of the child in well-being and inclusion good practice. There are many more perspectives on health and well-being that you could interlink with the summary table provided (Table 6.1). These perspectives could enable a range of supportive strategies to be adopted and implemented to enable you to be fully inclusive. This will help you to aim for supportive and inclusive health and well-being within your Early Years setting.

Further reading

Department of Health (2009) *Healthy Child Programme: Pregnancy and the First Five Years of Life*. London: DCSF. Available at: www.gov.uk/government/uploads/system/uploads/attachment_data/file/167998/Health_Child_Programme.pdf (accessed 20 July 2014).

NICE (National Institute for Health and Clinical Excellence) (2012) *Social and Emotional Well-Being: Early Years*. London: NICE.

Public Health England (2013) *How Healthy Behaviour Supports Children's Well-Being*. London: Health and Well-being Directorate, Public Health England.

The Children's Society (2013) *The Good Childhood Report*. London: The Children's Society.

TABLE 6.1 Summative reflection opportunity: summarising health and well-being perspectives with some strategies

	Psychological perspective–humanistic	Psychodynamic/psychoanalytic perspective (psychological perspective)	Holistic perspective	Medical perspective
View of the person's health and well-being	Inside each person is a real person trying to present who they truly are. (Key theorists are Maslow 1954 and Rogers 1961.) A person develops through the hierarchy of needs and aims towards self-actualisation with relationships being important in health and well-being areas.	Drives and instincts are present and these determine health/well-being. Id, ego and superego conflicts may occur according to Freudian theory. Defence mechanisms exist to deal with conflicts (Freud, 1937). Bowlby (1969) highlights attachment relationships and experiences are being crucial to health and well-being.	The child's health and well-being are created by numerous areas (emotional, spiritual, sexual, etc.) and these are interconnected and they interact to impact on the child.	A person is healthy when they are not physically unwell.
Cause of ill-health/poor emotional well-being	Unmet needs (Maslow, 1954). The inability to grow and aim towards self-actualisation (Rogers, 1980). Conditions of worth are imposed on a person and they may be unhealthy due to living up to these, as opposed to their own conditions of worth.	Conflicts, insecure attachments (Ainsworth and Bell, 1970) and internal working models of self, others and the world as being unsafe, unpredictable, and so on.	Influences on one area of the whole person can have an impact on the entire system. This impact can come from a range of influences or one specific influential element.	Disease or illness.
Supportive strategies and your role	Forming and maintaining effective relationships that enable the child to 'grow' and be who they truly are, i.e. presenting their real self. Respect, valuing children, aiming to understand and to be supportive by providing space to listen to children's voices. Self-esteem building opportunities. Child-centred opportunities and curriculum. Providing core conditions (Rogers, 1980). Giving choice and meeting needs within the setting.	Key workers and attachment opportunities to be created and available. Routines, predictability, consistency, safety. Environmental safety and internal safety via reassurance, praise etc. Opportunities for the expression of emotions from the sub-conscious, conscious and unconscious realms eg art, music, play, exercise and so on. Consideration of the unconscious or past impacts on well-being and be mindful of possible unconscious impacts on well-being and behaviour. Supporting attachment and loss. Loss not via bereavement but loss via change/transition.	Supporting the whole system by targeting one area or a few, e.g. space for meditation/peace/time out will target the spiritual area and have a knock-on effect on other areas. Holistic support may involve integrated approaches to enable specialists to support all of the areas within the model.	Medication. Support for physical ailments. The provision of specialist equipment, e.g. inhalers for asthma, Ritalin for some conduct disorders, medication for epilepsy/seizures. Designated staff for administering medication in a safe and secure place with risk assessed procedures.

References

Ainsworth, M. and Bell, S. (1970) Attachment, exploration, and separation: illustrated by the behaviour of one-year-olds in a strange situation. *Child Development*, 41(1): 49–67.

Amato, R. and Bruce, K. (1991a) Parental divorce and the well-being of children: a meta-analysis. *Psychological Bulletin* 110: 26–46, cited in W. Sigle-Rushton and S. McLanahan (2002) *Father Absence and Child Well-being: A Critical Review*. London: The ESRC Centre for the Analysis of Social Exclusion, London School of Economics and Political Science and Princeton, NJ: Princeton University, Center for Research on Child Well-being.

Amato, P. R. and Bruce, K. (1991b) Parental divorce and adult well-being: a meta-analysis. *Journal of Marriage and the Family*, 53: 43–58, cited in W. Sigle-Rushton and S. McLanahan (2002) *Father Absence and Child Well-being: A Critical Review*. London: The ESRC Centre for the Analysis of Social Exclusion, London School of Economics and Political Science and Princeton, NJ: Princeton University, Center for Research on Child Well-being.

Booth, T. and Ainscow, M. (2011) *The Index for Inclusion*, 3rd edn. Available at: www.csie.org.uk/inclusion (accessed 15 January 2015).

Bousted, M. (2013) Silenced and excluded, girls need to be heard. *TES* magazine, 13 Sept.

Bowlby, J. (1969) *Attachment and Loss*, vol. 1. New York: Basic Books.

Boxall, M. (2002) *How to use Nurture Groups to Promote Inclusion in Early Years*. Available at: www.optimus-education.com/how-use-nurture-groups-promote-inclusion-early-years (accessed 15 January 2015).

Bronfenbrenner, U. (1979) *The Ecology of Human Development*. Cambridge, MA: Harvard University Press.

Centre for Studies on Inclusive Education (CSIE) Available at: www.csie.org.uk/inclusion/what.shtml (accessed 15 January 2015).

Center on the Developing Child (2011) *In Brief: The Foundations of Lifelong Health*. Cambridge, MA: Harvard University. Available at: developingchild.harvard.edu/index.php/download_file/-/view/786/ (accessed 12 June 2014).

Compass (2007) *Commercialisation of Childhood*. London: Compass. Available at: www.compassonline.org.uk/publications/the-commercialisation-of-childhood/ (accessed 30 November 2013).

Crittenden, P. (1997) The effect of early relationship experiences on relationships and adulthood. In S. Duck (ed.) *Handbook of Personal Relationships*, 2nd edn. Chichester: John Wiley & Sons, pp. 99–119.

Department for Education (2011) *Letting Children be Children: Report of an Independent Review of the Commercialisation and Sexualisation of Childhood*. London: The Stationery Office. Available at: www.gov.uk/government/uploads/system/uploads/attachment_data/file/175418/Bailey_Review.pdf (accessed 12 June 2013).

Department of Health (2014) *Well-being: Why It Matters to Health Policy*. London. Health Improvement Analytical Team, Department of Health.

Ewles, L. and Simnett, I. (2003) *Promoting Health: A Practical Guide*. London: Baillière Tindall.

Freud, A. (1937) *The Ego and the Mechanisms of Defence*. London: Hogarth Press and Institute of Psychoanalysis.

Gerhardt, S. (2004) *Why Love Matters: How Affection Shapes a Baby's Brain*. Hove: Routledge.

Hurst, M., Dittmar, H., Bond, R., and Kasser, T. (2013) The relationship between materialistic values and environmental attitudes and behaviors: a meta-analysis, *Journal of Environmental Psychology*, 36: 257–69. Available at: www.sciencedirect.com/science/article/pii/S0272494413000704 (accessed 23 June 2014).

Kasser, T., Rosenblum, K. L., Sameroff, A. J., Deci, E. L., Niemiec, C. P., Ryan, R. M., Arnadottir, O., Bond, R., Dittmar, H., Dungan, N. and Hawks, S. (2014) Changes in materialism, changes in psychological well-being: evidence from three longitudinal studies and an intervention experiment. *Motivation and Emotion*, 38: 1–22. Available at: www.selfdeterminationtheory.org/SDT/documents/2014_Kasser_et_al_materialism.pdf.

Maslow, A. H. (1954) *Motivation and Personality* New York: Harper & Row.

Mothers Union (2010) *Bye, Buy Childhood: A Report into the Commercialisation of Childhood*. London: Mothers Union.

National CAMHS Support Service (2011) *Better Mental Health Outcomes for Children and Young People: A Resource Directory for Commissioners*. Available at: www.chimat.org.uk/camhs/commissioning (accessed 12 December 2013).

NHS (National Health Service) (2012) *A Primary Care Approach to Mental Health and Well-being*. Available at: www.nhsconfed.org (accessed 5 May 2014.).

NICE (National Institute for Health and Clinical Excellence) (2012a) *Social and Emotional Well-being: Early Years*. London: NICE.

NICE (National Institute for Health and Clinical Excellence) (2012b) Chapter 1 Recommendations. In *Social and Emotional Well-Being: Early Years*. Available at: http://publications.nice.org.uk/social-and-emotional-well-being-early-years-ph40/recommendations (accessed 19 June 2014).

Palmer, S. (2010) *The Commercialisation of Childhood*. Available at: www.suepalmer.co.uk/modern_childhood_info_the_commercial.php (accessed 31 Jan. 2014).

Public Health England (2013) *How Healthy Behaviour Supports Children's Well-being*. London: Health and Well-being Directorate, Public Health England.

Rees, G., Goswami, H. and Bradshaw, J. (2010) *Developing an Index of Children's Subjective Well-being in England*. London: The Children's Society.

Rogers, C. (1961) *On Becoming a Person: A Therapist's View of Psychotherapy*. London. Constable.

Rogers, C. (1980) *A Way of Being*. Boston: Houghton Mifflin.

Rush, E. and La Nauze, A. (2006) *Letting Children Be Children: Stopping the Sexualisation of Children in Australia*. Discussion Paper Number 93. Canberra: The Australia Institute.

Sigle-Rushton, W. and McLanahan, S. (2002) *Father Absence and Child Well-being: A Critical Review*. London: The ESRC Centre for the Analysis of Social Exclusion. London School of Economics and Political Science and Princeton, NJ: Princeton University, Center for Research on Child Well-being.

Statham, J. and Chase, E. (2010) *Childhood Well-being: A Brief Overview*. Briefing Paper 1. August. London: Childhood Well-being Research Centre.

The Children's Society (2013) *The Good Childhood Report*. Available at: www.childrenssociety.org.uk (accessed 28 June 2014).

The Economist (2001) Advertising to children: kid gloves, 4 January. Available at: www.economist.com/node/464997/print (accessed 21 July 2014).

The Scottish Government (2009) *Well What do you Think? The Fourth National Scottish Survey of Public Attitudes to Mental Well-being and Mental Health Problems*. Available at: www.scotland.gov.uk/Publications/2009/09/15120147/8 (accessed 21 July 2014).

Tiggemann, M. (2005) Body dissatisfaction and adolescent self-esteem: prospective findings. *Body Image* 2: 129–35.

WHO (1948) *Preamble to the Constitution of the World Health Organization as Adopted by the International Health Conference, New York, 19–22 June 1946*. Geneva: WHO.

Wollny, I., Apps, J. and Henricson, C. (2010) Can government measure family well-being? A literature review. In *Research & Policy for the Real World*. London: Family and Parenting Institute.

7

Practitioners' flexibility

Working with Gypsy, Roma and Traveller families

Jackie Braithwaite

The aims of this chapter are:

- To consider how inclusive practitioners' own settings are with regard to Gypsy, Roma and Traveller culture and heritage, regardless of whether a Gypsy, Roma or Traveller child attends the setting
- To offer a brief historical overview, which outlines the prejudices Gypsy, Roma and Travelling families have faced over centuries and continue to do so.

Introduction

> Educators can change the 'gazes' through which they 'read' children.
>
> (MacNaughton, 2003: 179)

The vast majority of Traveller pupils linger on the periphery of the education system and remain the group most at risk of failure – a situation highlighted (again) by Ofsted in 2003. One of Ofsted's concerns is the lack of visibility of the Traveller culture in the curriculum and it asserts:

> the curriculum in many schools provides good opportunities to celebrate and affirm different cultures and lifestyles. Too often, however, attempts to include those of Traveller communities are purely incidental and often divorced from the mainstream efforts of schools to promote race equality for all pupils. In too many schools, Traveller pupils are an 'unseen' minority ethnic group.
>
> (Ofsted, 2003: 6)

The main line of reasoning in this chapter is quite a simple one; that any educational curriculum, whether in schools or Early Years settings, should be representative of Gypsy, Roma, and Traveller (GRT) culture, regardless of whether there is a child from a GRT family on the roll or not.

It is evident that there are tensions with GRT families and settled communities and where GRT families are sited no doubt causes disputes, but as Lord Avebury (2012: vii) states:

> To achieve the goal of eliminating unauthorised encampments, financial support needs to be combined with obligations of local authorities to provide sites based on accurate and fair assessments of need with the prospect of government intervention where councils fail to act ... too often in the past, policy makers have sought to assimilate and eradicate the identity and unique lifestyle of Gypsies and Travellers.

Although there is no room in this chapter to accommodate a discussion of the injustice of inadequate site provision for GRT families, the notion of assimilation is raised as the chapter focuses on respect for the identities of GRT families in schools and Early Years settings.

This chapter encourages reflexivity regarding practitioners' own personal values and beliefs and a consideration of inclusive practice with regard to GRT culture and heritage.

The views sought from practitioners for the purpose of this chapter revealed little experience of working with GRT families and most practitioners' views had been strongly influenced by media reporting. One experienced practitioner reported: 'I haven't any experience of working with Travelling families but I would treat them like any other family – it's your duty.'

This response raises two points:

1. Does the notion that 'treating "them" like any other family' equate to inclusive practice – is inclusive practice about 'sameness'?
2. The second point is the use of the word 'duty'. How can that be defined? Is duty about being 'obliged' to do something, perhaps a burdensome task? Or is a commitment or a calling towards something worthwhile? How do you perceive your 'duty'?

Identifying Gypsies and Travellers

As Rogoff (2007: 5) suggests: 'cultural practices change across generations and vary within communities' and this is true of Gypsies, they are not one homogeneous group. Bhopal and Myers (2008) identify four groups of Gypsies in

Britain today, the largest being the English Romani. The other groups are a Nawkens (Scottish Gypsies or Travellers), Kale (Welsh Gypsies) and Minceir (Irish Travellers or Pavees). There are approximately 300,000 GRT families in Britain (Richardson and Ryder, 2012) and though most of these groups accept the term Traveller, many Gypsies, but not all, prefer to be called Gypsies. For families from Eastern and Central Europe, the term Roma is preferred and Fairground people prefer to be called Showmen. New Travellers were once referred to as New Age Travellers and they have been travelling since the 1960s. In the 1970s and 1980s as summer festivals emerged, there was more growth as the New Travellers, mainly consisting of young people and their families began to move between summer festivals in vehicles containing all their possessions (Derrington, 2011) and as Derrington explains, the homelessness of young people during the Thatcher government saw a surge in New Travellers as some young people adopted this life-style as an alternative to Thatcherite social policies. Each of these groups has its own heritage and history (Foster and Walker, 2009). To avoid making assumptions about the correct terminology, it is important to take the lead from children and their parents about how they wish to describe themselves (Derrington, 2011: 43).

For the purpose of this chapter the umbrella term of Gypsy, Roma and Traveller (GRT) is mainly used as it is a term used in most government policy documents, including The National Strategies (DCSF, 2009) and Ofsted documentation.

Although nomadism defines the characteristics of a Gypsy or a Traveller, not all GRT families live a nomadic life-style. Either by choice or because of no other legal option, most GRT families live in houses or on authorised sites (Derrington, 2011). Gypsies living in houses are often referred to as 'settled Gypsies' (Clark and Greenfields, 2006) but as the authors point out, the change of a dwelling does not equate to the loss of ethnic identity, instead 'it continues and adapts to new circumstances' (ibid.: 12).

Discrimination

The lives of Gypsy, Roma and Traveller families are surrounded by 'truths', 'untruths' and myths and they are constantly compared to society's wants and needs. Hawes and Perez (1996: xi) suggest there 'has been the unspoken, consistent presumption that Gypsies should, in the end, conform to a given range of behavioural norms'. The history of discrimination against Roma/Gypsies in Europe dates back to the fourteenth and fifteenth centuries where they were viewed as intruders at a time when states were trying to control their societies (Liegeois and Gheorghe, 1995). As Kendall (1997: 79) points out, because Travellers have the capacity to move across spatial boundaries, they were considered a direct threat by societies, which were sedentary, and because of this nomadic life-style they were positioned as 'strangers' within a spatial area. And Kendall adds, when deviant behaviour emerges, it is much easier to blame 'strangers' than your own people ... as strangers they provide the ideal scapegoat for undesirable behaviour such as criminal activity and the dumping of waste. This process also acts as an additional safety valve for the dominant group ... maintain[ing] their position of power and further weakening the position of the marginal group.

This view has resulted in Roma/Gypsies being mistrusted and feared and eventually 'denounced for living the life of a bohemian' (Liegeois and Gheorghe, 1995: 5). The authors highlight discrimination in all spheres, including housing, education and health and suggest that negative stereotyping has historically adversely affected policies against them. They note the views of Romani journalist, Jake Bowers who asserts that in most libraries and museums, there is no information that describes the history and culture of the Gypsy, Roma or Traveller.

Discrimination still affects Gypsy, Roma and Traveller families (Lloyd and McCluskey, 2008; Rose, 2011; Deuchar and Bhopal, 2012; Foster and Norton, 2012) and Foster and Norton (2012: 89) apportion some of the blame for this to the media, suggesting that negative newspaper headlines 'in the main characterise Traveller communities as dirty, thieving, scrounging, anti-social strangers in our otherwise well-ordered communities'. And as the authors point out, there is little in the way of either presenting positive information in the media or using any opportunity to celebrate the achievements and strengths of GRT communities. People rely on the media to inform them of topics of which they have no direct personal experience, and so assumptions are made and become part of daily chat (Morant, 1998). The failure in responsible and unbiased reporting results in 'othering', and as Richardson (2006: 114) states, 'the socially constructed truth through discourse replaces any evidence in reality' and the more 'othered' GRT families become, the more people want to read about them, which 'others' them even more and the cycle of 'othering' continues (ibid.).

Derrington (2011: 47) discusses racism against GRT children in schools and highlights it as 'a very common problem', which affects school attendance. According to Derrington, research shows that 'around one in three Traveller students dealt with racist name-calling by retaliating physically, often with encouragement from their parents' and by coping with this problem in a physical way attracts 'negative attention from teachers' and furthermore instead of teachers recognising this is an emotional response, they blame cultural traits.

An inclusive curriculum

'Inclusion' tends to be the term that educationalists in the UK prefer to use because it implies adjustments to policies and practice to take account of community needs and aspirations. Alternative terms 'integration' and 'assimilation' suggest greater degrees of cultural modification and suppression. If the square-peg-in-a-round-hole analogy were to be used, assimilation suggests that the child is reshaped, whereas inclusion implies an adjustment to the system.

(Foster and Cemlyn, 2012: 61, 62)

The view that education is a tool for empowering Gypsies and Travellers and facilitating an inclusive approach in schools is argued by Richardson and Ryder (2012), who suggest that the constant bullying, racism and clash of cultures can be viewed as an agent for assimilation. An inclusive approach to practice must be one where difference is considered both normal and wanted, as opposed to re-shaping children or being unresponsive to their individualism. Children should feel like they belong in the setting and have a voice that enables them to contribute to what goes on and a voice, which is listened to.

The Early Years Foundation Stage (DfE, 2012) seems to reflect a sociocultural outlook through its themed and principled approach. It sets out how the four themes: (1) a Unique Child; (2) Positive Relationships; (3) Enabling Environments; and (4) Learning and Development, and the four overarching principles, all inform what is viewed as best practice for children in Early Years care and education in England. *Development Matters* (Early Education, 2012: 2) refers to children's culture, using phrases such as 'value and respect all children and families equally', 'support babies and children to develop a positive sense of their own identity and culture' and 'offer stimulating resources, relevant to all children's cultures and communities'. Similarly in primary education, Nutbrown and Clough, (2009: 195) draw attention to the DCFS (2009, para 2.1) which states that 'differences are appreciated; everyone feels included', therefore there seems to be a strong assertion that children's cultures are both respected and embraced and that this notion is reflected in Early Years and primary pedagogy.

Case study 7.1: Jake's story

Jake is 5 years old and is an Irish Traveller boy and is in the Reception class. He lives on an authorised site in a trailer about 2 miles from his school with his 3-year-old sister, Janey and his parents. He is driven to school each day. His family travel from time to time for employment purposes.

The children are learning about Shapes and as part of this theme the teacher and the teaching assistant are taking small groups of children out of the school grounds and onto the local housing estate with the aim of identifying shapes outside. Each child has a clipboard with a sheet of paper showing common 2D shapes. They have been asked to make a mark next to each shape when they can match it with the same shape in their outdoor environment. They have been asked to focus on the surrounding buildings, which are mainly houses.

The children identify some of their own homes on the estate, shouting out, 'That's my house! That's my garden', and Samuel shouts, 'That's my bike outside my garage!' The teacher keeps them focused on the topic and asks the group of children what shape the wheels are on Samuel's bicycle and when they correctly suggest a circle, she encourages them to find a circle on their worksheet and to mark it with a tick. All the children, including Jake, are successful in completing their worksheets by identifying each shape from what they notice about the windows, doors and roofs of the houses and garages in the area.

At lunchtime, the teacher and the teaching assistant muse what a successful learning activity it was and how the children had enjoyed actively learning about shapes. The teaching assistant makes the suggestion that they could extend the activity by making houses through junk box modelling. This would consolidate the 2D shape learning and encourage the exploration of 3D shapes. The teacher agrees and says she will put a notice up in the classroom window to inform parents that the children were going to make model houses next week and to request 'junk' for the following week.

- Have the educators ignored Jake's culture intentionally or were they too focused upon the area of learning?
- What opportunities have been overlooked to promote a positive image of Jake's culture?
- If Jake's culture is ignored, what message does it send to other children and families?

Ofsted's report on provision and support for Traveller pupils (2003: 20) noted that there were only a few schools who had undertaken an audit of curriculum provision to identify any opportunities to promote positive images of Travellers and in a few cases they note 'a deliberate avoidance' and suggest that 'schools resort to the argument "we do not see any differences and we respond to them [Travellers] in the same way as we do any other children"'. As Ofsted quite rightly posit, 'such statements would not be made or accepted about other minority ethnic groups' and suggest that despite schools having equal opportunities policies, this attitude amounts to 'cultural blindness' (ibid.: 20).

Little seems to have changed from the warnings of Ofsted (2003), as one practitioner recently expressed:

No, there was no mention of GRT culture in the history topic of The Homes We Live In we were doing in Year One but there should have been because 'they' [Gypsies, Romas and Travellers] do exist in our society, don't they?

(Continued)

(Continued)

Another practitioner, working in a different setting involved in the same topic in a Year One class, commented:

> We did it in PE too with the children ... the teacher called out a type of home and the children had to respond to it. For instance, if she called 'Terraced', the children held hands in a row. If she called 'Semi-detached', they held hands in a pair, if she called 'detached', they found a space and stood by themselves, but no, there was no reference to a caravan or trailer but we have no GRT children in our school although we could have done caravans anyway.

These practitioners have identified a history topic taught in schools to Year One children and it is called 'Homes We Live In'. The learning objectives are:

1. To understand that people live in different sorts of homes.
2. To talk about homes using appropriate vocabulary.

The intended overall Learning Outcome is: 'Recognise and name different types of homes'. Therefore, despite curricular documents containing possibilities to explore cultural diversity, it is left to educators to recognise such opportunities and in this instance, both educators in different settings overlooked the chance to embrace difference.

According to Siraj-Blatchford (1994: 150) 'the first step to racial equality in early years settings is to recognise that educators are not objective, value-free beings', and personal histories influence beliefs, thinking and actions. As an early childhood practitioner, part of your role is to make judgements about children and their families on a daily basis and to help you to do this, you will undoubtedly draw upon your own accumulated knowledge and professional experiences, your own cultural practices and what you have been 'trained' to think which will influence the decisions you make. This, whether consciously or not, will include your own personal biases. Rather than complying with 'existing practices, rules, traditions and understandings' (MacNaughton, 2003: 146) that are deemed to be true (Durand, 2008), practitioners need to become inquirers instead of followers. As Waage (2006: 25) argues, when educators become more concerned about the subjects children are learning instead of the child inside, they fail 'to value what is different about them and the capacity of their communities' and then there is an opportunity missed to promote 'participation as a learning opportunity'.

Reflection on Case Study 7.1

House, Osgood and Simpson (2012) identify that the word 'must' is present in over 200 instances in 26 pages of the EYFS (2012). Children in the Early Years

Foundation Stage of learning are constantly observed and tracked against the seven areas of learning. This tracking system is continued throughout children's schooling, checking for competences and, as Luff (2012) suggests, if assessment is viewed as checking competence, children are positioned in terms of the economy and how they will eventually benefit society. In terms of GRT children, the question may have to be asked, whom their 'economic status' might benefit. The second question, which arises, is whether politicians and educators find the GRT pupil a good enough investment.

Education

Derrington (2011: 43) points out the complexities of GRT in the education system and suggest that though a generalisation of GRT culture cannot be made, educators need to gain a better understanding of GRT families. Some of the points Derrington highlights are:

- The child centredness of GRT families and the high level of protection they feel for their children – therefore there may be a reluctance to allow trips and extracurricular activities.
- Many parents are anxious about the welfare of their children – physically, morally and psychologically.
- Some parents may find school jargon difficult if they themselves are not able to read and write well.
- Due to their own unhappy school experiences a feeling of intimidation and wariness can develop.
- If the parents avoid meetings in school because of such feelings, this can be misconstrued as not caring about their child's education.

However despite these dilemmas, Gypsy and Traveller parents are keen to educate their children to at least a basic literacy level but some parents see little relevance in further schooling once these skills have been acquired (Kiddle, 1999).

Research results

The perceptions of early years practitioners sought for this discussion were that GRT families did not need Early Years education because 'their culture is very traditional, mothers stay at home and fathers work'.

When asked what they perceived was the purpose of Early Years provision, for instance, was it solely to meet the needs of working parents, one response was: 'It's about school readiness too.'

The omnipresent notion of 'school readiness' permeates Early Years thinking and links directly to government agendas, policies and the investment in early education in preparation for what children will 'become'. It is a term which GRT children are not used to. Instead their economic status may need to support the traditional Traveller economy.

Under Section 7 of The Education Act 1996 in England and Wales, parents are required to make sure that their children have a full-time education once they reach compulsory school age. It is an offence under Section 444 to fail to do so. Parents of GRT children will not be convicted of non-attendance if they can demonstrate certain evidence, such as being engaged in a family business that requires them to travel from place to place or to cultural events, which some GRT parents may place before education.

Attendance is interrupted for children from Fairground Showmen families during the summer months. During the winter months children are enrolled at a base school and when they travel they are provided with distance learning packs (Derrington, 2011). According to Marks and Woods (2008), cited in Derrington (2011), it is thought there are around 1,000 children from Fairground families accessing this flexible education which is personalised to meet individual needs.

Similarly, Circus communities travel, and the frequency of this makes it difficult for children to access school, therefore they may have tutors who will travel and live with them but again, the children will have a base school with distance learning packs an option (Derrington, 2011).

Although there is a criterion which sets out how many days children GRT pupils must attend school over an academic year, this allowance gives the families the option to home school while they are travelling (Deuchar and Bhopal, 2012). Therefore, attendance can be erratic and this has been widely identified as a disruption to schooling, which can create a barrier to building positive relationships with teaching staff (Wilkin *et al.*, 2009).

If children are absent for travelling for work purposes, the code of 'T' is used in the register. However, as Derrington (2011: 50) points out, as for any other pupil, absences should be followed up. If not, it 'may be interpreted as an act of passive condoning that encourages further disengagement (self-fulfilling prophecy)'.

Nationally, Buckinghamshire is recognised as a leader in developing mainstream inclusion by supporting schools on a strategic level. According to Buckinghamshire Services for Children and Young People, local authorities around England tend to have Traveller Education Support Services (TESSs) and in Buckinghamshire the Minority Ethnic and Traveller Education Services (METAS) carry this out. However, as Foster and Walker (2009) explain, some authorities are members of a consortium who receive support from a lead borough who will employ and manage staff for them. Therefore, there are many ways that the TESS are managed and it is important to know how your local authority supports GRT education services and how you would contact them.

According to Myers, McGhee and Bhopal (2010: 539), the TESS is 'a friendly, familiar and non-judgemental presence ... act[ing] as a gateway between parents and schools'. Besides creating effective links, they provide training for practitioners, facilitate a mechanism to exchange information between the setting and parents with literacy difficulties and support the induction of new GRT children. Foster and Walker (2009: 35, 36) explain that the TESS usually

> maintain a database of all GRT children and young people from birth to 19 living or attending schools in the area ... the database is the primary means of recording and sharing information of Gypsy, Roma and Traveller children and families with the TESS and other departments of Children's Services ... when families arrive in the LA, the TESS supports their access to schooling.

Although Pre-School education is not compulsory, a member of the TESS will visit all families with children who are reaching nursery school age to discuss the value of Early Years education and their entitlement to it.

Foster and Walker (2009) express concern for the future of Traveller education because of cuts and the withdrawal of ring fencing funding, and more recently Lord Avebury (2012: vi) confirms 'cuts in local and national funding are seeing the loss and erosion of valuable targeted services for Gypsies and Travellers, notably in the shrinkage of the national network of Traveller Education Services'. This can do little to help GRT children move from the periphery of the education system to the mainstream.

Early Years and the transition from home to pre-school

'Children's chronological age has become a powerful social marker shaping children's lives in the modern world, linked as it is to ideas about stages and developmental readiness' (Vogler *et al.*, 2008: 17). By the time children reach three or four years of age, it is assumed that they will be attending Early Years provision of some description as they begin the long haul through the education system until they leave work-ready. For some children they will have been attending nurseries since babyhood. By the time they reach middle childhood they will be engulfed in schoolwork, homework and, for some, be in a school environment from 8 a.m. until 6 p.m.

For GRT children, the markers in their childhood are somewhat different. Derrington (2011: 48) notes 'young children tend to be perceived and treated as "babies" for several years', therefore there may be a resistance to the mainstream view that early education is a valuable one. Similarly Derrington (ibid.: 48) highlights that middle childhood is not the same for GRT children. Traveller children tend to adopt some adult responsibilities, which include 'childcare duties, gaining financial independence, using tools and learning to drive'.

However, some GRT children do attend Early Years provision and Case Study 7.2 explores the transition process for Janey.

Case study 7.2: Janey's story

Christine is a member of the TESS team. She has worked with Jake's family (see Case study 7.1) since he started school. Christine is keen for Jake's sister, Janey, to enrol at the Pre-School as she is now approaching 4 years of age. Christine is supporting Janey's mother and the setting during the enrolment and transition process. Although Janey and her mother are familiar with the school site, they have not visited the Pre-School because Jake did not attend. Janey has no experience of being apart from her mother or her community and the setting has no previous knowledge of working with the family.

- What does the setting need to consider?
- What would the setting's long- and short- term plans look like?
- How will partnership working enhance a positive transition process for Janey and her mother?

Building positive relationships with parents is of utmost importance in Early Years education, and of equal importance is working in partnership with any other professionals who are working with a family. Therefore, for Janey and her mother, the Reception class teacher and Christine will all play an essential role in the transition and settling-in process. However, the importance of the physical environment should not be underestimated in the transition to a new setting. Cleave *et al.* (1982: 39), cited in Fabian and Dunlop (2002: 3), identify three critical features as 'the *scale* of the setting, the *range* of [a child's] territory, and the limitations on [the child's] *movements* within it' (authors' italics). These points are important as GRT children often have freedom to explore outdoors, and Janey may have been used to spending a lot time outside and may view her new environment as being a confined space which limits her freedom to play and explore as she is used to.

- How will Janey's key person work with her family and Christine to plan an appropriate learning environment for her?
- Consider your own resources. How inclusive are they? Would they reflect Janey's culture?

The text, *Bender Tents and Bumper Cars: Celebrating Gypsy, Roma and Travellers in the Early Years* (Buckinghamshire Services for Children and Young People, 2014) sets out a long list of points for consideration when supporting transition and includes the following:

1. Children may be entering a setting where, for the first time, most of the adults they encounter are not family members and are not Travellers.
2. Some GRT parents are very protective of their children and may be reticent about leaving them in a school or setting, particularly if they have had no or little experience of the education system themselves.
3. Children may need to be shown how to use running water and flush toilets as there may be no running water in the home.
4. If the parents are not literate, the children will have had few opportunities at home to hear stories read to them and to handle books. However, in many GRT families, there is a strong tradition of oral story telling.
5. As circuses and fairgrounds operate in the evenings, children from these backgrounds may not go to sleep until quite late.

How could you address these points?

Moving to a culture of mutual respect: children learning from each other and with each other

All learning should be play-based, regardless of whether it is adult-led or not. Developing a topic from a child's interests through purposeful observation; listening as well as looking, allows the practitioner to develop meaningful learning with children. As Nutbrown and Clough (2009) suggest, current pedagogy discourse could be constructed in the context of raising achievement, on one hand, while considering the promotion of inclusion on the other. The following short account is presented as a case study in *Building Futures: Developing Trust* (DCSF, 2009a) and it shows how practitioners managed to do this, following the EYFS model.

Case study 7.3: Trailers

The topic began with a practitioner listening to children discussing with each other where creatures might live. One child told another that he did not live in a house – he lived in a trailer. The practitioners decided to build upon this and introduced the rest of the children to a large wooden caravan they had in the construction area. Consequently two of the GRT children became leaders of the developing play. The theme of 'Homes' developed and caravans and trailers became the emphasis. The setting equipped the GRT children with a camera to

(Continued)

(Continued)

photograph where they lived. Through further discussion in the setting, this idea developed into the children deciding that they wanted some role-play trailers in their setting and with the help of the practitioners, the group designed two trailers by using pictures and models of trailers to help develop their ideas. Once they had a plan, they drew up a list of what was needed and eventually their design came to fruition. The garden accommodated the large cardboard trailers. The parents of the GRT children who had led this project were invited to the setting where they had refreshments inside the completed trailers.

This shows that attuned practitioners can recognise potential for learning for all children and foster a culture of mutual respect where *all* children are empowered. It also shows that the practitioners had the will to use all opportunities to welcome GRT parents into the setting.

The importance of developing positive images that fosters self-esteem is frequently highlighted in *Bender Tents and Bumper Cars: Celebrating Gypsy, Roma and Travellers in the Early Years* (Buckinghamshire Services for Children and Young People, 2014), and a powerful message is presented in the following vignette.

'*I* was in school today, Mammy!'

'Yes, I know you were in school today, I took you.'

'No, Mammy, *I* was in school today!'

When the mother of this excited Irish Traveller child questioned her daughter's teacher the next day, it emerged that the setting had bought some jigsaws reflecting Gypsy, Roma and Traveller culture which the little girl had been delighted and proud to play with, seeing her way of life reflected for the first time.

If you completed an audit of your resources, what would it show?

Involving parents

Research shows that where GRT parents have been invited into school to share their knowledge and skills, it has raised awareness, developed trust and raised confidence (Kiddle, 1999; Ofsted, 2003). Consider the following two examples presented in *Bender Tents and Bumper Cars: Celebrating Gypsy, Roma and Travellers in the Early Years* (Buckinghamshire Services for Children and Young People, 2014), which promotes cultural knowledge.

1. A village school was doing a topic, Wheels. A parent was invited in with their horse and cart. Later in the year when the school fete was held, the parent showed the wagon and gave pony rides.
2. For the Christmas Bazaar, a parent demonstrated the craft of making paper flowers and the children were invited to join in.

These are quite simple illustrations of celebrating GRT culture by involving parents of GRT children in a school or Early Years setting. However, to represent GRT culture in your setting, regardless of whether you have GRT children on roll, you could also celebrate Gypsy, Roma, Traveller History month in June.

Gypsy, Roma, Traveller History Month (GRTHM)

Gypsy, Roma, Traveller History Month is an annual event held in the month of June. It was an initiative of the Labour Government and was launched in June 2008. The Foreword in *The Inclusion of Gypsy, Roma and Traveller Children and Young People* document (DCSF, 2008) by Lord Andrew Adonis, the then Parliamentary Under-Secretary of State for Schools states:

> I have endorsed a national Gypsy, Roma and Traveller History Month in June – the first will be in 2008. This will offer us all the chance to raise awareness and explore the history, culture and language of these communities, which is not usually included in the curriculum for all pupils. We can challenge myths, tackle prejudice and be in a position to offer a balanced debate about the issues. We will be able to celebrate the richness that Gypsy, Roma and Traveller communities bring to our everyday lives through their many varied academic and artistic achievements.
>
> (Adonis, 2008: 6)

Therefore the aims of the GRTHM are:

- to promote knowledge of the Gypsy, Roma and Traveller history, culture and heritage;
- to disseminate information on positive Gypsy, Roma and Traveller contributions to British society;
- to heighten the confidence and awareness of Gypsy, Roma and Traveller people of their cultural heritage;
- to celebrate Gypsy, Roma and Traveller history, culture and heritage.

The GRTHM began with a few events and grew into a nationwide celebration. Although due to funding cuts, the GRTHM website is not kept as up to date as it once was, it is an interesting website to visit. However, the National Teachers of Travellers + Other Professionals (NATT+) also promotes GRTHM and it is a useful place to gain information and ideas to celebrate in June. It is also a useful website to gain information about inclusive GRT resources for schools and Early Years settings.

The GRTHM is a celebration, which could be embedded into a long-term plan in a school, or Early Years setting for all children to take part in and its timely month of June makes it even more accessible. The possibilities of what could be celebrated are endless, such is the vibrancy of the GRT culture.

- Consider Case study 7.1 and Case study 7.2. Would you expect to see GRTHM embedded in the setting's long-term plan?
- Consider your own practice. How could your setting celebrate GRTHM?
- If you have celebrated it in the past, how could you improve upon it?
- Would you choose to advertise your celebration locally? If not, why not?

Conclusion

The basis of the education system in England is built on the understanding that all children are in it for the long haul and they progress through each phase of the system until they finally enter the world of work.

For most GRT children, the education system is for the short haul. As they move through each phase, especially to secondary education, different dilemmas emerge and different priorities take over, in particular, those concerned with family roles and responsibilities.

Some may view this in the discourse of non-conformity but GRT families have practices that are fundamental to who they are and their identities should not succumb to the rigid target-driven ethos of the education system which may not consider them a good enough investment.

The important points of this chapter are:

- The prejudices that GRT family incur both in school and as a minority community continue to prevail.
- GRT culture should be represented in all settings, regardless of whether there is a GRT child on roll.
- An audit should be carried out to check whether GRT culture is visible through books and other resources, regardless of whether there is a GRT child on roll.
- Self-esteem for a GRT child will be fostered when the their culture is embedded in the curriculum.

- GRTHM should be celebrated each June, regardless of the demographics of settings and whether a GRT child is attending.

There are no straightforward answers to the tensions that arise but some considerations can be made:

- Educators should 'change the "gazes" through which they "read" children' (MacNaughton, 2003:179) so that children are not ignored or simply assimilated into the mainstream.
- Educators should take the time to develop relationships with families despite the interruptions for travelling. As Foster and Walker (2009: 53) state: 'Schools will need to be flexible, to be Willows rather than Oaks.'
- In an attempt to promote the awareness of GRT history and culture to help to dispel untruths, settings should be representative of the GRT culture regardless of their demographics or whether GRT children attend.
- Finally, when a child from a Gypsy, Roma and Traveller family does attend a setting, their uniqueness needs to be swathed in an ethos which values difference, rejects assimilation and tackles racism fairly.

Further reading

Cemlyn, S., Greenfields, M., Burnett, S., Matthews, Z. and Whitwell, C. (2009) *Inequalities Experienced by Gypsy and Traveller Communities: A Review, Equality and Human Rights Commission*. Available from: www.equalityhumanrights.com.

DCSF (Department for Children Schools and Families) (2008) *The Inclusion of Gypsy, Roma and Traveller Children and Young People*. Nottingham: DCSF. Available at: www.lanc-sngfl.ac.uk/projects/ema/download/file/Inclusion%20of%20Gypsy%20Roma.pdf.

DCSF (Department for Children, Schools and Families) (2009a) *Building Futures, Developing Trusts: A Focus on Provision for Children from Gypsy, Roma and Traveller Backgrounds in the Early Years Foundation Stage*. Nottingham: DCSF. Available at: http://webarchive.nationalarchives.gov.uk/20130401151715/https://www.education.gov.uk/publications/eOrderingDownload/00741-2009BKT-EN.pdf.

DCSF (Department for Children, Schools and Families) (2009b) *Moving Forward together: Raising Gypsy, Roma and Traveller Achievement. Booklet 4: Engagement with Parents, Carers and the Wider Community*. Nottingham: DCSF. Available at: www.cosiv.cz/wp-content/uploads/2013/11/National-Strategies-Roma-Young-People-4.pdf.

Derrington, C., Lewins, L. and Wormington, P.(n.d) *Raising the Attainment of Gypsy Roma and Traveller Pupils, Guidance for Initial Teacher Education Students, Trainees and Newly Qualified Teachers*. NATT+. Available at: www.natt.org.uk/.

Foster, B. and Walker, A. (2009) *Traveller Education in the Mainstream: The Litmus Test*. London: Hopscotch.

Save the Children (n.d.) Early Gypsy, Roma and Traveller Project. Available at: www.savethechildren.org.uk.

Save the Children (n.d.) Early Years Outreach Practice. Available at: www.savethechildren.org.uk.

References

Adonis, Lord (2008) Foreword. In *The Inclusion of Gypsy, Roma and Traveller Children and Young People*. Nottingham: Department for Children Schools and Families.

Avebury, Lord (2012) Foreword. In J. Richardson and A. Ryder (ed.) *Gypsies and Travellers Empowerment and Inclusion in British Society*. Bristol: Polity Press.

Bhopal, K. and Myers, M. (2008) *Insiders, Outsiders and Others: Gypsies and Identity*. Hatfield: University of Hertfordshire Press.

Buckinghamshire Minority Ethnic and Traveller Achievement Service (METAS) (n.d.) *Buckinghamshire Services for Children and Young People*. Available at: https://democracy. buckscc.gov.uk/Published/C00000127/M00002798/AI00005891/$METASreport. docA.ps.pdf (accessed 11 May 2014).

Buckinghamshire Services for Children and Young People (2014) *Bender Tents and Bumper Cars: Celebrating Gypsy, Roma and Traveller Cultures in the Early Years*. Services for Children and Young People: Buckinghamshire County Council. Available at: www. buckscc.gov.uk.

Clark, C. and Greenfields, M. (2006) *Here to Stay*. Hatfield: University of Hertfordshire Press.

DCSF (Department for Children, Schools and Families) (2009a) *Building Futures, Developing Trust: A Focus on Provision for Children from Gypsy, Roma and Traveller Backgrounds in the Early Years Foundation Stage*. Nottingham: DCSF.

DCSF (Department for Children, Schools and Families) (2009b) *Moving Forward Together: Raising Gypsy, Roma and Traveller Achievement. Booklet 4: Engagement with Parents, Carers and the Wider Community*. Nottingham: DCSF. Available at: www.cosiv.cz/wp-content/ uploads/2013/11/National-Strategies-Roma-Young-People-4.pdf.

Derrington, C. (2011) Supporting Gypsy, Roma and Traveller pupils. In G. Richards and F. Armstrong (eds) *Teaching and Learning in Diverse and Inclusive Classrooms*. London: Routledge.

Deuchar, R. and Bhopal, K. (2012) 'We're still human beings, we're not aliens': Promoting the citizenship rights and cultural diversity of Traveller children in schools: Scottish and English perspectives, *British Educational Research Journal*. doi: 10. 1080/01411926.2012.679252.

DfE (Department for Education) (2012) *Statutory Framework for the Early Years Foundation Stage*. Available at: www.gov.uk/government/uploads/system/uploads/attachment_ data/file/271631/eyfs_statutory_framework_march_2012.pdf.

Durand, T. (2008) Celebrating diversity in early care and education settings: moving beyond the margins. *Early Child Development and Care*, 180(7): 835–48.

Early Education (2012) *Development Matters in the Early Years Foundation Stage (EYFS)*. The British Association for Early Childhood Education. Available at: www.early-education.org.uk (accessed 10 February 2014).

Foster, B. and Walker, A. (2009) *Traveller Education in the Mainstream: The Litmus Test*. London: Hopscotch.

Foster, B. and Cemlyn, S. (2012) Education, inclusion and government policy. In J. Richardson and A. Ryder (eds) *Gypsies and Travellers: Empowerment and Inclusion in British Society*. Bristol: The Policy Press.

Foster, B. and Norton, P. (2012) Educational equality for Gypsy, Roma and Traveller children in the UK. *The Equal Rights Review*, 8.

Hawes, D. and Perez, P. (1996) *The Gypsy and the State*, 2nd edn. Bristol: The Policy Press.

House, R., Osgood, J. and Simpson, K. (2012) The revised EYFS: still too much, too young. *Early Years Educator*, 14(2): 18–20. Available at: www.earlychildhoodaction. com/docs/EYE%20June12%20House.pdf (accessed 10 February 2014).

Kendall, S. (1997) Sites of resistance: places on the margin – the Traveller 'homeplace'. In T. Acton (ed.) *Gypsy Politics and Traveller Identity*. Hatfield: University of Hertfordshire Press.

Kiddle, C. (1999) *Traveller Children: A Voice for Themselves*. London: Jessica Kingsley.

Liegeois, J. and Gheorghe, N. (1995) *Roma/Gypsies: A Minority Report*. London: Minority Rights Group.

Lloyd, G. and McCluskey, G. (2008) Education and Gypsies/Travellers: 'contradictions and significant silences'. *International Journal of Inclusive Education*, 12(4): 331–45.

London GRTHM. Available at: www.grthmlondon.org.uk/grthm/about-grthm/ (accessed 10 April 2014).

Luff, P. (2012) Challenging assessment. In T. Papatheodorou and J. Moyles (eds) *Cross-Cultural Perspectives on Early Childhood*. London: Sage.

MacNaughton, G. (2003) *Shaping Early Childhood*. Maidenhead: Open University Press.

Minority Ethnic and Traveller Services, *Buckinghamshire Minority Ethnic and Traveller Achievement Service – METAS*. Available at: http://democracy.buckscc.gov.uk/ mgConvert2PDF.aspx?ID=5183 (accessed 25 April 2014).

Morant, N. (1998) Social representations of gender in the media: quantitative and qualitative content analysis. In D. Miell and M. Wetherell (eds) *Doing Social Psychology*. Milton Keynes: The Open University.

Myers, M., McGhee, D. and Bhopal, K. (2010) At the crossroads: Gypsy and Traveller parents' perceptions of education, protection and social change. *Race, Ethnicity and Education*, 13(4): 533–48.

Nutbrown, C. and Clough, P. (2009) Citizenship and inclusion in the Early Years: understanding and responding to children's perspectives on 'belonging'. *International Journal of Early Years Education*, 17(3): 191–206.

Ofsted (2003) *Provision and Support for Traveller Pupils*. HMI 455. London: Ofsted. Available at: www.ofsted.gov.uk/resources/provision-and-support-for-traveller-pupils (accessed 11 April 2014).

Richardson, J. (2006) *The Gypsy Debate*. Exeter: Imprint Academic.

Richardson, J. and Ryder, A. (2012) Setting the context: Gypsies and Travellers in British society. In J. Richardson and A. Ryder (eds) *Gypsies and Travellers: Empowerment and Inclusion in British Society*. Bristol: The Policy Press.

Rogoff, B. (2007) The cultural nature of human development. *The General Psychologist*, 42(1).

Rose, A. (2011) Building on existing informal learning in Traveller communities through family literacy programmes: an Irish case study. *International Journal of Inclusive Education*. doi:10. 1080/13603116.2011.629688.

Siraj-Blatchford, I. (1994) *The Early Years: Laying the Foundations for Racial Equality*. Stoke-on-Trent: Trentham Books.

Vogler, P., Crivello, G. and Woodhead, M. (2008) *Early Childhood transitions research: A review of concepts, theory and practice*. Working Paper No. 48. The Hague: Bernard van Leer Foundation.

Waage, T. (2006) Modern childhood: the image of the child in our society: The Seventh Kilbrandon Lecture. Available at: www.scotland.gov.uk/Resource/ Doc/136953/0034036.pdf (accessed 14 April 2014).

Wilkin, A., Derrington, C. and Foster, B. (2009) *Improving the Outcomes for Gypsy, Roma and Traveller Pupils*. Research Report No. DCSF-RR077. London: NFER.

Web resources

Equality and Human Rights Commission: www.equalityhumanrights.com

Gypsy Roma and Traveller History Month: www.grthmlondon.org.uk/grthm/about-grthm/

Gypsy, Roma and Traveller Resources: www.natt.org.uk/

National Association for the Teachers of Travellers + Other Professionals: www.natt.org.uk/

Save the Children: www.savethechildren.org.uk

8

Gender and sexuality

The experiences of families/carers and Early Years practitioners

Cora Rooney and Karen Taylor

The aims of this chapter are:

■ To explore existing and inherent beliefs about gender and sexuality
■ To identify issues and dilemmas from your own practice
■ To develop strategies for inclusive practice in relation to equality and diversity.

Introduction

We have separated gender and sexuality to enable you to explore each area in detail but in reality they are interconnected. Without inclusive practice, the well-being of children, parents/carers and practitioners is affected. For further information about well-being, see Chapter 6 (Nangah and Mills) in this book.

This chapter will enable you to make informed and inclusive decisions about the way that you work relating to gender and sexuality. This chapter will build on your existing knowledge, skills and values and raise awareness that will support you in developing strategies for the promotion of diversity and equality in your practice in this field. The issues raised in this chapter will enable you to consider how everyone is affected. By developing your practice you will provide a safe, inclusive, equal and diverse Early Years environment for all.

To put this in context, the Office for National Statistics (ONS) found that 'approximately 97.3 per cent of three and four year olds were in early years placements' (ONS, 2012: 2) and that lifelong learning is a key factor to well-being. In other words, Early Years settings are key to the child's holistic development. The Early Years experience is likely to impact on future educational expectations for both the child and parent/or carer. It is imperative, therefore, to get this right for present and future outcomes that are in the best interests of all children.

The Early Years Foundation Stage (EYFS) framework (DfE, 2014) sets the standards for the Early Years provision in England. Key components of the EYFS are: consistency, quality, security, partnership and equality and, from 1 September 2014, safeguarding and welfare requirements. Throughout this chapter you will find activities, which are based on real-life scenarios from Early Years practitioners. It may be helpful to consider the EYFS standards as you work through these activities.

Standards are helpful as they can enable you to assess, plan, intervene, review and evaluate (Sutton, 2006) both for the individual child's needs and for the overall running of your setting. The use of the audit tools at the end of this chapter will also help you with some of your processes. Two audit tools have been provided, one for gender and one for sexuality.

Ofsted, which is the organisation responsible for the regulation and inspection of Early Years settings, measures your Early Years setting against these standards. Inspection reports by Ofsted about your setting are published as a public document. Consequently, parents and carers may read these reports in order to make decisions about whether their child or children should come to your setting. Therefore, it is important to consider how your Early Years setting evidences inclusive practice in relation to equality and diversity in general, and gender and sexuality in particular, as analysed in this chapter.

Legislation

Legislation provides a statutory framework to support the child, the parent/carer, you and your setting in achieving inclusive practice. The following pieces of legislation are included here because they are specifically linked to equality and diversity. This is not an exhaustive list and you will need to consider other legislation, policy and guidance. This may include the Children Act 1989, the Children Act 2004 and the Childcare Act 2006 (National Archives, 2014a).

It is 25 years since the establishment of the United Nations Convention on the Rights of the Child (UNCRC) and UNICEF is the only organisation to be named in relation to the convention (UNICEF, 2014). UNICEF is a global organisation that specifically advocates on behalf of children by targeting governments to facilitate changes in policy and legislation which promote the rights of the child. UNICEF encourages and supports governments, communities, individuals and organisations to respect the rights of the child:

> In advocating to protect children's rights, to help meet their basic needs, and to expand their opportunities to reach their full potential, UNICEF helps to strengthen laws and policies and to improve understanding of the Convention at all levels of society.
>
> (UNICEF, 2014)

The above quote provides a useful starting point for you to ensure that you, your colleagues and your setting are acting in the child's best interest.

Furthermore, the Equality Act 2010 (National Archives, 2014b) is a single anti-discriminatory piece of legislation, which makes it illegal to discriminate against anyone on the grounds of gender, religion, disability, sexual orientation, ethnicity, race, marriage and age. The Equality and Human Rights Commission (EHRC) has been assigned the role by government to promote equality and challenge discrimination.

This chapter will enable you to consider case studies and your own practice in relation to gender and sexuality. The Equality Act 2010 will facilitate your discussions and decisions. A link can be found under Web resources at the end of the chapter.

When making decisions in your setting it is also important to consider Article 8 of the Human Rights Act 1998, 'The right to respect for private and family life, for home and correspondence' (National Archives, 2014c), in particular, recognising and celebrating the fact that children live within a diverse range of families.

The above pieces of legislation highlight similar themes, which are important to consider when exploring issues about gender and sexuality, such as dignity, respect, rights and inclusion.

Ethics

In order to be able to develop inclusive practice, you need to be aware of your personal ethics and values and how these might impact on your professional ethics and values. Therefore, the chapter will start with a definitions exercise. Following this, throughout the chapter, there are case studies and audit tools together with signposting to further reading. As you progress through the chapter, you are encouraged to revisit the definitions exercise to reflect on your personal and professional development.

Your Early Years setting provides the foundation for lifelong learning. The experience for the child, parent/carer, staff and wider community should be a positive one that embraces diversity and promotes inclusion, which supports the well-being of the child, parent/carer, staff and wider community.

Read the following words and definitions (Table 8.1).

- What do these definitions mean to you?
- How do you relate to them?

(Continued)

(Continued)

TABLE 8.1 Definitions for gender and sexuality

Term	Definition
Gender	Relates to the roles, behaviour, expectations and identity assigned to women and men. It is socially constructed and as such changes over time (Robinson and Diaz, 2006; Leith *et al.*, 2011; Thompson, 2011).
Sex	The physical and biological differences between men and women (Yuill and Gibson, 2011).
Sexuality	'Human sexuality is much more than intercourse and reproduction; it encompasses many components, including a person's identity, gender, behaviors, values, and ideas about intimacy. Young children learn about these components either directly or indirectly from trusted adults' (Sciaraffa and Randolph, 2011: 33). In other words this relates to human sexual development.
Sexual orientation	The definitions of 'Lesbian', 'Gay', 'bisexuality' and 'heterosexuality' are better expressed as 'sexual orientation towards people' rather than 'sexual attraction to'. This reflects the fact that people build committed, stable relationships and is not purely a focus on sexual activity (Stonewall, 2014).
Lesbian	It is a term used exclusively with women and comes from the Greek Island of Lesbos, where the Greek poetess Sappho lived in the seventh century BC and was known for her passionate poems, which were dedicated to women. The term has been used in English since the nineteenth century (Stonewall, 2014).
Gay	This term describes a man who has an emotional and/or sexual orientation towards men. Some women describe themselves as gay rather than lesbian; it is a generic term for lesbian and gay sexuality (Stonewall, 2014).
Bisexual	This is a term which relates to men and women who have a sexual orientation toward men and women.
Trans and transgender	Defines children and adults who identify themselves with the opposite gender or non-gender and can include cross-dressing and gender reassignment (Sparkle, 2014).
LGBT	This term refers to Lesbian, Gay, Bisexual and Transgender people.
Homosexual	This term was coined by a Hungarian Doctor Karoly Maria Benkert in 1869 and introduced into English by sexologist Havelock Ellis in the 1890s. Originally scientists and doctors used homosexual to describe same sex attraction and behaviour as a sign of mental disorder and moral deficiency. The American Psychiatric Association officially declassified homosexuality as a mental illness in 1974 but it was not until 1992 that the World Health Organisation followed suit. To distance the term from such medical labels the terms gay and lesbian are now used (Stonewall, 2014).
Heteronormativity	Where the only acceptable form of sexuality is heterosexuality. This reduces the status of other forms of sexuality, particularly homosexuality (Yuill and Gibson, 2011).
Family	Most families are based on kinship, a social bond of blood ties, marriage or adoption, but who is included under the umbrella term 'family' changes over time and across different cultures. Rather than being a 'natural' unit, therefore, the family could be said to be another example of a social construction. What traditionally has been known as the sociology of the family (with a focus of the structure of the idealised, white, nuclear family) is increasingly being conceptualised as the sociology of the intimacies and relationships (Smart, 2008). As such, it then becomes possible to include a variety of relationships between friends, sexual partners, family and kin instead of perceiving the traditional family as the only possible model of personal relationships (Todd *et al.*, 2011).

Parental responsibility (PR)	Parental responsibility (PR) is defined in s.3 (1) of the Children Act 1989 as all the rights, duties, powers, responsibilities and authority which by law a parent of a child has in relation to the child and his property. This means that the person who holds parental responsibility has the power to be able to make decisions, for example, regarding the child's name, to consent to medical treatment, decide religion and give financial support of the child. More than one person may hold parental responsibility, the child's birth mother will automatically have parental responsibility (but this would no longer apply if an adoption order has been granted). The birth father automatically has PR if he is married to or subsequently marries the child's mother. If the birth father is not or does not get married to the child's birth mother, he can obtain PR by jointly registering the birth of the child or by making a PR agreement with the child's mother, he may also apply to the court for a PR order. PR is also granted to anyone with a Residence Order (RO), a prospective adopter when a child is placed for adoption; a step-parent by agreement or court order;or the local authority under a care order or emergency care order. PR can be complicated so practitioners should seek appropriate advice and follow procedures accordingly.
Anti-discriminatory practice (ADP) Anti-oppressive practice (AOP)	Challenges organisational, socio-political, social and personal processes and cultures which discriminate against an individual or group on the basis of class, race, gender, age, disability and sexuality (Thompson, 2006). 'Addresses social divisions and structural inequalities in the work that is done with clients (users) or workers. AOP aims to provide more appropriate and sensitive services by responding to people's needs regardless of their social status. The practice embodies a person centred philosophy. It aims to empower people who are oppressed and excluded' (Dominelli,1993, cited in Okitikpi and Aymer, 2010: 100–1).
Inclusive practice	'Respectful educators will include all children; not just children who are easy to work with, obliging, endearing, clean, pretty, articulate, capable, but every child – respecting them for who they are, respecting their language, their culture, their history, their family, their abilities, their needs, their name, their ways and their very essence' (Nutbrown et al., 2013: 92).
Social construct	This can relate to identity that includes: gender, sexuality, disability, age, ethnicity, and can change over time and within different cultures (Stonewall, 2014; Yuill, 2011). Social constructs can be used to challenge or reinforce stereotypes. Inclusive practitioners will explore how different identities are oppressed through social constructs, thus enabling the practitioner to challenge stereotypes.
Well-being	Mental health is defined as a state of well-being in which every individual realizes his or her own potential, can cope with the normal stresses of life, can work productively and fruitfully, and is able to make a contribution to her or his community (World Health Organization, 2013).
Multiple discrimination	Most of us belong not to one community but to several. We have multi-faceted identities – being Black and gay, or disabled and transgender and a woman. The different aspects of our identity are a source of pride and strength. But they can also make us the target of prejudice on more than one level. For example, a Black gay child might experience homophobia from some parts of the Black community, racism from some parts of the gay community, and racism and homophobia from everyone else! This is known as multiple discrimination (Stonewall, 2014).

(Continued)

(Continued)

- What is your first response?
- What does it mean in practice?
- What might the impact be on children, families/carers, and other staff members?

You may understand what the word means or you may not. You might feel comfortable or uncomfortable with some or all of these definitions.

- Why do you think this is?
- Who do you talk to about this?
- What does your setting policy say?
- What barriers might there be to discussing these terms?

You may have noticed that some of the definitions relate to men and women rather that children and young people. This could be important when developing your parent partnerships in your setting. This does not mean that the terms cannot apply to children and young people also.

It is important to understand these words and definitions for a number of reasons. First, so that you can recognise oppression and discrimination, and have the confidence to challenge them appropriately. Second, to think about what is age-appropriate language. Third, to help you to follow and implement legislation and codes of practice. Fourth, to consider how definitions, context and impact may change over time. Finally, it helps to develop your own skills knowledge and values, which gives you the confidence to challenge oppression and discrimination and promotes inclusive practice in your Early Years setting.

Reflection is an important part of inclusive practice and it is advisable, therefore, to reconsider these definitions and your responses to them once you have completed the activities about gender and sexuality.

Gender

Legislation, poverty and the media all have an impact on the social construct of gender. How gender is viewed affects everyone, either in a positive or negative way, depending on whether you are perceived as being in the 'in group' or as 'other', where 'Other is defined as those groups that have been marginalised, silenced, denigrated or violated' (Kumashiro, 2002, cited in Robinson and Diaz, 2006: 24).

Despite equality legislation, women in the UK are under-represented in local and national government and therefore under-represented in decision-making processes that shape our lives (Oxfam, 2007; Fawcett Society, 2010). The Oxfam ReGender briefing paper (Oxfam, 2007: 2) states: 'These issues are compounded for ethnic minority women, women with disabilities, Lesbian, Bisexual and

Transgender women and women from lower socio-economic backgrounds.' If women from all backgrounds are socially excluded from decision-making processes, it means that the voices of women and girls are not heard. The mechanisms to challenge exclusion on the grounds of gender are harder to navigate without a visible and consistent channel of communication from the private, voluntary and statutory sector to national government and the international community.

Women are more likely to live in poverty in the UK. This is due to a number of factors, including being paid a lower wage than men (Fawcett Society, 2010). Ninety per cent of lone parent families are headed by women (The Poverty Site, 2009, cited in Fawcett Society, 2010) and 40 per cent of ethnic minority women live in poverty (Fawcett Society, 2009). Therefore, if women are living in poverty, their children will be too and it is likely that these children are attending your Early Years settings. The Child Poverty Action Group (CPAG) use figures from the Department of Work and Pensions (2013) which state that more than 1 in 4 children are living in poverty. Cooper and Stewart (2013: 5) found that children in low-income households do less well than their better-off peers on many outcomes in life, such as education or health, 'simply because they are poorer'. It is important to note that in the current economic climate; '63% of children living in poverty are in a family where someone works' (Barnardos, 2014). The impact of living in poverty can result in fewer life opportunities, which in turn can perpetuate the cycle of poverty for future generations.

If gender is linked to poverty and adversely affects women and their children, another adverse effect is the role that the media has to play. A lack of positive female role models in the media, a stereotyped view of women as victims who need to be rescued and the continuation of portraying women as passive objects all contribute to the social construct of gender. Women are more likely to be described in terms of their age, physical appearance or marital status than men (Fawcett Society, 2010).

Stereotypes of specific gender roles for men and women can result in exclusion for men and women, girls and boys if they are not fulfilling that stereotypical role.

Reconsider the definitions in the previous exercise.

- How can discrimination and oppression occur?
- Consider your own responses to the definitions.

The engagement of fathers is key to the development of children in schools (Cullen *et al.*, 2010). It therefore seems appropriate that Early Years settings consider ways of engaging fathers, and other male role models, in order to develop better outcomes for children.

Equality between women and men will not occur through legislation alone, it has to change in partnership through inclusive societal attitudes. This means that equality in law has to be backed up with practical guidance. Equality has to occur in order to benefit all. Article 5 of the UN Convention for the Elimination of all Forms of Discrimination Against Women (CEDAW) calls on states:

> To modify the social and cultural patterns of conduct of men and women, with a view to achieving the elimination of prejudices … and all other practices which are based on the idea of the inferiority or the superiority of either of the sexes or on stereotyped roles for men and women.
>
> (Fawcett Society, 2010: 29)

The UK Government has made a commitment to report to CEDAW every four years on the outcome of implementation of recommendations made by CEDAW. The Government Equalities Office (GEO) is responsible for equality strategy and legislation across government. This office works with non-governmental organisations (NGOs) to produce reports for CEDAW (the most recent being in 2013). As well as reporting to CEDAW, the GEO is responsible for 'taking action on the government's commitment to remove barriers to equality and help to build a fairer society, leading on issues relating to women, sexual orientation and transgender equality' (Government Equalities Office, 2014).

There are some compelling reasons as to why you and your setting should be aware of these issues. You might be affected with regard to being paid a low wage. Parents and carers of the children who use your service may be in low paid jobs, in jobs where they cannot get time off or on benefits. This is more likely to affect women.

Key factors that may need to be considered regarding gender are:

- How do you ensure that everyone is included?
- What concurrent, integrated and proactive planning do you and your setting need to consider in terms of promotion of gender equality, which is not at the expense of girls or boys?
- What is your role as a practitioner at this early stage to challenge inequality and promote positive gender role modelling?
- How will this contribute to greater life opportunities for all children?

In this task you need to recognise that gender is not a homogeneous term but it includes factors such as ethnicity, sexuality, disability, socio-economic status and culture. These factors will influence your perceptions and the perceptions of others. Great skill is required to ensure that every voice is heard.

This is particularly pertinent in the Early Years sector in the UK, because the vast majority of Early Years practitioners are women. The consequence of this is that gender issues, stereotyping and discrimination can disproportionately affect the Early Years workforce.

It is a constant challenge and the key is not to be complacent. It is important to remember that inclusion and equality for all helps everybody.

Case study 8.1: 'I'm not allowed to play with that toy'

A child-led play session is taking place in your setting. A group of ten children (five girls and five boys) are engaged in a variety of activities. The area is divided into smaller areas, which contains the following:

- a dressing-up box
- teddy bears, dolls and dinosaurs
- chairs and tables
- paper, crayons, paints
- water and sand
- a play kitchen
- a play farm
- building blocks
- books
- a train set

Four of the girls are playing with the dolls or kitchen equipment or the fairy and princess costume in the dressing-up box.

Four of the boys are playing with the farm or building blocks or the pirate costume. The fifth boy picks up and puts on a blue tutu. The fifth girl is playing with a dinosaur and a train set. The dinosaur is the driver of the train.

After a short time one of the other girls comes over to the girl playing with the train and the dinosaur. She is offered the train but she says, 'I'm not allowed to play with that toy.'

It is now time for the children to go home. Parents, carers and guardians are arriving. One of the parents, upon seeing one of the boys dressed in the blue tutu, says, 'I wouldn't let my son be dressed in that.'

Activity 1: Identifying issues

Write down which issues are raised here:

- for the children both individually and as a group;
- for the parents, carers, guardians;

(Continued)

(Continued)

- for you as a practitioner;
- for your setting.

Activity 2: Balancing needs

How do you respond in an inclusive way to any issues raised, which meets the needs of the following?:

- the children both individually and as a group;
- the parents, carers, guardians;
- you, as a practitioner;
- your setting.

Activity 3: Practitioner-led play

This scenario above described child-led play.

- What would be similar and/or different in practitioner-led play?
- What challenges are there?
- How would you resolve them?

Activity 4: Legal framework

Consider which policies, legislation and guidance are relevant to support you in working inclusively to challenge perceptions of gender roles, gender stereotypes and gender assumptions. How do you and your setting put these into practice?

Audit tool: gender

Consider the Early Years setting that you work in and do a gender audit using Table 8.2.

TABLE 8.2 Audit tool: gender

How many people work there?
How many are women (full-time/part-time)?
How many are men (full-time/part-time)?
What role do you have in your setting?
Which roles happen as part of your or others' job description?
Which roles happen by default?
How are different job roles displayed in your setting?
What links does your setting have with guest speakers, e.g.
    people who come in to speak about their job, promote sport,
    do craft activities or language classes?
What impact does this have on inclusivity around gender on
    the children, parents, carers and guardians?

What training opportunities either in-house or externally can
be accessed to explore issues of gender?
How can training opportunities relating to gender be
developed, achieved and sustained?
How does your setting work in participation with parents,
carers and guardians?
How could your setting work in participation with parents,
carers and guardians?
Where do governors, board of trustees and/or funders fit in?
How are women and men supported and encouraged in your
setting?
Is this equitable?
If it is not equitable, how is this challenged?
Where is good practice shared between settings?
How can good practice be shared between settings and the
wider community?
What reviewing and evaluation processes are in place in
relation to inclusive practice and gender/gender issues?
Who is responsible in your setting to implement, monitor,
review and evaluate inclusive practice relating to gender?

Summary of key points around gender

■ Gender roles are socially constructed.
■ Challenging oppression and discrimination on the grounds of gender creates an equal and inclusive environment for all children, parents/carers,
staff and the wider community.
■ An inclusive environment promotes positive self-esteem, outcomes and life
chances for all.
■ Attitudes, legislation and theory can help to promote an inclusive environment.
■ This is an on-going process and complacency is not an option.

Sexuality

It is important to remind ourselves that early years' development and life
outcomes are dependent on a number of factors including the socio-economic
status (SES) of parents, the parents' education and the quality of the Early Years
provision. As highlighted earlier in this chapter, if families and children are
perceived as 'other', this may have a detrimental effect on life outcomes. When
the setting is inclusive, this enables children to develop social skills, which will
support them throughout their lives in order to achieve the best outcomes possible (Yaojum *et al.*, 2008). A literature review commissioned in 2008 about Early
Years life chances by the Equality and Human Rights Commission (ERCH)
found that there was little evidence in relation to LGBT issues 'because the
datasets that contain information both on early years and on life outcomes do
not collect information on sexual orientation' (Johnson and Kossykh, 2008: v).

This absence of information highlights issues of invisibility and exclusion by omission. If children, parents/carers and staff feel invisible or 'other', they are more vulnerable to oppression and discrimination and will be disadvantaged in life opportunity choices.

The ERCH literature review summarised that, though there had been no link with Early Years and later years outcomes, that students who identified as LGBT chose careers that were perceived as more gay friendly rather than those they wanted to choose. Another point to note was that other students who were not gay, but did not conform to the norm, were also subject to homophobia. This highlights the fact that tackling homophobia is everyone's responsibility. If these attitudes can be challenged from the Early Years onwards, then this will provide a more inclusive learning environment in primary school and secondary school.

Stonewall, the lesbian, gay and bisexual charity, carried out a schools report in 2007 and a subsequent schools report in 2012, relating to questions about homophobic bullying. Following the report in 2007, Stonewall launched a series of events and resources aimed at supporting schools to challenge homophobia. Some elements of homophobia have decreased; reports of homophobic bullying are down from 65 per cent in the 2007 report to 55 per cent in 2012 (Stonewall, 2012). However, homophobic insults and language are just as common as in 2007. Unfortunately, the number of children who have self-harmed has increased; out of the 1600 children who identified as LGB, in the survey, 1 in 4 said that they self-harmed as a result of homophobic bullying. Teachers appear to be unsure about whether they can teach about same sex relationships, despite the fact that Section 28 of the 1998 Local Government Act was repealed in 2003 (Greenland and Nunney, 2008).

So where do you as Early Years practitioners fit into this issue about sexuality? Some of you may identify as LGBT and may or may not be out in your setting. You may have already had situations within your setting, for example, name calling, of a homophobic nature and have not been sure what to do. You may have parents/carers who are from the LGBT community.

While attention to diversity and difference is now widespread in schools, particularly under the rubrics of 'multiculturalism' and 'equal opportunities', sexuality is notable for its absence. This is particularly the case in primary schools where notions of childhood 'innocence' add to other social and cultural processes to mark the primary school as 'asexual' and sexuality as 'inappropriate' or even 'dangerous' in it. We argue that sexuality (especially heterosexuality) is not only present but crucial to the organisation of primary schools, both explicitly and implicitly. Recognition of this fact is necessary not only to protect children from (sexual) abuse, but also to construct a truly diverse society. Lack of attention to sexuality in its diversity constructs a present (and a future) in which homophobia is tolerated and in which teenagers and adults have difficulty 'coming out' as lesbian, gay or bisexual later in life and may even commit suicide (Douglas *et al.*, 1997). It also fails to recognise the diversity of households and families in which children live and creates a situation where lesbian and gay couples are considered 'inappropriate' or 'second-best' homes for children due, in part, to the difficulties their sexuality may pose for their children (Wallis and Van Every, 2000: 410). However, Sciaraffa and Randolph (2011: 34) suggest that educators 'can promote healthy sexual development by using words, behaviours, and even facial expressions that communicate acceptance'. While Wallis and Van Every are talking about primary schools, we argue that there is no reason why age-appropriate conversations and adaption of resources from Stonewall could not be used in Early Years settings to provide the best possible opportunity for all. Links to Stonewall and their resources (such as 'different families') can be found at the end of the chapter.

When considering Case study 8.2, reflect on the definitions exercise and you may also find the links to web sites useful.

Case study 8.2: 'What is normal?'

A fundraising event is taking place in your Early Years setting one Saturday morning in December. The main room has several stalls, which include cake, tombola, jumble, craft, etc.

Geoff and Pete are the fathers of Emily, who started to attend your setting in September, and are running the tombola stall. You notice that the parents, carers and guardians are moving their children away from the tombola stall and when Emily goes over to talk to the children, you hear them say, 'Go back to your daddies.'

On the Wednesday morning, a letter arrives which is signed by several of the parents/carers/guardians stating that they object to the promotion of homosexuality and they have concerns about Emily being brought up by two men, saying that it is not normal. The signatories are saying that they are looking at alternative Early Years settings for their children if nothing is done about this.

- What would you do?
- When considering this scenario, who would you talk to?
- Where would you go for guidance and advice?
- What policies would you consider?
- What are your personal and professional values in relation to this scenario in particular and in relation to LGBT issues in general?

Theories and models into practice

Theories help us to predict and to anticipate how children might behave and react. They help us structure what we observe. Theories help us to make sense of what we see. When we analyse play, we find ourselves linking what we have found with what other people (theorists) have found. We may find our observations fit with theories. We may find that we do not. This will help us think deeply.

(Bruce, 2001: 19)

Theories may also be used as a way of implementing legislation, policy and guidance and good practice, for example, child-centred practice. Theories can also be challenged as society changes, for example, Bowlby's attachment theory (Bowlby, 1969). Theories can also be used to challenge practice, such as discriminatory practice. This can help you to understand why someone might be exhibiting homophobic, sexist, racist beliefs or behaviour and then you can challenge the behaviour.

It is important to remember that theories do not work in isolation and one theory does not fit all circumstances. We all have different perceptions, perspectives and experiences and need to practise with emotional intelligence. Developing a holistic approach to working with children will help in understanding their well-being needs. For example, thinking about key dates in the calendar such as Mother's Day or Father's Day. It would be more inclusive to ask children to 'make a card for someone special' rather than for 'dad' or 'mum'. A secure key person system will support your understanding of who is important to the child.

When approaching potentially challenging areas of practice such as gender and sexuality, it is important to recognise that you might be challenging your own and others' perceptions of what is 'normal'. Ultimately, using theories inclusively promotes positive outcomes for all. Below you will find an introduction and outline to a method and a theory, which relates to challenging discrimination and oppression in order to promote inclusion. This list is not exhaustive and it is expected that you will go on to explore other theories.

Consider how you could apply the following to enable you to practise inclusively in relation to gender and sexuality.

The PCS (Personal, Cultural and Structural) model

PCS stands for Personal, Cultural and Structural levels in their broadest terms (Thompson, 2006; Teater, 2010). This model can be used as a tool to understand where discrimination and oppression come from and how to challenge them. Using the PCS model will enable you as an Early Years practitioner to empower children, families and other practitioners who have experienced discrimination or oppression or who could potentially experience discrimination and oppression. It can help you to reflect on your Early Years practice and enable you to analyse your own belief systems in relation to gender and sexuality. You can start by highlighting where your personal beliefs (the 'P' in the PCS model) might be contributing to the discrimination and oppression of children, parents/carers and colleagues. It may also help you to identify other people's personal beliefs about gender and sexuality (use the exercises in this chapter to identify personal beliefs).

The cultural level (the 'C' in the PCS model) includes a personal set of norms, values and beliefs, which are shared within a group, for example, in a work, family or social setting. This collective way of 'seeing, thinking and doing' (Thompson, 2006: 27) establishes what is perceived as 'normal'. This could be a positive in that it provides structures, boundaries and a sense of identity, but what if you are perceived as 'other'? It is important therefore to understand cultural influences in order to challenge them when they exclude. Reflect on the exercises in this chapter and identify which cultural norms, values and beliefs are being demonstrated. What is discriminatory or oppressive and what is inclusive?

The structural level (the 'S' in the PCS model) refers to divisions within society. This reflects on who has the power and influence and who is oppressed. Consider this in relation to sexuality and gender. Where does legislation empower or disempower?

In this chapter, we have asked you to consider Thompson's PCS model in relation to gender and sexuality. You can also use this powerful model to consider other areas such as age, disability, ethnicity and religion.

Feminist theory

There are many types of feminist theory, including Marxist, post-structuralist, post-modernist and liberal feminism (Robinson and Diaz, 2006). This can be feminist theory's strength and its vulnerability. The strength is because feminism covers a wide range of perspectives, as feminist theorists and writers have a wide range of experiences and perceptions. Its vulnerability is that it can become difficult to navigate through the many different perspectives. However, the common themes that emerge from feminist theory are that feminists want to highlight the oppression and exclusion of women. It is political in nature in terms of structures within society (patriarchy) (Thompson, 2006). Feminists highlight that the private and public sphere are interconnected, that 'the personal is political'. Both women and men need to be engaged in the fight for equal rights.

Therefore, we want you to consider feminist theory as a theory that seeks to obtain equality for women and ultimately equality for all. Feminist theory can support girls and boys, women and men in achieving their potential by removing socially constructed barriers in relation to gender. Thompson (ibid.: 66) explains how both men and women 'can feel alienated and disaffected' as a direct result of gender roles that are defined in their culture. Most significantly, it is the limitations that these expectations generate that are worrying. Professor Thompson goes on to expand on how it is necessary to reflect on the personal level, in order to avoid 'reinforcing and reproducing the sexism inherent in the C and S levels'.

> The theories introduced above are not the only theories.
>
> ■ Research some other theories, using the further reading references.
> ■ What other theories you might use and why?

Audit tool for sexuality

Consider the Early Years setting that you work in and do a sexuality audit using Table 8.3.

TABLE 8.3 Audit tool: sexuality

How does your setting ensure inclusive practice in relation to
   challenging homophobia?
What training is required to raise awareness about LGBT issues?
How can you work in partnership with children, parents, carers,
   guardians, LGBT organisations and the wider community?
What resources does your setting have which celebrate difference
   and promote an inclusive community?
How can these resources be developed and sustained?
How does your setting support a child who is gay?
How does your setting support a child whose parent(s), carer(s),
   guardian(s) are gay?
How could inclusive practice in relation to LGBT issues be
   developed and sustained?
Are LGBT staff in your setting seen as role models, are they
   supported, are they outed? How do you ensure dignity at work?
Human sexuality development: how can barriers be broken down
   to talk about sexuality with children?
How is homophobic language challenged in your setting? How
   would you challenge children, parent(s), carer(s) staff and
   visitors?
How do you ensure there is no complacency and constant
   reflection?

Summary of the key points – sexuality

■ What is family? Who is in a family?
■ What are the issues of coming out as a parent/carer to school or as a child of LGBT parents or as a member of staff in an Early Years setting
■ If a child and their family/carer feel included and valued, this enables children to thrive and achieve.
■ Developing a holistic approach to working with children in understanding their well-being needs will support all areas of learning and development.
■ Human sexual development is a lifelong process.

Strategies to develop inclusive practice in relation to gender and sexuality

- Build on existing positive working relationships with children, parents/ carers and staff to develop partnership working about gender and sexuality.
- Undertake sustained professional development for staff which includes on-going training about gender and sexuality.
- Keep up to date and implement relevant legislation, policy and guidance.
- Share good practice with other Early Years settings within your local, national and global communities.
- Develop links with primary schools, secondary schools, colleges and universities to establish and maintain a dialogue about positive role modelling in relation to gender and sexuality.
- Forge alliances with women, men, the LGBT and the wider community to challenge discrimination and oppression. (Stonewall has a diversity champion programme, for example).
- Build on, establish and maintain links with local businesses/employers who can provide positive role models.
- Develop existing resources through the strategies suggested above and by liaising with organisations which are listed in the web resources section.

Conclusion

Inclusive practice in relation to gender and sexuality in an Early Years setting should be supported by legislation, policies and guidance. Managers and practitioners in Early Years settings need to have access to on-going training, resources and other sources of support to enable them to provide an inclusive environment, which benefits all.

It is important to work in partnership with children, parents/carers, colleagues, other Early Years settings and the wider community to share good practice and to challenge discrimination and oppression. Inclusive practice and a sense of well-being provide the opportunity for positive life chances.

Goldschmied and Jackson (1994) refer to 'people under three', not babies, toddlers, or even children, but people with rights, which includes being treated with dignity and respect. They also emphasise the importance of good quality care being based not just on knowledge. It is also on the ability of those adults to empathise with their children, and to understand the experiences and feelings of young children imaginatively, especially when they are separated from their parents (David *et al.*, 2003).

References

Barnardos (2014) *Child Poverty*. Available at: www.barnardos.org.uk (accessed 30 July 2014).

Bowlby, J. (1969) *Childcare and the Growth of Love*. London: Penguin.

Bruce, T. (2001) *Learning Through Play*. London: Hodder Education.

Childcare Act 2006, c.21, Part 1 Section 1. Available at: www.legislation.gov.uk/ukpga/2006/21/section/1 (accessed 15 January 2015).

Cooper, K. and Stewart, K. (2013) *Does Money Affect Children's Outcomes?* London: Centre for Analysis of Social Exclusion, London School of Economics and Political Science.

Cullen, S., Cullen, M., Band, S., Davis, L. and Lindsay, G. (2010) Supporting fathers to engage with their children's learning and education: an under-developed aspect of the Parent Support Advisor Pilot. *British Educational Research Journal*, 37(3): 485–500.

David, T., Goouch, K., Powell, S. and Abbot, L. (2003) *Birth to Three Matters*. Nottingham: DfES Publications.

Department of Work and Pensions (2013) *Households Below Average Income: An Analysis of the Income Distribution, 1994/95–2011/12*. London: Department for Work and Pensions.

DfE (Department for Education) (2014) *Statutory Framework for the Early Years Foundation*. Available at: www.gov.uk/government/uploads/system/uploads/attachment_data/file/335504/EYFS_framework_from_1_September_2014__with_clarification_note.pdf (accessed 30 July 2014).

Douglas, K. A., Collins, J. L., Warren, C., Kann, L., Gold, R., Clayton, S., *et al.* (1997) Results from the 1995 National College Health Risk Behavior Survey. *Journal of American College Health*, 46(2): 55–66.

DSCF (Department for Schools Children and Families) (2007) *Cyberbullying Safe to Learn: Embedding Anti-Bullying Work in Schools*. Nottingham: DCSF.

Emerson, J. A. (2011) Chalk talks: who's in a family? Parental rights and tolerance promoting curriculum in early elementary education. *Journal of Law and Education*, 40(4).

Fawcett Society (2009) *Poverty Pathways: Ethnic Minority Women's Livelihoods*. London: Fawcett Society.

Fawcett Society (2010) *What About Women?* London: Fawcett Society.

Goldschmied, E. and Jackson, S. (1994) *People Under Three: Young Children in Day Care*. London: Routledge.

Government Equalities Office (2014) *What we do*. Available at: https://www.gov.uk/government/organisations/government-equalities-office (accessed 30 July 2014).

Greenland, K. and Nunney, R. (2008) The repeal of Section 28: it ain't over till it's over. *Pastoral Care in Education*, 26(4): 243–51.

Johnson, P. and Kossykh, Y. (2008) *Early Years, Life Chances and Equality: A Literature Review*. Manchester: Equality and Human Rights Commission (EHRC).

Knowles, G. (ed.) (2006) *Supporting Inclusive Practice*. New York: Routledge.

Leith, V., Sutherland, M. and Gibson, N. (2011) Gender. In C. Yuille and A. Gibson (eds) *Sociology for Social Work: An Introduction*. London: Sage.

National Archives (2014a) Children and Families Act 2014. Available at: www.legislation.gov.uk (accessed 30 July 2014).

National Archives (2014b) Equality Act 2010. Available at: www.legislation.gov.uk/ukpga/2010/15/contents (accessed 30 July 2014).

National Archives (2014c) Human Rights Act 1998. Available at: www.legislation.gov.uk/ukpga/1998/42/contents (accessed 30 July 2014).

Nutbrown, C., Clough, P. and Atherton, F. (2013) *Inclusion in the Early Years*, 2nd edn. London: Sage.

Office for National Statistics (ONS) (2012) *Measuring National Well-being, Education and Skills*. Available at: www.ons.gov.uk/ons/dcp171766_268091.pdf (accessed 30 July 2014).

Okitikpi, T. and Aymer, C. (2010) *Key Concepts in Anti-Discriminatory Social Work*. London: Sage.

Oxfam (2007) *Not Seen and Not Heard? Gender, Community Engagement and Representation*. Oxfam ReGender Briefing Paper. Available from: www.oxfam.org.uk/resources/policy/gender/ (accessed 30 July 2014).

Robinson, K. and Diaz, C. (2006) *Diversity and Difference in Early Childhood Education*. Maidenhead: Open University Press.

Sciaraffa, M. and Randolph, T. (2011) Responding to the subject of sexuality development of young children. *Young Children*, 66(4): 32–8.

Smart, C. (2008) 'Can I be bridesmaid?': combining the personal and political in same-sex weddings. *Sexualities*, 11(6): 763–78.

Sparkle (2014) *National Transgender Celebration*. Available at: www.sparkle.org.uk (accessed 30 July 2014).

Stonewall (2014) *Education for All: Primary School*. Available at: www.stonewall.org.uk/at_school/education_for_all/primary_schools/default.asp (accessed 15 January 2015).

Sutton, C. (2006) *Helping Families with Troubled Children: A Preventative Approach*, 2nd edn. Chichester: John Wiley & Sons.

Teater, B. (2010) *An Introduction to Applying Social Work Theories and Methods*. Maidenhead: Open University Press.

The Poverty Site (2009) Available at: www.poverty.org.uk/07/index.shtml (accessed 15 January 2015).

Thompson, B. (2011) Reassessing gender issues in the primary classroom. In G. Knowles (ed.) *Supporting Inclusive Practice*. London: Routledge.

Thompson, N. (2006) *Anti-Discriminatory Practice*, 4th edn. Basingstoke: Palgrave Macmillan.

Todd, M., Hothershall, S. and Owen, J. (2011) Intimacies and relationships. In C. Yuille and A. Gibson (eds) *Sociology for Social Work: An Introduction*. London: Sage.

UNICEF (2014) United Nations Convention on the Rights of the Child. Available at: www.unicef.org/crc/ (accessed 30 July 2014).

Wallis, A. and Van Every, J. (2000) Sexuality in the primary school. *Sexualities*, 3(4): 409–23.

World Health Organization (2013) *Mental Health: A State of Well-Being* Available at: www.who.int/features/factfiles/mental_health/en/ (accessed 30 July 2104).

Yaojum, L., Devine, F. and Heath, A. (2008) *Equality Group Inequalities in Education, Employment and Earnings: A Research Review and Analysis of Trends over Time*. Manchester: Equality and Human Rights Commission.

Yuille, C. and Gibson, A. (2011) *Sociology for Social Work: An Introduction*. London: Sage.

Web resources

Challenging Violence, Changing Lives, Womankind Worldwide's UK Schools Programme: www.womankind.org.uk

Child Poverty Action Group: www.cpag.org.uk/child-poverty-facts-and-figures

Daycare Trust: www.daycaretrust.org.uk

Disability Rights UK: http://disabilityrightsuk.org

Equality and human rights: www.equalityhumanrights.com

Fair Play South West: regional gender equality network: www.fairplaysw.org.uk

Fatherhood Institute: www.fatherhoodinstitute.org

Gingerbread, Single parents, equal families. Providing expert advice, practical support and campaigns for single parents: www.gingerbread.org.uk/policy

Grandparents Plus: www.grandparentsplus.org.uk

Oxfam Paper and Reports on Gender: www.oxfam.org.uk/resources

Pinkstinks is a campaign that targets the products, media and marketing that prescribe heavily stereotyped and limiting roles to young girls. www.pinkstinks.co.uk/campaign.php

Save the Children: www.savethechildren.org.uk

Sparkle for transgender information and support: www.sparkle.org.uk/

Stonewall: the lesbian, gay and bisexual charity: www.stonewall.org.uk/

The Equality Trust: www.equalitytrust.org.uk

The Fawcett Society, working for women's rights since 1866: www.fawcettsociety.org.uk

The Lesbian and Gay Foundation: www.lgf.org.uk/

UNICEF: www.unicef.org/crc

Women in film and TV: www.wftv.org.uk

9

Challenging the assumptions of multiculturalism and inclusion

Kathy Brodie

The aims of this chapter are:

- To consider and explore your own culture and what this means to you
- To analyse some aspects of multiculturalism and how this may affect the inclusion of children in your care
- To review some inclusive strategies to use in your own practice in your setting.

Introduction

> The fact is that no single, unproblematic definition of 'culture' is to be found here. The concept remains a complex one – a site of convergent interests, rather than a logically or conceptually clarified idea.
>
> (Hall, 1980: 59)

The UK is becoming steadily more ethnically diverse, with 80.5 per cent of people identifying themselves as having a white ethnicity in 2011, down from 94.1 per cent of people in 1991 (ONS, 2012). Every ethnic group showed a percentage increase since 2001, excepting the White Irish category. There are also more categories of ethnicity being added to the census each year, with Gypsy or Irish Traveller and Arab categories being added in 2011.

The increase in ethnic diversity will naturally mean an increase in cultural diversity and a more multicultural society. This is reflected in our Early Years settings, both in the children who attend and also the practitioners who work in Early Years. Inclusion, integration and multiculturalism are becoming more prominent issues in settings around the UK. There is a need to examine how Early Years practice is developed that genuinely recognises and includes different cultures, one that goes beyond cultural tourism.

These issues will be analysed through the lenses of inclusion and good inclusive practice. A specific focus is on self-reflection and how important this is in being able to recognise and respond to differences or, more importantly, similarities in a culture. Focus groups were held to discuss practitioners' experiences of inclusion and multiculturalism, to help understand how this manifests itself in practice.

Background

The United Nations Conventions on the Rights of the Child (UNCRC, 1989) is a ratified convention that aims to set up special safeguards and care for children. Article 30 declares that:

> In those States in which ethnic, religious or linguistic minorities or persons of indigenous origin exist, a child belonging to such a minority or who is indigenous shall not be denied the right, in community with other members of his or her group, to enjoy his or her own culture, to profess and practice his or her own religion, or to use his or her own language.

This is a clear statement of a child's right to inclusion in a multicultural, or pluralist, society. Note that there is no qualifier to this statement – it is the right of every child, everywhere.

For compulsory education, the school report, *Education for All*, also known as the Swann Report (DES, 1985) reported that multicultural understanding had to be evident throughout all school practices. This was to combat the inequality of opportunity that pupils suffered in the late 1970s and early 1980s. Since then there has been a more proactive awareness of good practice and multiculturalism is evident in subsequent curricula, such as the National Curriculum (DfE, 2013).

In addition to these legal requirements, practitioners have a moral and ethical duty to all children in their care to include and integrate children into all aspects of the setting's daily life. This is an essential element for all children's personal, social, emotional, moral and spiritual development. Without this inclusion, there is a danger that children will not learn to appreciate other cultures. Equally, this has to be done sensitively, to ensure that children still value their own, unique, cultural heritage. From a practitioner's perspective, learning about other cultures, ideologies and beliefs can be hugely interesting personally. As a reflective and curious practitioner, this will be very beneficial for your continued professional development.

A note on some terms used

We use some terms in everyday language, with the presumption that others know what they mean and have a similar understanding to ourselves. However, this is not always the case. For clarification, included here are some frequently used words and their meanings as they have been used in this chapter.

■ *Culture*: the definition of culture used here is all-encompassing and includes artefacts, food, clothing, housing, as well as less tangible aspects of culture such as philosophy, language, beliefs and attitudes.
■ *Multiculturalism*: multiculturalism is used here to mean the integration of different cultures into a community or setting. It is typified by tolerance, and is supportive of cultural heritage and diversity. Children will still have a unique identity within this multicultural paradigm and celebrate positive difference. Cultural pluralism is a form of multiculturalism, but it is the coexistence of many cultures, within a dominant culture.
■ *Cultural diversity*: this is used here to denote the respectful acknowledgement that there are other cultures, noting the differences and the similarities.

Pappamihiel (2004: 540) describes culture as having two states: a surface culture and deep culture. Surface culture is the most obvious aspects of cultural difference, for example, food, dress and language, whereas the concept of 'deep culture' is defined as ideology and beliefs of a culture. Often the surface culture is embraced, and even welcomed, but it is at the deep culture level that conflicts may occur. This may be due to misunderstandings about ideology or a strong opposing belief system.

Case study 9.1: The Christmas Show

Michelle comes from a family who are Jehovah's Witnesses. Part of their religious doctrine is not to celebrate birthdays or Christmas.

When Michelle started at nursery, it was explained that her mum and dad did not want her to take part in any birthday celebrations or any Christmas activities. They felt it would be too confusing for Michelle to do this at nursery, but then not at home.

This caused some concern with the practitioners, because everyone's birthday was celebrated with the 'Birthday Song' and usually with cake or sweets. There was a lot of discussion about how this could be managed on a practical level and also the effect it might have on Michelle's self-esteem if she had to be excluded on a regular basis.

(Continued)

(Continued)

One solution to this was to celebrate birthdays just before lunchtime, when one practitioner would stay in another room with Michelle, playing a game or doing an activity. This relied on having a supernumerary practitioner and space in order to do this. Michelle was also aware that she was being excluded from something that all the other children were involved in.

The nursery celebrated Christmas by having a small show, which usually consisted of the children dressing as characters from the Nativity and singing Christmas songs. This had to be rehearsed and practised several times before the performance. This was a greater concern to practitioners because the practices sometimes took up to an hour and everyone was involved, so there were no supernumerary staff.

Some practitioners felt that Michelle's mum should keep her at home on the Nativity days, so there would be minimum disruption at nursery. Some practitioners thought that Michelle should be involved and that the songs and costumes could be chosen to be more secular and thus, possibly, less unacceptable to her parents. All the practitioners wanted to ensure that Michelle could be included as much as possible.

- Consider your own, personal thoughts on this. Do they differ from your professional ideology?
- Do these beliefs differ from your own about birthdays and Christmas? What does this tell you about your own cultural beliefs?
- Explore some solutions to this problem with a critical friend.

Understanding our own culture

Reflection

Before we can discuss multiculturalism, it is important to understand your own culture and how this affects your practice. Everyone has a culture. It could well be that you've not thought about your own culture before, because it is around you and part of you all the time. Your culture will include obvious physical signs, such as the clothes you wear, the items you have in your home and the type of food you cook. There will also be less obvious signs, such as your beliefs about a woman's role in the home or childcare practices, which would be as a result of your cultural heritage. This is not to say that one way is 'right' and the other is 'wrong', it is simply a difference as a result of how you were raised as a child, or the community that you live in, or the family that you are a part of. It is because there are so many complex and subtle influences all around us in our daily lives that cultural pressure is difficult to define and sometimes difficult to recognise. The sort of television programmes that we watch, the types of food that are available in our local shops or the choice of friends in our social circle may influence us.

It could be that you have considered your own culture for a number of reasons. For example, you may have experience of living abroad or have family with a different cultural heritage. In this case you may have noted how different people do things differently. It may be as simple as the timing of the evening meal – many Mediterranean countries have their evening meal much later than in northern Europe. Or it could be a much greater difference such as how much independence children are given or how gender roles are defined in the home.

Whether you have already thought about your own culture before or not, it is worth taking a few minutes just to reflect on your culture and the sorts of things in it you consider normal. Imagine that you are an alien from outer space who has no idea about human behaviour or beliefs. How do you think they would view the following?:

- what you had for breakfast;
- who lives in the house with you;
- the clothes that you wear for work;
- how you got to work;
- the community that you live in.

How do you think these things may vary around the world?

Reflecting on the things that you find normal and seeing them from a different point of view, 'making the familiar strange' (Mills, 1959), is a powerful way of understanding your own culture, and the sort of effects that this has on your day-to-day life.

Reflexivity

When you have reflected on your own culture, you can then use this experience to inform your practice with children. It is important to recognise that others have cultures different to your own, but it is even more important to use this information to support good practice. Being able to make reflections and then use them in your practice, is called being reflexive. Bolton (2010: 9) suggests that this is not so much a technique, but an 'on-going constituent of practice … a pedagogical approach'. Considering multiculturalism and inclusion, it is only by appreciating and understanding your own culture that you can begin to see the differences with others' culture. This is vital if you are going to be more than tokenistic in your setting. It could be that you are not fully including a child, purely because you have not appreciated there are differences in culture. Once you have identified these differences, then you can consider what this means for inclusion. For example, are you aware of any differences in the way that children eat food at home and in your setting? It may be perfectly normal for your child to eat food with their hands at home, but then be asked use a knife and fork in your setting.

It is important to understand this first because elements of inclusion are about seeing the setting, routines, food and attitudes from the child's point of view. Until you understand these things yourself, you will not be able to understand what the child sees.

Use of language

The language we use to describe multiculturalism sends out message to adults and children about our attitudes. Heritage is often associated with racial backgrounds. For example, dual heritage is a positive term, reflecting the fact that children benefit from two different types of cultural influences. In fact, many children will have multiple heritages as globalisation means that people travel further and more frequently from their birthplace. 'Culture' is more often used to describe the type of activities that people are involved in, such as traditions, food, dress and music. This tends to be more fluid as new influences exert themselves. This can be as simple as fish and chips being replaced by Chinese food as Britain's favourite takeaway food. It may be more personal, such as a family tradition. It is likely that many traditions are similar across many cultures, for example, celebrating a child's birth or coming of age. In this sense of the word 'culture', we are all multicultural because we have the traditions from our family, the community we live in, the place where we work and our own social groups.

Ethnicity is a little harder to pin down because it refers to a group who identify with each other on a number of very different commonalities, for example, ideology, religion, place of birth or language spoken. Ethnic groups often have sub-groups, and the use of 'ethnic group' as a term is only a relatively recently phenomenon. The term 'ethnic minority' should be used with care, as it implies difference rather than similarity and may be seen by some as being derogatory.

For inclusion, the importance of knowing which terms are preferred by each different family is twofold:

1. You need to know the preferred terms that parents and families would like you to use, for example, dual heritage. It may be that the family do not regard themselves as an 'ethnic minority' but as a family within the community.
2. A positive way of starting a parent partnership is by opening this dialogue about preferred language and to find the similarities in traditions, food, etc. as well as the diversity.

Family culture

A significant difference in culture, which may not be immediately obvious when children attend your setting, is that of family culture. This is the way that families interact and is more deeply embedded than simply food or clothes. It is probably something that most families do not consciously think about, but evolves over time. For example, Durand (2010) explains how some families value individualism, while others value collectivism. A culture of individualism values the independence, self-reliance and unique nature of each person. Conversely, a culture of collectivism is more focused on the family as a whole unit, made of interdependent people working together for the common good. These two perspectives are not culturally specific, though there is a tendency for Western cultures to value the individual, support unique thoughts and focus on an individual's self-esteem. Some Asian cultures are more likely to value collectivism, which will include undisputed respect for elders and a common understanding of a child's place in the family. At any one time, a family is likely to be on a continuum between individualism and collectivism. For example, sometimes we do things we don't want to do, for the good of the family and sometimes our own individual view overrides others.

Children's development is likely to be affected by their parents' beliefs and cultures at home. The amount of 'autonomy and relatedness' (Cruz de Carvalhoa *et al.*, 2014: 3), or individualism and collectivism, which children experience at home will affect their attitudes towards interpersonal and intrapersonal relationships in your setting or school. For example, if children live in a family which values collectivism, they are going to be bewildered about making individual choices for activities. Conversely, if individualism is the norm at home, children may not appreciate the need for everyone to go and wash their hands at the same time.

It is essential to understand that children may be experiencing something very different in their family culture at home to things they are experiencing in your setting. This may be confusing for the children in your care, though some older children may be able to reconcile the two different cultures. As an inclusive practitioner, you will need to first of all recognise this, and then take it into consideration and support children who may have to make adjustments in order to fit in with the culture of the setting.

The culture of your setting

The way that families prioritise, organise and cooperate can be viewed through the lens of ecocultural theory (ECT). This theory has its roots in sociocultural theories (Tonyan, 2014: 2) and analyses how families use their ecology (resources) with their culture (beliefs or values) and the requirements of the family as a whole. As a very simple example, with limited time (resource), how would a parent's culture (belief) sway their choice between reading to a child at bedtime or watching TV? The answer would depend on the type of dominant ecoculture in the family. Those parents, who believe that reading to children is more important, will forgo their TV time. On the other hand, those who believe that children should be able to settle themselves to sleep may choose to watch TV.

Ecocultural theory can also be used to analyse the dominant culture in settings and schools. Tonyan's (2014) research focused on how the structure of the day within a childcare setting reflected the beliefs and views of the practitioners within the setting. She also explored the type of language used to describe settings as a reflection of the setting's inherent culture. The findings showed that 'asking providers to describe their daily activities provides insight into their cultural models' (ibid.: 11). Thus, the culture and belief systems in the setting can be determined by analysing the types of descriptions and language that practitioners use about their setting. For example, many childminders advertise their childcare as being like a 'home from home'. Large private day nurseries emphasise the many opportunities for children to 'socialise with other children' and their range of resources. Some educational philosophies are associated with particular aspects of child development, such as children's independence in a Montessori setting or self-expression in a Reggio Emilia approach. All these will influence the culture of the setting and consequently the experiences that children will have.

The culture of school

There are many dilemmas when children transition into school. One of which is for children to adapt to the different ethos or culture at school. This is exacerbated by the fact that the school curricula in the UK is based on the white, middle-class perspective of what is required knowledge, with other views marginalised or simply not represented (Duncan, 2014). Duncan goes on to highlight how tokenistic and superficial multiculturalism in school actually 'serves to draw a line even more firmly between "them" and "us"' (ibid.: 119). She then discusses the perspective that multicultural policy for schools ignores the reality of aspects such as economic and political struggles and that, until entire social structures are changed and political power is redistributed, the core problem will not have been addressed. Anything without this is merely demonstrating differences, rather than tackling them.

- What is a cultural 'norm' to you?
- How and why did you play when you were a child?
- How much freedom did your parents allow you?
- Was it similar to your friends?
- How would you describe your setting? Would you use words such as 'homelike' or 'preparation for school'? What does this tell you about the culture of your setting? What conflicts may there be between the culture of your setting and that of the child's home life? How may this hinder or help inclusion?
- Go back to Case study 9.1. Does your setting celebrate birthdays and Christmas? How would you deal with this situation? If you do not celebrate birthdays and/or Christmas, could you relate more to the practitioners or the parents? What will happen when Michelle goes to school?

Understanding another person's culture

Once you have explored and have an understanding of your own culture, and the culture of your setting or school, it is beneficial to understand some of the many facets of the culture of others. At a surface level this may be considered to be race, language or religion. However, understanding another's culture is much more complex than this. Being able to anticipate and interpret the differences in culture, you can start to adapt your practice to be more inclusive on a much deeper level.

A difference in language is a very obvious cultural difference. It may well be that you have bilingual, or multilingual, children in your setting. Their parents and carers may be multilingual. The challenges and opportunities that language presents is discussed elsewhere in this book, but from a cultural point of view, you will need to know how language is used in the home and how this may include, or exclude, children in the setting. It is advisable to discuss this with parents and carers before children start at the setting. It may even be that the parents or carers have chosen to send their child to your setting so that they can learn the cultural norms and English language while there. Therefore, trying to communicate in a child's home language would be counter-productive and may cause tensions.

It is useful to be aware that communication is more than just spoken, or written language. You should also be conscious of your own body language, which may be culturally different from the child's expectations. Research has suggested that emotions and the way that emotions are expressed facially may not be universal and in fact people may have facial 'accents' in parallel with verbal accents (Merluzzi, 2014). These nuances may be cultural and it is theorised that these evolved because this would have given the cultural group an advantage over those who are not part of the group. This could be viewed as the inclusion of those in the group, for example, in the family or community group. Extending this theory to children in a setting, the disadvantage of this is evident when a child moves out of that group (their family) into your setting. He or she may not understand the way that non-verbal signals are being given in this new group of people in the setting. The research concluded that it was the smiles and scowls that were likely to be most culturally specific. This is particularly important for young children because so much of the Early Years are highly emotional. In the fast pace of an Early Years setting, it is essential that children pick up on these non-verbal clues quickly to be able to understand the situation, for example, when they have transgressed a rule or have done something good. Pappamihiel (2004: 543) describes these as 'display rules' and explains how Americans may use a smile for happiness readily, the Japanese are more circumspect about smiling and for Koreans this may be a sign of embarrassment.

Fortunately, contextual or situational factors and body language are as important as the cultural nuances of facial expressions. Training can also help understanding about the culturally specific elements of facial expression and how to modify these for the children in their care to improve inclusion and mutual understanding.

Some further thoughts

Some families who are new to the country, such as recently arrived immigrant families or refugees, may bring a 'distinct world-view' (Durand, 2010: 838). This may be very different from those of children already in the setting and indeed may be alien to the practitioners, who have no knowledge of the sorts of experiences these families might have had. It would be tempting, as an inclusive practitioner, to encourage homeland traditions and customs for these families to help the children settle in. However, you should be sensitive to the fact that some families, especially refugees, may not want to carry on these traditions as they may be painful reminders of what they have left behind (Keat *et al.*, 2009).

Early Years practitioners are usually very aware of the importance of self-esteem and the vital role of specific praise in supporting self-esteem. It should be noted that, culturally, the type of phrase used might be more influential than others. For example, using a phrase that emphasises social identity ('Your mum and dad will be proud') could be more effective than 'You should be proud of yourself' in cultures where the societal identity is more important than the personal. Han and Thomas (2010: 474) call this a 'skilled dialogue', where practitioners are respectful and culturally responsive to the needs of the children and their families.

- How would your body language look to a child with a different cultural background? Would making eye contact with an adult be seen as disrespectful or expected in their home culture? And in your setting?
- What sort of conversations do you have with families who are recent immigrants or refugees?
- Do you look beyond the surface level into the deep level of cultural differences? How do you do this?

Including others and their culture successfully

Although multiculturalism is complex and multi-faceted, there are some inclusive approaches and ideas that you may find useful to consider.

In order to fully understand the complexity of a family's culture, you will need to have an open and honest dialogue with them. It is much better to ask the question first, rather than risk offending the family or confusing their child. When asked sensitively and genuinely, most parents and carers are very happy to discuss their cultural identity, especially if the emphasis is on helping their child to be happy in the setting. One way to start this conversation is to ask which festivals or celebrations they have in their calendar, and how best to celebrate these to include their child. Children's individuality should be respected and treasured. Hovdelien (2014: 10) points out that children should not be seen as representatives of 'Somalian, Muslim or British culture' but as individuals, unique and simply themselves.

Another way of approaching this is giving the child agency, as they become more confident in the setting. After all, they are the experts in their home life and the cultural beliefs that they hold. Do be aware of the power imbalance, as you are the adult and some children may find this too much responsibility. Power relationships between children and adults vary in different cultures. In some cultures it is seen as being disrespectful for a child to make eye contact with an adult (Han and Thomas, 2010), whereas in Western culture, this is an expectation of being ready for good conversations.

> - Do you know the power relationships in the cultures you have in your setting?
> - Do you know and understand the expectations of the adults for the children? For example, girls will wait on boys? That children have to listen quietly to the 'teacher' and not move?
> - What problems could this cause? How could you resolve these?

Critical analysis of multiculturalism

Societal values

There is much debate on whether multiculturalism is fostered at the expense of societal values, and where this balance lies (Hovdelien, 2014). This can be especially problematic when considering the role of women and girls in society. If the society that you live in values education for both boys and girls, for example, but the cultural background of the family attending the setting is that only the boys get an education, would you still encourage the girls to learn to read and write? And how far would you go to impose your own, ethnocentric ideas? It could be that you encourage behaviour that is considered normal within your community or society, without considering that it is outside the bounds of the normal cultural behaviour some families. A typical example of this might be the tradition of sitting on Father Christmas's knee to tell him what you would like for Christmas. When considered out of context, by somebody who has never seen this before, it seems very eccentric to encourage a young child to sit on a stranger's knee. It is sensible to try to find the balance between a family's indigenous culture, the culture of the society or community they live in and the culture of the setting. You must have good understanding of all three cultures in order to do this.

Race

When you ask practitioners about inclusion and race, you will often hear the phrase 'We are colour blind here', meaning that practitioners treat all children the same, whatever the colour of their skin. This very much fits with the idea of the unique child in the Early Years Foundation Stage (EYFS) (DfE, 2014), where each child is treated as an individual, with their own strength and needs. Children are not stereotyped or put in a box according to, for example, their background, skin colour or gender. While there are very many advantages to this, such as not making assumptions, labelling or being pigeon-holed, there is some debate as to whether this is useful when trying to support and include children from a wide range of all races and cultures.

Boutte, Lopez-Robertson and Power-Costello (2011: 337) suggest that between the ages of 3 and 5 that children start to become racially aware. They suggest that if practitioners choose to ignore this, that 'stereotypes and misconceptions are likely to be magnified' as children construct their own world-view with limited or inaccurate knowledge. This is not to suggest that you have to be an expert on every race, racial history or culture. It is likely that you will need to talk to parents and other family members to understand the family history. Kaufman and Wiese (2012: 288) suggest that practitioners should provide 'affirmative images and resources' to support children in embracing their own skin tone. Husband (2012: 366) argues that anti-racist education depends on an 'intensive critique and reflection' of all aspects of early education, along with a critical self-awareness, political awareness and praxis (action as a result of reflection and reflection on that action). This suggests that being 'colour blind' actually allows racial and cultural stereotypes to proliferate, because they are not challenged or explored with young children.

Ideology

Postmodern theories explore the idea of pluralist thinking, where there is more than one, single 'truth' and there are multiple perspectives (Dahlberg *et al.*, 2006). Any judgement of what a 'truth' is depends on the cultural context in which it occurs. The theories also suggest that your 'self' is not one, single thing, but has been formed from your social, cultural, emotional and other experiences in life.

In many respects, postmodern ideologies and multiculturalism are inevitably bound together. Multiculturalism may look and mean something very different from person to person, depending on their life experiences. Using the postmodern perspective of multiple truths, this is totally acceptable. However, this can cause tension when there are debates on whether we are living in a 'multicultural society', for example. This phrase may have many, contradictory meanings for practitioners. It is worth reflecting on this with practitioners, to be able to comprehend each other's understanding of ideas and ideology around multiculturalism.

Pluralist monoculture

Baldock (2010: 27) explores whether multiculturalism is truly integrated in some areas. He talks about 'pluralist monocultures', which he describes as many cultures, existing side-by-side tolerantly, but not interacting or learning about each other – or from each other. This could be defined as coexisting rather than co-constructing. There are few benefits to this sort of 'multiculturalism' because there is no exchange of ideas or beliefs. This limits the quality and quantity of creative ideas, learning opportunities and collaboration.

Go back to Case study 9.1.

- How could you use your discussion about the Nativity to strengthen parent partnership?
- How could you use this to demonstrate or role model reflective practice with other practitioners?
- How could you balance the needs of the family with those of the Nursery, other parents and practitioners?

The voice of practitioners

The focus group used in the research for this chapter consisted of practitioners on a Foundation Degree, with a range of ages, backgrounds and numbers of years experience. The research was conducted using a semi-structured interview technique. The practitioners, with minimal intervention, led it so there was plenty of opportunity for an open and candid exchange of views.

The general consensus of the focus group was that being multicultural was good practice and that 'the world has got smaller'. All of the practitioners in the group celebrated a range of multicultural festivals, such as Diwali and Chinese

New Year. Most of the celebrations seemed to focus around food. The level of engagement, when including multicultural ideas, was on a continuum, as you would expect. This ranged from celebrating a few festivals during the year (pre-planned rather than responsive to children's needs) to including multicultural dressing-up resources in the role-play throughout the year. At the end of this continuum there was consideration given to all types of multicultural activity, as part of the continuous provision and reflecting the authentic multicultural nature of the setting at that particular time. This was then varied as the children left or joined the setting.

- Where would you put your setting on the multicultural continuum?
- Do you fully understand the meaning and symbolism of the festivals that you celebrate?
- How could this be improved?

From the focus group, the conversations started with the concept of the individual, unique child, but this quickly moved on to wider aspects, following Bronfenbrenner's (1979) pattern: parents, language, location and cultural values. However, the larger societal and political influence was noticeable by its absence. As you would expect, the practitioners were very focused on their own setting, in their own specific geographical area, but the wider societal implications were almost negligible during the conversation. Only one student identified her own culture and the effects it has had on her practice and perspective. She could also describe her own cultural background clearly and had evidently thought about this in her own practice, as well as when her own children were growing up.

The practitioners in the focus group came from a variety of setting types and cared for children in the whole Early Year age range, i.e. newborn to 5 years old and above. This highlighted an interesting disparity in the treatment of multiculturalism in different age ranges. The practitioners felt that private, independent settings were more genuine in engaging in multicultural activities, including parent liaison and partnership. Schools, especially compulsory education, were considered to be more tokenistic in their treatment, even though they had access to additional and more varied resources, such as multilingual books, interpreters and toys. One explanation for this may be the autonomy that private settings have, compared to the more rigid curriculum imposed by the school timetable. At odds with this finding was one childminder's experience. She was very inclusive across her practice, but found that parents 'excluded' themselves by not wanting to participate in multicultural activities.

The focus group highlighted how multiculturalism has both a surface level of understanding, as well as a deeply personal meaning for some. I found the practitioners had very positive attitudes and a willingness to discuss multiculturalism. There was acknowledgement that there may be many ways to be inclusive and this could differ from setting to setting, practitioner to practitioner. Practitioners seem to be less concerned with the wider political, social and economic debate that other cultures may have. This could be explained by the fact that the concept of the unique child, as described in *Development Matters* (Early Education, 2012), is well embedded in most settings, as demonstrated by the very child- and family-centred discussions.

Practical strategies

Meinert and Winberry (1998: 12) suggest that multicultural inclusion needs to be both 'integrated and infused'. For example, multiculturalism should be integrated into all Early Years continuous provision throughout the curriculum from home corner to outdoors. Specific multicultural activities should be woven through the planned curriculum as well, infusing these into your children's experiences. One practical strategy would be to have experiential events for your youngest children, such as festivals and celebrations, which children can relate to easily. As your children become more culturally sophisticated, you can add specific lessons or learning outcomes about your own culture and others' culture. Finally, probably when your children are school aged, you can start to compare and contrast cultures for your children to evaluate.

Durand (2010: 845) suggests some ways to support cross-cultural competence, from the first meeting with the family, to your own continued professional development, which have been adapted here:

1. Parent partnership and getting to understand their beliefs and ideologies will take time. You are not going to be able to capture it all on the registration form and you will almost certainly have to revisit some ideas during the time they are with you. Try to ensure that the relationships you have with families are sensitive, honest and helpful.
2. Being reflective and reflexive will help you to understand your own point of view and to then use this to support your children. It is much easier if you are able to do this before the children start in your setting.
3. Making assumptions will almost certainly lead to difficulties later on. Check your own assumptions and maybe talk these through with someone who can act as a critical friend; for example, your expectations about making eye contact with a child.
4. Find out about your children's cultural background, in partnership with the parents, so you have a bank of knowledge to call on.

5. Remember to share your cultural background with children and families. Think of times that are culturally important to you and how you can make this meaningful to the families you work with.

6. Share your experiences, knowledge and attitudes with other practitioners and professionals. This is good professional practice and helps to embed the knowledge you have gained.

The practitioners at Liyah's Early Years setting wanted to celebrate the Hindu festival Diwali, or Festival of the Lights. Although they celebrated this every year with the children, making tea light holders, this was the first year that they had a Hindu family attending the setting.

Liyah excitedly told the mum about celebrating Diwali and asked if she could bring in some food for the celebrations. When the day came, Liyah was surprised to find that the food that had been brought in was crisps and shop-bought cakes. On further investigation, she found that the family were the third generation in the UK, and though they had listed Hindu as their religion, they followed few of the traditions.

- What assumptions have you made as a practitioner?
- Do the children in your setting now feel more included (or just confused)?
- How could this be handled differently?
- What are the similarities here? For example, do you celebrate every festival equally (Halloween, Valentine's Day, Summer Solstice)?

Being similar

Multiculturalism is more than just festivals and celebrations; this can become too tokenistic, and may deny children the opportunity of exploring their culture. It is just as important to explore similarities and how these bind us together. It should be remembered that every child is unique, an individual, whatever their culture. Making assumptions about a child or a family because of their cultural background is rarely useful and may even be a hindrance. We have a common humanity, our need for food, living space, security and friendship (Maslow, 1943) and practitioners should not forget this.

It is good reflective practice to consider the purpose of the activity when emphasising cultural distinctiveness. Practitioners may want to ask whether singling out someone else's cultural distinctiveness will encourage inclusion and human solidarity, or whether it will make that culture exotic and different.

Multicultural competence is a 'process' (Durand, 2010: 845) just as being inclusive is also a 'relative, shifting, organic set of processes' (Nutbrown *et al*., 2013: 3). There are no short cuts and your policy, procedures, attitudes and daily practice should be constantly reviewed.

- How do your routines, caregiving and education reflect your own culture?
- Is there greater emphasis on home, school or enrichment (as defined by Honyan, 2014)?
- Does your setting reflect the attitudes towards multiculturalism of the society in which it exists?
- What does it mean to 'have a positive sense' of your own culture and beliefs? (Early Education, 2012)

Conclusion

At the beginning of this chapter, I discussed how you should first understand your own culture, so you can appreciate the impact that this could have on your inclusive practice. This is a vital starting point because your individuality, experience and knowledge will influence your choices when approaching multiculturalism in your setting and how you approach inclusion.

Genuinely understanding the culture of the children in your setting will help inclusion to be deep level, and not tokenistic. This is just as important even if it appears on the surface that the children's culture and background are the same as your own. It is possible that their family culture or community culture will differ. Understanding and finding the similarities between cultures, as well as appreciating cultural diversity, support inclusive practice and stop multiculturalism becoming tokenistic.

Inclusion cannot be achieved in a day. It is a process that needs to be continually reviewed, having clear strategies for all practitioners and implemented equally across the whole setting. Similarly, the cultural diversity and ethos of the setting need to be regularly reviewed. You can improve your daily practice by critically analysing multiculturalism in your setting, and challenging any assumptions. Each child is an individual who should be included and valued for who they are.

Further reading

Tina Durand's article 'Celebrating diversity in early care and education settings: moving beyond the margins' (2010) addresses some interesting challenges in the USA.

Caroline Bath's 'Conceptualizing listening to young children as an ethic of care in early childhood education and care' (2013) focuses on the ethical practices when listening to children. As stated in this chapter, it is essential to have genuine, respectful conversations with families and children to fully understand their inclusion needs. This paper explores how your pedagogical practices can support this.

References

Baldock, P. (2010) *Understanding Cultural Diversity in the Early Years*. London: Sage.

Bath, C. (2013) Conceptualizing listening to young children as an ethic of care in early childhood education and care. *Children & Society*, 27: 361–71.

Bolton, G. (2010) *Reflective Practice: Writing and Professional Development*. London: Sage.

Boutte, G., Lopez-Robertson, J. and Power-Costello, E. (2011) Moving beyond color-blindness in early childhood classrooms. *Early Childhood Education Journal*, 39(5): 335–42.

Bronfenbrenner, U. (1979) *The Ecology of Human Development: Experiments by Nature and Design*. Cambridge, MA: Harvard University Press.

Cruz de Carvalhoa, R., Seidl-de-Mouraa, M., Dal Forno Martins, G. and Vieirac, M. (2014) Culture and developmental trajectories: a discussion on contemporary theoretical models. *Early Child Development and Care*, 1(1).

Dahlberg, G., Moss, P. and Pence, A. (2006) *Beyond Quality in Early Childhood Education and Care: Languages of Evaluation*. London: Routledge.

DES (Department of Education and Science) (1985) *Education for All: Report of the Committee of Inquiry into the Education of Children from Ethnic Minority Groups* (The Swann Report). London: HMSO.

DfE (2013) *The National Curriculum in England: Key Stages 1 and 2 Framework Document*. Available at: https://www.gov.uk/government/uploads/system/uploads/attachment_data/file/260481/PRIMARY_national_curriculum_11-9-13_2.pdf (accessed 1 July 2014).

DfE (2014) *Statutory Framework for the Early Years Foundation Stage*. Available at: https://www.gov.uk/government/uploads/system/uploads/attachment_data/file/299391/DFE-00337-2014.pdf (accessed 15 January 2015).

Duncan, M. (2014) Reflecting on racism in predominantly White settings. In C. Hayes, J. Daly, M. Duncan, R. Gill and A. Whitehouse (eds) *Developing as a Reflective Early Years Professional: A Thematic Approach*. Northwich: Critical Publishing.

Durand, T. (2010) Celebrating diversity in early care and education settings: moving beyond the margins. *Early Child Development and Care*, 180(7): 835–48.

Early Education (2012) *Development Matters in the Early Years Foundation Stage* (EYFS) London: Early Education.

Hall, S. (1980) Cultural studies: two paradigms. *Media, Culture and Society*, 2: 57–72.

Han, S. H. and Thomas, S. (2010) No child misunderstood: enhancing early childhood teachers' multicultural responsiveness to the social competence of diverse children. *Early Childhood Education Journal*, 37: 469–76.

Hovdelien, O. (2014) The limitations of multiculturalism in Norwegian early childhood education. *International Journal of Inclusive Education*, 18(11): 1107–19.

Husband, T. (2012) 'I don't see color': challenging assumptions about discussing race with young children. *Early Childhood Education Journal*, 39: 365–71.

Kaufman, E. and Wiese, D. (2012) Skin-tone preferences and self-representation in Hispanic children. *Early Child Development and Care*, 182(2): 277–90.

Keat, J., Strickland, M. and Marinak, B. (2009) Child voice: how immigrant children enlightened their teachers with a camera. *Early Childhood Education Journal*, 37: 13–21.

Maslow, A. (1943) A theory of human motivation. *Psychological Review*, 50: 370–96.

Meinert, R. and Winberry, S. (1998) The multicultural debate and the K through 8 curriculum challenge. *Early Child Development and Care*, 147(1): 5–15.

Merluzzi, A. (2014) Nonverbal accents: cultural nuances in emotional expression. *Association for Psychological Studies Observer*, 27(4).

Mills, C. W. (1959) *The Sociological Imagination*. Oxford: Oxford University Press.

Nutbrown, C., Clough, P. and Atherton, F. (2013) *Inclusion in the Early Years*. London: Sage.

Office for National Statistics ONS (2012) *Ethnicity and National Identity in England and Wales 2011*. London: ONS.

Pappamihiel, E. (2004) Hugs and smiles: demonstrating caring in a multicultural early childhood classroom. *Early Child Development and Care*, 174(6): 539–48.

Tonyan, H. A. (2014) Everyday routines: a window into the cultural organization of family childcare. *Journal of Early Childhood Research*. doi:10.1177/1476718X14523748.

United Nations (1989) *United Nations Convention on the Rights of the Child*. Available at: www.ohchr.org/EN/ProfessionalInterest/Pages/CRC.aspx (accessed 1 June 2014).

10

Using research to develop inclusive practice in the Early Years

Sean Creaney

The aims of this chapter are:

- To explain different approaches to research; namely positivism, interpretivism and action research
- To provide an overview of the challenges involved in research in the Early Years, notably the importance of finding ways of capturing the authentic voice of the child in research investigations
- To outline a range of child-friendly methods of inquiry appropriate for research in the Early Years.
- To examine some of the issues to be resolved when conducting research with children who have Special Educational Needs (SEN)
- To examine the implications of the children's rights agenda and its relationship to research, most notably the United Nations Convention on the Rights of the Child (UNCRC).

Case study 10.1: SEN inclusion

You are an Early Years professional working in a pre-school. The setting prides itself on its inclusive practice and is committed to promoting the views and rights of children. The team works hard to recognise and value different languages used by practitioners, children and families and makes good use of published policies that acknowledge a range of family structures.

However, you are concerned that the level of support given to children who have Special Educational Needs (SEN) fails to enable them to access the full range of play and learning opportunities. You are not sure how to gather the views, opinions, perspectives and experiences of children in the setting who have SEN. You are aware of participatory action research as a possible approach; however, you are unsure of the practicalities and ethics, particularly with regard to the possibility of these young children expressing their needs and experiences unambiguously.

- How do you know what the needs of the child are?
- Does this knowledge incorporate the child's point of view?
- How can you know what the child feels or wants?
- What makes the child happy or causes the child anxiety?
- How do you ensure that the child is listened to and what the child says is acted upon?
- As a researcher, what forms of data collection are available to you to capture the perspectives and experiences of the child?
- How can you be sure that your interpretation of the evidence is consistent with the needs of the child and the family – rather than convenient for the Early Years team?

Looking at Case study 10.1, answer the following questions:

- What concerns would you want to identify and address to make sure that your research is ethical? How would you monitor the research process to ensure an ethical approach?
- Your research starts from an assumption – an aspect of team practice can be improved on. How can you be sure that this assumption does not lead and shape your research?
- How can your findings be shared with children and their families?
- Addressing one aspect of practice that could be improved might lead to subsequent neglect of – or lower priority being given to – other areas. How can the team guard against this?

These are a lot of questions! You may not feel able to answer them all right now – but discuss some of them with those whom you work with and make some notes about how you might begin to answer these questions. If you have any initial thoughts about how you would tackle this issue as a reflective practitioner, note those too. At the end of the chapter return to your first thoughts and add to them.

Types of social research

Early Years practice is necessarily creative and innovative. An enquiring, investigative culture should be encouraged (Ingleby and Oliver, 2008). This increases the likelihood that practitioners are clearer about 'what works' and 'what does not' with children and families (ibid.).

Practitioners have an intuitive understanding of this. I met with a group of experienced Early Years practitioners and Stacey, one of the focus group participants, said, 'We need to understand what works and why – research can help us in that.'

Research is important. It helps to develop inclusive practice. It has real benefits for children and young people. As Hayley, another focus group member said, research is 'not something we do only when we have the time for it – we do it all the time to improve our practice'.

Two of the most significant theoretical perspectives on research will be outlined before investigating the types of research methods appropriate for generating data on what does and does not work. In addition, a third approach, namely action research, is discussed, as it has become influential among Early Years practitioners.

Two broad approaches to research are commonly identified and, unhelpfully, are often presented as alternatives in that as a researcher it is suggested that you must adopt one stance or the other. In reality, most care and education research combines some elements of both.

Positivist approaches (or *positivism* in general) derive from the methods developed by natural scientists over hundreds of years and are represented as objective, scientific and free from bias. Following this approach, any data collected should be carefully controlled (to measure the significance of identified variables) to allow for the testing of theories and hypotheses and to enhance the capacity to make reliable predictions (McKechnie, 2002: 48). Some social scientists – including those working in Early Years care and education – have borrowed from the practice of chemists, physicists, and other natural scientists. Positivist social scientists seek – often through the collection of observed and measured statistical data – to test ideas and concepts and to produce findings that can be generalised (Denzin and Lincoln, 1994). For example, 'if we want to know how many children have experienced the death of a parent, we must collect appropriate statistics' (Green and Hogan, 2005: 5). Or if we want to know how much time boys spend in the book corner (compared to at the sandpit), we would observe and record our findings. As Green and Hogan acknowledge, though, statistics do not 'account for the rich variety of experience within the early years context' (Ingleby and Oliver, 2008: 103). It is for that reason that some researchers in education, and other social sciences, start from another perspective.

An *interpretative* theoretical perspective differs somewhat in its outlook to positivist research; rather than starting from a hypothesis to be tested, interpretative approaches allow the 'theory to emerge from the data once it has been gathered, and may be constantly adjusted as more data emerges' (McKechnie, 2002: 48). It is an approach that focuses on experiences, viewpoints and perspectives of the 'social world' (Ingleby and Oliver, 2008). Indeed, it is argued that 'The creativity of children and Early Years practitioners may be captured [best] by placing an emphasis on researching the process of interaction' (ibid.: 103). Critics of this approach to research argue that since two different researchers can offer two different interpretations, what value can we attach to any reported 'findings'?

It has been argued that interpretative, qualitative research approaches are more appropriate to early childhood research than positivist, quantitative-based investigations (Lewis and Lindsay, 2000). There is, however, a third approach to research that differs to positivism and interpretivism and which has become influential. Action research is committed to the idea of 'improving practice'. Rather than gathering data and generalising the research findings (which is central to the positivist approach), action researchers start from the presumption that what they are looking at is 'particular' and 'specific'. Reflective practice is at the heart of action research: problems are identified, data is gathered and analysed, and then different ways of working are described and implemented. This process is then repeated where the 'new' approach is evaluated in a cyclical process.

This approach to Early Years research may be important for a number of reasons. If a planned intervention or strategy is not working as intended or as expected, the reasons for this can be explored, and identifying and implementing alternative strategies or improvements can be made. In addition to this, promising approaches can be highlighted, shared and used to inform practice. Optimists might argue that this research may have an impact on government policy and guidance.

If Early Years practitioners are to be aware of new initiatives, and the potential they offer in practice, they need to engage in reflective research. This point was raised and discussed by the focus group.

Sarah explained how only by action research could she explore solutions to challenges in the work place. The challenge Sarah referred to was behaviour management. More specifically, Jess suggested that it would be valuable to 'look at how children are included holistically to see if they are struggling and to see if additional support or a planned intervention is appropriate'.

Of course, Early Years practitioners do not work in a political or economic vacuum and it is not sufficient to 'wish' for something to happen. Claire reminded the group of the frustrations and cautioned that 'sometimes though we have to wait for the money before we implement any support strategies'. There are further challenges too in the workplace. For example, Molly reflected upon her experiences attempting to conduct research with children who have speech and language delay. Despite her extensive professional experience, Molly still finds that there are instances when she has difficulty understanding what children are saying. Molly drew on her undergraduate studies to develop a research strategy that might produce the most helpful data. Recognising that for young children especially being 'tested' can be stressful – and that might further limit communication skills – she opted to use non-participant observations as a research method.

The action research approach has, at its heart, a desire to transform practice for the better, 'providing the space for participants to review activities and achievements and to carry out ongoing tasks of evaluation and revision' in order to inform future practice (Smith, 2009: 128). This may be especially significant as we seek to develop and improve an inclusive practice that recognises the needs and contributions of individuals. More specifically, ideally the child identifies their own needs, and is given power and control over the research process by having responsibility for devising the research questions, through to analysing the findings and the implementation of new forms of practice intervention. I will return to participatory approaches later on in this chapter. However, before that, I want to explore the ideas behind involving young children in research.

Involving young children in research

Research results

Jess: We sometimes underestimate children … we shouldn't be afraid to ask them what they think.

Sarah: Your researching should be natural, whilst the children are in play.

Early Years practitioners are more aware than most that young children are innately capable of 'processing' and 'understanding' information, yet this capacity is frequently underestimated by researchers who presume that young children 'cannot understand' (Gray, 2012: 69).

Over the last 20 years or so an approach that recognises and values the capacity of young children to give voice to their feelings and experiences has gained momentum. This is reflected in some measure in statements such as the United Nations Convention on the Rights of the Child (UNCRC) and this has helped challenge the presumption that children are objects to be studied and are the passive subjects of the application of the findings (Kirby *et al.*, 2003).

Indeed, one of the focus group participants, Rosie, stressed the importance involving children in research. During discussions Rosie referred to the importance of adhering to the UNCRC and more specifically honouring 'freedom of speech'. Rosie went on to argue that 'you shouldn't not involve children; you should always ask for their opinion'. However, in relation to the case study, how much involvement and say can children have over the research process? A further question is relevant here: if is it important to 'act upon' what a child has said, how can we know what young children with communication difficulties tell us?

In relation to children's rights, though the UNCRC purports to be a 'legally binding international instrument', in the UK it has no legal basis: the principles set out are more 'aspirational' than 'enforceable' (Greig *et al.*, 2013: 204). Nevertheless, one of the four core principles outlined within the UNCRC is respect for the view of the child. Article 12 is most relevant for research purposes as it promotes the active involvement of children in matters that affect them and deems the child to be the key decision-maker: 'state parties shall assure to the child who is capable of forming his or her own views the right to express those views freely in all matters affecting the child' (UN, 1989).

Furthermore, in relation to participation in research, Article 12 states that 'children have the right to be consulted and taken account of' (Morrow and Richards, 1996, cited in Roberts-Holmes, 2005: 54). In addition to the UNCRC, the Children Acts of 1989 and 2004 advocate the involvement of children in the research process, especially when it concerns their welfare. However, too often adults – sometimes researchers, sometimes politicians and policy-makers – are only too ready to decide that a child is not 'capable of forming his or her own views' and, as a result, the 'views, opinions, feelings and wishes, are neither sought nor acted on. Children are effectively silenced and ultimately oppressed by the adults who are in charge of them' (Greig *et al.*, 2013: 205).

There are some more hopeful and encouraging signs. In recent years there has been a shift in thinking regarding the involvement of children in research. Rather than being viewed as the 'developmental child' or 'child that needs protecting', children are now deemed to be socially active decision-makers (Hendrick, 1997), regarded as 'knowers' (Palaiologou, 2012: 1) and invited to partake in research 'on the basis of who they are, rather than who they will become' (Moss and Petrie, 2002: 6).

Prior to this relatively new way of thinking, it was adults who decided what was best for the child (James and Prout, 1990). The child was considered to be a human *becoming* rather than a human *being* (Quortrup, 1987) as they were deemed to be unable to express an informed opinion due to their age and perceived social incompetence.

In this model of childhood, first and foremost, it is the failings of the child that are identified, starting from the belief that children do not have anything of value to add to the research process (David, 1992). However, the need to listen to the child and deem them to be 'experts in their own lives' (Langsted, 1994) has developed as a perspective out of a critique of the child as a passive non-participant model. This is evident with the emergence of 'the new sociology of childhood' (James and Prout, 1997) and the subsequent promotion of participatory research methods.

This 'new sociology' emphasises the practice of reflection. Here practitioners are expected to reflect not only on the choice of methodology but also the research methods chosen and interpretation of the findings (James, 1999). Importantly this sociological paradigm prompts researchers to be mindful of the appropriateness of the research techniques used to gather data. Indeed, it is argued that to prevent a lack of participation and engagement in the research process (and arguably to help ensure that children enjoy partaking in the study) 'researchers need to employ methods that tap into the different skills, or competencies, that children have, for example, drawing, stories and written work' (McKechnie, 2002: 45).

Furthermore, from an epistemological perspective (that is the theory of knowledge), by 'attending to what children say, we gain access to the meaning they themselves attach to their experiences' (ibid.: 45). These methods are used with children in their 'natural settings', to uncover authentic knowledge, with a view to 'making sense' of the thoughts expressed by the research participants (Denzin and Lincoln, 1994: 2).

In other words, these qualitative approaches strive to help the researcher reveal and report the attitudes or actions of individuals from the subjective perspective of the participant involved in the study (Bryman, 1988). Description and context are important in qualitative research and in relation to the child's voice, these approaches allow for the child to 'have a say' and 'be heard' (Grieg and Taylor, 1999: 46).

For some, the notion that research is 'subjective' is counter-intuitive. Surely the whole point of research, some will say, is to 'find out, to establish what is true and what is false'? If that is the case, researchers should strive to be objective. In the fields of education and social science, most qualitative researchers doubt that there is an objective reality. Rather, 'multiple realities' exist within society. What is 'good' and 'successful' for some may be interpreted as 'damaging' by others. It really is very difficult, if not impossible, to have objective measures of achievement when it comes to care and education.

It is the role of the researcher to study these socially constructed realities by exploring the experiences, viewpoints and perspectives of the research participants (Cresswell, 1998). Subjectivity is prioritised in this approach and deemed to be highly important.

However, it must be acknowledged here that Early Years practitioners face many challenges initiating activities 'with children' and giving them a voice:

> [Practitioners] who are asked on the one hand to adhere to an ideological shift of actions 'with children' while on the other they are required by officialdom to measure children against models and a set of standards laid down in regulations.
>
> (Palaiologou, 2012: 4)

As Palaiologou (ibid.: 4) notes, a 'mismatch' exists, where the emphasis is on giving voice and adhering to the wishes and needs of the child alongside practice that is 'laid down' by 'officialdom' and deemed to be in the child's best interest. The dilemma here is that practitioners try to act according to reason and hence attain ethical practice, yet external practices are imposed upon them in the name of the good of the children.

In other words, though practitioners are required to involve children in activities, and promote shared decision-making, the 'audit society' (Power, 1997) has crept into Early Years where practitioners have to comply with the statutory framework (Williamson, 2012: 180). This has resulted in developmental progress being measured against prescribed standards of learning, development and welfare – as set out in the Early Years Foundation Stage (EYFS) in England.

In our focus group discussion Leah emphasised that the EYFS acknowledges that 'every child is different', though Sarah questioned how 'fair' and 'inclusive' the EYFS actually is, as it requires that children are 'doing this at this stage and this age'. (Jo Basford's Chapter 2 in this book on assessment is relevant here.)

The EYFS has many strengths, not least the enhancement of the child's welfare (safeguarding and child protection issues are given priority in the framework). However, though the intentions of the framework are benevolent, arguably it can be counter-productive as it may constrain a practitioner when it comes to giving the child a voice.

Ethical and inclusive research practice with children who have Special Educational Needs

> Even children with severe learning disabilities or very limited expressive language can communicate preference, if people who understand their needs and have the relevant skills to listen ask them in the right way.
>
> (Department of Health, 1991: 14, cited in Ellis and Beauchamp, 2012: 48)

Early Years practitioners will need to draw on all their skills and experience if they are to involve young children in research. Children may be unwilling or unable to engage directly with the research process and if researchers infer messages from observed behaviour that message ceases to be the child's voice. This whole process may be more complex when working with children who have Special Educational Needs (SEN) (Ellis and Beauchamp, 2012). This may result from the limited experience that practitioners have when it comes to specific additional needs when much learning takes place 'on the job'. Before discussing these challenges and identifying ways to address them, it is important to define key terms that form the next part of this chapter.

Although the concept of SEN is contested, put simply, a child with a SEN is defined to be a person who has a difficulty or disability that impacts on their ability to learn – that can be specific, moderate, severe, profound or multiple – and demonstrates a need for special educational provision (DfES, 2001). Children who have SENs (for example, behavioural or social difficulties, dyslexia, or attention deficit hyperactivity disorder) may, because of ill-considered or designed provision, experience problems in accessing learning opportunities (ibid.).

Insufficient professional training, poor communication with the family, or inadequate support from other professional services may all contribute to the failure of effectively communicating with children. There is a heightened risk that assumptions will be made about what is 'said' and how it is understood, recorded and reported (Ellis and Beauchamp, 2012).

However, with regard to engagement and participation, the Children Act 1989, along with formal ratification of the UNCRC, provided a platform for the child's voice to be heard and in turn for child-centred practice to flourish through a focus on allowing children individually to be respected 'in their own right' (Green, 2012).

Article 12 of the Convention provides that the views of children are to be taken seriously through 'active participation'. The competence of a child to express those views is determined in accordance with 'the age and maturity of the child' (DOH, 1999: 46). This notion of 'competence' is likely to be problematic; it might well be that young children under the age of 5, for example, may be prevented from taking part and having their voices heard because they are presumed to be 'incompetent'.

Article 13, on the other hand, differs somewhat in its focus 'valuing a child's participation in any shape or form relative to the individual' (Green, 2012: 21). This Article also demonstrates a 'commitment to conducting research with children, rather than on [them]' (O'Kane, 2008: 125). In order to ensure that this commitment is realised, researchers should not employ research methods that are designed for adults. Rather, careful consideration should be given to the appropriateness of the techniques for use with children. In particular, ethical considerations are important here and the methods chosen need to be fit for purpose – capable of capturing children's experiences and understandings of the social world effectively (Thomas and O'Kane, 1998).

However, there are further ethical considerations that need to be made when researching with younger children with SEN. Although there are various codes of practice in existence that offer guidance (see British Educational Research Association (BERA, 2004) and the British Psychological Society (BPS), for example) on the process of gaining informed consent, and adhering to matters of confidentiality and anonymity, the challenges involving young children with SEN in research remain.

Some children, with diagnosed and defined SEN, may have cognitive and emotional difficulties and may be unable to understand the elements that make up the research process. In such circumstances researchers should remain committed to the task of building a relationship by 'getting to know' the child and understanding their needs and wants, demonstrating a firm desire to include the child fully (Hart, 1992) in the research process. There are difficult balances to be struck when it comes to carrying out research that is believed to be in the best interests of the child's care and education, yet there is no certainty that the child understands what is happening or what they are a part of.

If that is the case – and clearly with very young children that must be true – then it is imperative that the parents or carers are fully involved and consent to the proposed research. It is also important to establish a good working relationship with parents or carers, as they may be able to offer valuable insight into the child's wants and needs and in turn may be able to help the child understand the research process, and in particular what is to be expected of them as a participant:

> Parents hold key information and have a critical role to play in their children's education. They have unique strengths, knowledge and experience to contribute to the shared view of a child's needs and the best ways of supporting them.
>
> (DfES, 2001: 16)

This is another possibility, however, as Hayley explained in the focus group discussion; 'sometimes parents and carers can make inclusive practice difficult'. Rosie amplified when suggesting that undoubtedly the intentions of the parent or carer may be benevolent – and acting in what they perceive to be 'the best interest of the child' – they may prevent their child from expressing their own opinion or may 'withdraw their child' from the study. The parent or carer may not want the child to be seen in a 'negative light' or they may deem the child to be incapable of answering the question/s asked. In some instances parents do not accept that their child may have additional needs or may resist what they see as the stigma of being identified as having SEN. However, as the researcher, you may believe the child is capable of understanding the question and you may wish to explore this possibility with the parent or carer.

- Think of a child with whom you have worked closely, who has clearly defined additional needs. How do you know what she thinks and feels about her care and education?
- What information do you share with her parents (remember this is a two-way process, each of you 'gives' and 'receives')?
- You want to review the effectiveness of your planning when it comes to meeting the child's needs – how would you involve the child and the parents in that review?

It is good practice to invite relevant professionals and family members to take part in the research, at the earliest opportunity, to help with designing appropriate child-friendly methods of engagement. It is important to develop a trusting relationship early on. Some researchers are nervous that by getting too close to the child and the family – and developing an emotional attachment – it becomes even harder to be objective or balanced. It follows, from this view, that the validity of any findings may be challenged. However, developing a relationship with the participant/s will be vital in deciding how to communicate effectively with the child.

There will be a number of specific and practical matters to be resolved in any event. For example, it is important to decide when and where the research will take place. All parties must agree the venue, including, if at all possible, the child. Any change in routines or established patterns can be disturbing and affect the child's 'normal' behaviour or responses.

When it comes to finding ways of capturing the 'voice' of the child, when the spoken word is not an option, it may be that photographs or scrupulously observed body language are valid. Though there is always a risk that adults will place their interpretation, their language, and their values on what they see a child do.

There are additional matters to consider, such as the unequal power relationships that may exist between adults and children. It should not be presumed, though, that adults always hold power over children. Even very young children learn how they might manipulate adults. Researchers have a responsibility to look at where power is held and is exerted and must take care to empower the child participant. This mirrors the idea discussed earlier that children should be treated as 'subjects', invited, or rather actively encouraged to take 'ownership' rather than 'objects' where research is done 'to' children. This is at the heart of participatory approaches in research.

With regard to ethics, information regarding the purpose/s of the study needs to be properly communicated with the child or the parent. Only then is it possible to make an informed decision regarding whether to participate or not. Consequently, alternative forms of communication may be necessary; these include sign language and/or Braille. In addition to these techniques, some researchers may ask the child to produce a handprint in paint to demonstrate approval of participation. However, questions may be asked regarding whether the child understands the process, including the implications of taking part in the study.

There are further ethical issues to consider. For example, children may not wish to inform the researcher that they do not want to answer a certain question or even withdraw from the study (Ellis and Beauchamp, 2012). One way of overcoming these difficulties would be to introduce a 'traffic light' activity. Although this activity would need to be designed as appropriate to the child's age and ability, here children 'hold up' yellow cards (if they wish not to answer a question) or a red card (if they wish to withdraw from the session or study completely) (Knight *et al.*, 2006). This activity would need to be practised beforehand in order to ensure that the participants fully understand the mechanics of it.

Participatory approaches

It has been argued that there is a lack of convincing evidence that being involved in research, even in a 'truly participatory' sense, has any actual benefits for the children participating (Hill *et al.*, 2004). Despite this, there are a number of potential benefits (Jones and Welch, 2010) including increasing the effectiveness of the service, the enhancement of the child's political voice, and the opportunity for the vulnerable child to 'speak out' against forms of oppression and be listened to.

For participatory approaches to capture the voice of the child 'effectively' there are certain standards that should be upheld, namely adherence to a value base consisting of trust and respect; and appropriate training and supportive mechanisms for participation on how actually to contribute in a meaningful way (Lansdown, 2001).

As Tilly, one of the focus group members, said: 'We have to rely a lot on observations for our data.' When using observations, though, as a research tool, they should be interactive, and child-centred. Indeed, as part of a participatory approach to research, the child should be given power and control, to a certain extent, over the research agenda and given a say regarding the activities deemed most suitable. The Mosaic approach to research is a good example of this. This is multi-method, comprising a range of 'tools' – verbal and visual (Greig *et al.*, 2013), designed to elicit the perspective of the child participants in creative ways to adhere to differential levels of engagement. The Mosaic approach plays to a child's strengths rather than focusing on 'deficits' (Clark, 2004: 144), using fun, engaging methods, to help children express their views comfortably.

Although the Mosaic way of researching can be successful when contributing to service evaluations, for example, it is an approach that may not be completely free from adult control over the research agenda. Concerns may still be raised over a child's privacy, and whether an accepted culture of 'listening' actually occurs in practice (Clark and Moss, 2001). Furthermore, though the participatory skills of the participants can be enhanced by the use of various tools (namely maps and photos, for example), these methods are not without practical challenges.

Other methods may be advocated, namely drawing workshops and diaries. Some children may enjoy partaking in these exercises but others may have had negative experiences and be nervous or reluctant to take part. This is just another example of the importance of knowing the child and being sensitive to her feelings and responses. Having said that, if the method of a diary is well designed prior to its use for research purposes (Punch, 2002), it may provide a fascinating insight into what it is like to be a child.

Rather than an adult deciding the most suitable methods to be used, in accordance with the children's rights movement, researchers should empower children to have a say on suitable methods. Traditional research techniques, such as focus groups, and individual interviews (though they will need to be age-appropriate and be consistent with the development of the child) can prove a useful consultative platform for encouraging child participation. With regard to children who have severe and complex difficulties learning, and more specifically those younger than, say, 5 years of age, written exercises may not be suitable. In turn, role-play exercises may provide a better basis for the children to express themselves.

Another example of how to make the research process child-centred is to find ways of allowing children to select or provide their own images – be they drawings or photographs – rather than asking children to comment on images provided by the researcher.

Related to the above techniques is the ethnographic approach. Proponents argue that it is the most appropriate way of grasping the perspective from 'the point of view' of those being studied (Denscombe, 2007). In this approach the method of (participant and/or non-participant) observation is often used. However, there are clearly difficulties note-taking when observing children directly. A further implication of this approach (linked to action research – noted at the beginning of this chapter) is that, as a researcher, you may experience difficulties remaining 'impartial' (Chambers, 1983) as a result of the intimate relationship you may have formed with the participants.

You may choose to observe at a distance, in order to remain more objective and increase the validity of the findings. Though in Early Years settings children may be more comfortable and more familiar with adults sharing their play and learning at close quarters. Having a note-taker sitting in the corner may be more disturbing for a child and she or he may question why you are there.

There will be other issues that experienced researchers are familiar with in their work with children (though adult participants may respond similarly!). In the focus group Gemma reminded us that researchers should be aware that a child may say what they think the researcher wants them to say and, in turn, may be unwilling to express their opinions openly. As Leah said: 'Children may act differently if there is someone new in the room.' Furthermore, there are ethical, power-related issues to consider, as Leah also pointed out: 'Children might feel they are doing something wrong if you're watching them.'

There are other factors that experienced researchers will be aware of. For example, the child may feel compelled to answer in a certain way due to their parent or carer being present during the research study. However, one way potentially to overcome this issue is to encourage the child to discuss the thoughts and feelings of others rather than their own.

In our focus group discussions, Stacey said that with regard to research findings, ultimately, 'it is our interpretation. It is not what the children are saying.' An awareness of this is critical if as researchers we are to review our findings and report and share them as honestly as we can, taking care to be clear about what we are inferring from the evidence we have collected. Interpretation must be ours – but we should explain our evidence as clearly as possible to leave open the prospect of other interpretations.

Conclusion

Researchers adopting a quantitative position focus on 'the measurement and analysis of causal relationships' rather than the process of social experience (Denzin and Lincoln, 2005: 10). On the other hand, qualitative researchers 'seek answers to questions that stress the socially constructed nature of reality, the intimate relationship between the researcher and what is studied' (ibid.: 10).

Early childhood studies researchers use research studies that are interpretative and qualitative widely. However, because of the subjectivity or 'intimate relationship' building, it becomes difficult for a researcher, operating from within this paradigm, to demonstrate the validity, reliability and repeatability of research findings: 'would two different researchers interpret a participant's voice in the same way?' (McKechnie, 2002: 10). To counteract these criticisms, qualitative researchers note the importance of being reflective throughout the process. They argue that these reflections should be documented, in the form of a research diary, to add credibility to the findings of the study. Indeed, the focus group participants noted the importance of reflecting on practice. To quote the words of one participant, Leah: 'You need to reflect on what worked and what didn't.'

It would be rather naïve to suppose that the process of research is 'neat' and 'uncomplicated'. Trying to collect the experiences and views of young children with varied communication skills, different degrees of self-confidence and trust; trying to engage parents and carers in the research process all make for complexities that can only represented by approximation. This is not – and should not be represented as – an exact science.

Go back to the notes that you made in response to the initial questions in this chapter. Having worked through this material, review and revise your first notes and draw up an action plan for the next piece of action research you plan to carry out in your setting. In particular, identify how you will include the child's authentic voice and show where your own interpretation will be evident.

References

BERA (2004) *Revised Ethical Guidelines for Educational Research*. Available at: www.bera.ac.uk/publications/pdfs/ETHICA1.PDF.

Bryman, A. (1988) *Quantity and Quality in Social Research*. London: Unwin Hyman.

Chambers, R. (1983) *Rural Development: Putting the Last First*. London: Longman.

Clark, A. (2004) The Mosaic approach and research with young children. In V. Lewis, M. Kellett, C. Robinson, S. Fraser and S. Ding (eds) *The Reality of Research with Children and Young People*. London: Sage.

Clark, A. and Moss, P. (2001) *Listening to Young Children: The Mosaic Approach*. London: National Children's Bureau and Joseph Rowntree Foundation.

Cresswell, J. W. (1998) *Qualitative Inquiry and Research Design: Choosing among Five Traditions*. Thousand Oaks, CA: Sage.

David, T. (1992) 'Do we have to do this?': the Children Act 1989 and obtaining children's views in early childhood settings. *Children and Society*, 6(3): 204–11.

Denscombe, M. (2007) *The Good Research Guide for Small-scale Social Research Projects*, 3rd edn. Maidenhead: Open University Press.

Denzin, N. K. and Lincoln, Y. S. (eds) (1994) *Handbook of Qualitative Research*. London: Sage.

Denzin, N. K. and Lincoln, Y. S. (2005) Introduction: the discipline and practice of qualitative research. In N. K. Denzin and Y. S. Lincoln (eds) *The Sage Handbook of Qualitative Research*, 2nd edn. Thousand Oaks, CA: Sage.

DfES (Department for Education and Skills) (2001) *The Special Educational Needs Code of Practice*. London. HMSO.

DoH (Department of Health) (1999) *Convention on the Rights of the Child: Second Report to the UN Committee on the Rights of the Child by the United Kingdom. Executive Summary*. London: TSO.

Ellis, C. and Beauchamp, G. (2012) Ethics in researching children with special educational needs. In I. Palaiologou (ed.) *Ethical Practice in Early Childhood*. London: Sage.

Gray, C. (2012) Ethical research with children and vulnerable groups. In I. Palaiologou (ed.) *Ethical Practice in Early Childhood*. London: Sage, pp. 64–83.

Green, D. (2012) Involving young children in research. In I. Palaiologou (ed.) *Ethical Practice in Early Childhood*. London: Sage.

Green, S. and Hogan, D. (2005) *Researching Children's Experiences: Approaches and Methods*. London: Sage.

Greig, A. and Taylor, J. (1999) *Doing Research with Children*. London: Sage.

Greig, A., Taylor, J. and MacKay, T. (2013) *Doing Research with Children*, 3rd edn. London: Sage.

Hart, R. (1992) *Children's Participation: From Tokenism to Citizenship*. Florence: UNICEF International Child Development Centre.

Hendrick, H. (1997) Constructions and reconstructions of British childhood: an interpretative survey, 1800 to the present. In A. James and A. Prout (eds) *Constructing and Reconstructing Childhood*. London: Falmer Press.

Hill, M., Davis, J., Prout, A. and Tisdall, J. (2004) Moving the participation agenda forward. *Children and Society*, 18(2): 77–96.

Ingleby, E. and Oliver, G. (2008) *Applied Social Science for Early Years*. Exeter: Learning Matters.

James, A. (1999) Researching children's social competence: methods and models. In M. Woodhead, D. Faulkner and K. Littleton (eds) *Making Sense of Social Development*. London: Routledge.

James, A. and Prout, A. (eds) (1990) *Constructing and Reconstructing Childhood*. London: Falmer.

James, A. and Prout, A. (eds) (1997) *Constructing and Reconstructing Childhood*, 2nd edn. London: Falmer.

Jones, P. and Welch, S. (2010) *Rethinking Children's Rights: Attitudes in Contemporary Society*. New York: Continuum.

Kirby, P., Lanyon, C., Cronin, K. and Sinclair, R. (2003) *Building a Culture of Participation*. London: Department for Education and Skills.

Knight, A., Clark, A., Petrie, P. and Statham, J. (2006) *The Views of Children and Young People with Learning Disabilities about the Support They Receive from Social Services: A Review of Consultations and Methods. Report to DCSF*. London: Thomas Coram Research Unit.

Langsted, O. (1994) Looking at quality from the child's perspective. In P. Moss and A. Pence (eds) *Valuing Quality in Early Childhood Services: New Approaches to Defining Quality*. London: Paul Chapman.

Lansdown, G. (2001) *Promoting Children's Participation in Democratic Decision-Making*. London: UNICEF.

Lewis, A. and Lindsay, G. (eds) (2000) *Researching Children's Perspectives*. Buckingham: Open University Press.

McKechnie, J. (2002) Children's voices and researching childhood. In B. Goldson, M. Lavalette and J. McKechnie (eds) *Children, Welfare and the State*. London: Sage.

Moss, P. and Petrie, P. (2002) *From Children's Services to Children's Spaces: Public Policy, Children and Childhood*. London: RoutledgeFalmer.

O'Kane, C. (2008) The development of participatory techniques. In P. Christensen and A. James (eds) *Research with Children: Perspectives and Practices*, 2nd edn. London: Routledge, pp. 125–55.

Palaiologou, I. (ed.) (2012) *Ethical Practice in Early Childhood*. London: Sage.

Power, M. (1997) From risk society to audit society. *Soziale Systeme*, 3(1): 3–2.

Punch, S. (2002) Research with children: the same or different from research with adults? *Childhood*, 9(3): 321–41.

Quortrup, J. (1987) Introduction: the sociology of children. *International Journal of Sociology*, 17(3): 3–37.

Roberts-Holmes, G. (2005) *Doing your Early Years Research Project: A Step by Step Guide*. London: Sage.

Smith, R. (2009) *Doing Social Work Research*. Maidenhead: McGraw-Hill.

Thomas, N. and O'Kane, C. (1998) The ethics of participatory research with children. *Children and Society*, 12: 336–48.

United Nations (UN) (1989) *United Nations Convention on the Rights of the Child*. New York: United Nations.

Williamson, J. (2012) Ethics when inspecting early years practice. In I. Palaiologou (ed.) *Ethical Practice in Early Childhood*. London: Sage.

11

Some practical steps towards a more inclusive practice

Keith Savage and Kathy Brodie

When we started planning this book, we knew that we did not want to present it as a 'How to do inclusion' manual, to be skimmed by stressed practitioners anxious about an imminent inspection. Rather we hoped that we would encourage people to take a fresh look at their practice – preferably in association with peers and team workers. In this book we have made a point of including the voice of experienced Early Years workers – and we are grateful to them for sharing their thoughts with us so directly and honestly. All this has been done in the belief that as professionals there is nothing more important than honest and continual reflection on the work that we do. 'The reflective practitioner' can be used as a rather glib label, something of a cliché that has no real meaning. We know that it is sometimes hard to make time to reflect and to write up the journal that you promised yourself you would. As professionals, we are guilty of breaking those sorts of promises too.

In the daily hustle and bustle of work, when dozens of decisions are made – often with the minimum of consideration – it is difficult to be persuaded that it matters to find space to pause, and to consider. Yes, the children that you are working with today may be in your nursery, home or class for just a few weeks or months, and you want to make the most of every session you have. But your career may last for another 20 or 30 years. You can't conduct it all at break-neck speed and you owe it to yourself, the children and their carers to stop and think through the impact of your work. Over the course of a long career, life-styles change, society's expectations change. The practice that made sense 10 years ago no longer does today.

When it comes to inclusive practice – and we insist that any practice worth doing must be inclusive – there will always be fresh challenges to respond to. It is only in recent years that we have come to understand about new conditions affecting very young children – such as foetal alcohol spectrum disorders – that have caused us to rethink what we know about early learning. We have emphasised in this book that inclusion is multi-dimensional. It follows that we will have to take account of wide-ranging new ideas and information to maintain an inclusive practice that is fit for purpose today and tomorrow. This is another reason why this book is not intended to be a manual of tick-lists and tables to provide comfort in advance of the next inspection. Dahlberg and Moss (2005) have argued persuasively that Early Years practitioners must take responsibility for their decisions and actions – certain that they will sometimes get it wrong – rather than hiding behind files full of policies, guidelines, flow charts and tick lists. They describe the reliance on schedules and written instruction as the function of technicians, not professionals (though this might be a bit hard on technicians). They suggest that the human and social worlds in which we live and work are full of uncertainty and that our knowledge of them can be provisional at best. We must be ready to interpret and understand anew in the light of fresh experiences.

Trained professionals should have the confidence to use their judgement, drawing on their experience, what they have seen and heard, and informed by the work of others. There will seldom be a single, 'correct', answer to the challenges we deal with and the 'best' answer must take account of the wishes of the child, the family, other children and practitioners across a range of services. So we make no apologies for not giving you all the answers in this book. Our hope is that through reading and sharing the case studies and reflective activities in the first 10 chapters you will gain in confidence when it comes to resolving the issues you face.

It is important to remember that you are not alone when it comes to making practice more inclusive – whatever problems you find, they are not your problems alone. Trying to 'solve' these problems on your own is almost doomed to fail anyway. As we have already said, inclusive practice needs to take account of the views, perceptions, hopes and fears of many people – and thus many people are likely, at some stage or another, to be involved in resolving questions.

So, even if you have an obvious leadership or management role where you work, you should expect to listen to others, both in identifying challenges to your practice, and in finding ways of adapting to those challenges. Depending on the relationships you have with others – and how they see you as a leader – this may be a challenge in itself. If you are used to solving problems and informing the team accordingly, you might need to re-think your approach when it comes to inclusion. Let's consider this example:

> You are the manager of a privately owned day nursery. You have a well-established team; team members get on well, the children enjoy being at the nursery and you receive many compliments about the quality of care from parents. You overhear a conversation between a parent and an Early Years practitioner, in which the parent of a 3-year-old says, 'I'd rather my daughter was kept away from that new girl. Her parents are a bit rough and are not the sort I want my daughter to meet.' You can't hear the reply clearly, but it is brief and sounds something like, 'OK. We'll do that.'

As a manager, there are a number of possible responses here. At the very least you would want to talk to the practitioner to be sure of what was said and agreed. Would you want to talk to the parent? If so, what would you say? (If not, why not?) Would you want to meet with the whole staff and/or organise some training? Would you want to alert the setting owner? What record of this incident would you keep for future reference? Would you ask the staff to keep an eye on interactions between the two girls lest any complaints be made? Bearing in mind the content in earlier chapters about children having views about their own lives and 'agency', would you want to find out what they think and feel?

No doubt you would want some control over these events – so that they didn't get out of hand – but necessarily other people would become involved and that makes outcomes less certain or predictable. Spend 10 minutes or so working out how you think that you would want to try and manage this issue; identify the priority actions and who you would involve. Be clear about the outcomes you are looking for and how you would try to follow up the incident to see what impact it might have had on the nursery.

Now look at your 'action plan' and put yourself in the position of the practitioners. How would you feel about what your manager is proposing to do? Do you feel that she is worrying too much about something that has been said in an unguarded moment? Is this going to distract you from your core work? Or do you feel, 'About time. These posh parents who think they are better than the rest of us need to be told'?

There is always the possibility that squashed between these adult worries are two young children who have views and opinions of their own – but is anyone actually concerned or interested?

Maybe we are labouring the point, but what we seek to make clear is that trying to be the wise counsel in situations of this sort can never be easy and that there is nothing to be gained in rushing to resolve matters. We would encourage you to start with the children rather than the adults though. If it is not a problem for them, is it one for you? (Your answer might be 'Yes'!)

There may be instances where you feel out of your depth or isolated – this latter state may well be the case sometimes for practitioners who tend to work by themselves, such as nannies and childminders. Whatever your role, you should be able to find practical advice and support not too far away. You may, of course have a SENCO or other specialist on site. If you are part of a nursery chain, you should have a senior manager, adviser or trainer to talk to; if you work in a school, then the Local Education Authority should have specialist staff. The Professional Association for Childcare and Early Years (PACEY) can offer training and support to its members, including nannies and childminders. Most LEAs have Gypsy, Roma and Traveller Education Teams. Stonewall have some excellent and accessible resources.

Of course there are many networking possibilities on-line – though these should be used with some care. There are plenty of specialist sites for different aspects of inclusion. For example, for Special Educational Needs (SEN), there is the well-established and reputable on-line starting point, Special Needs Jungle. This is written and presented from a parental viewpoint – and there is nothing wrong with that. From a professional, child-centred perspective, the Council for Disabled Children is a trustworthy source of news and information.

As ever, it is better to be familiar with those that you might turn to in advance of any crisis. As part of any continuing professional development (CPD) you, and your team, should plan internal or external training events, perhaps starting from resources that you might find in any of the above sources or sources detailed throughout this book.

Depending upon the size of your staff team, you may want to identify someone to take particular responsibility for monitoring changes in the political, cultural and economic environments that might impact on inclusive practice. Part of the intended role of those with Early Years Professional Status was that they act as 'change agents' so that change was identified and planned for strategically rather than being dealt with as it happened – possibly at times of heightened stress. Even though this Status has been reshaped several times since its inception, this is still a desirable and admirable aspiration.

There are some aspects of our work as Early Years practitioners where there is a clear consensus – though the more closely we examine even the most 'obvious' statement, we find there are potential questions to 'unpick'. While there is general agreement that Early Years practice should be inclusive, that is a statement that can quickly unravel. You are unlikely to find anyone who advocates that children should learn to judge one another – positively or negatively – by the colour of their skin, the sound of their voice or their home address. In the same way that we can agree, as a society, that we need to build more houses – so long as they don't block my view or eat into the green belt – we can also agree that we want inclusivity, until it challenges our prejudices or wishes for our children. Most of us would say that we want our children to grow up to be tolerant and respectful of others, to accept differences and to choose friends for who they are, not what they are. If we are honest, are we really as broad-minded and as tolerant as we might like to think we are?

One of us (all right, it is Keith) finds the speech pattern used by many younger people, especially in the south of England, known as 'high rise terminals' or 'uptalk' almost unbearable. It is a trivial thing, but can an intelligent person really speak like that? The answer, obviously, is 'Yes, they can and do' and both Keith and Stephen Fry will have to learn to overcome their prejudices here. If we can admit to this prejudice what others might we hold? We are not at a meeting of Alcoholics Anonymous, nor is this a confession to a priest, so let us pass on that last question.

Our point is a simple one – we aspire to an idea because we recognise that it is a good one. The words 'idea' and 'ideal' are obviously closely related; the idea of 'inclusivity' is a good one but we should not be forever chastising ourselves because we find ourselves reluctant to endorse another's decisions when it comes to tattoos, diet, faith or sex life. As professionals, however, we do have an obligation to allow others to make their own choices and judgements. We have come to our own conclusions by our own routes but in our work with children, we want to open up possibilities not close them down.

We hope that this book has encouraged you to stop, pause and look at your world of work from a number of angles. We hope that while the picture that you have constructed may be complex, it is, at least, manageable. Finally, we hope that you have more confidence than ever to work for a world that puts a premium on openness, equality, respect and the joy of diversity.

References

Dahlberg, G. and Moss, P. (2005) *Ethics and Politics in Early Childhood Education*. London: RoutledgeFalmer.

PACEY (2014) *Training: The Key to Success*. Available at: www.pacey.org.uk (accessed 10 August 2014).

Special Needs Jungle (2014) *Parent-Led Information, Resources and Informed Opinion about Children and Young People with SEN*. Available at: www.specialneedsjungle.com (accessed 10 August 2014).

The Council for Disabled Children (2014) *Our Networks*. Available at: www.councilfordisabledchildren.org.uk (accessed 10 August 2014).

Index

Index